A Guide to
Successful Employment
for Individuals with Autism

A Guide to Successful Employment for Individuals with Autism

by

Marcia Datlow Smith, Ph.D.
Psychologist

Ronald G. Belcher, Ph.D.
Research Associate

and

Patricia D. Juhrs
Executive Director

Community Services for Autistic Adults and Children
Rockville, Maryland

·P·A·U·L·H·
BROOKES
PUBLISHING Cº

Baltimore • London • Toronto • Sydney

Paul H. Brookes Publishing Co.
Post Office Box 10624
Baltimore, Maryland 21285-0624

Typeset by Brushwood Graphics, Inc., Baltimore, Maryland.
Manufactured in the United States of America by
The Maple Press Company, York, Pennsylvania.

The cases described in this book are based on the actual experiences of
the authors. The names of individuals have been changed, and certain
aspects of the situations have been altered, to protect confidentiality.

Library of Congress Cataloging-in-Publication Data
Smith, Marcia Datlow, 1951–
  A guide to successful employment for individuals with autism / by
Marcia Datlow Smith, Ronald G. Belcher, and Patricia D. Juhrs.
     p.   cm.
Includes bibliographical references and index.
ISBN 1-55766-171-5
  1. Mentally handicapped–Vocational guidance–United States.
2. Autism—Patients—Vocational guidance—United States.
3. Autism. I. Belcher, Ronald G. II. Juhrs, Patricia D. III. Title.
HV3005.S65 1994
331.7'02'0874—dc20   94-8826
                                                   CIP

British Library Cataloguing-in-Publication data are available from the
British Library.

Contents

About the Authors

Marcia Datlow Smith, Ph.D., is a psychologist who works with individuals with autism in integrated community settings. She received her Ph.D. from the University of Maryland and has worked for 15 years in assisting people with autism to achieve community integration despite challenging behaviors. Her research interests have included autism, community integration, management of challenging behaviors, and supported employment, and she has lectured and published extensively. Among her publications is *Autism and Life in the Community* (1990, Paul H. Brookes Publishing Co.).

Ronald G. Belcher, Ph.D., is a consultant who provides psychological evaluation, behavioral intervention plans, staff training, and psychotherapy to individuals with developmental disabilities and mental illness. Dr. Belcher has 15 years of experience working with people with autism, and completed a position as Research Coordinator on a 3-year federal grant researching supported employment for individuals with autism. He received his doctoral degree in clinical psychology from The American University. He has presented programs throughout the country on behavioral intervention, staff training, and quality assurance as related to autism, and has also coauthored papers on supported employment, facilitated communication, instructional procedures, and leisure activities for individuals with autism.

Patricia D. Juhrs directs a nationally recognized organization serving individuals with autism, Community Services for Autistic Adults and Children (CSAAC). She developed the first supported employment services for people with autism at CSAAC, and has directed several federal grants from the U.S. Department of Education to provide training and assistance to professionals establishing supported employment programs for people with autism. Ms. Juhrs has participated as a member of the President's Health Reform Committee as an expert concerning long-term financing of supported employment programs. In addition, she is a member of the State of Maryland's Rehabilitation Advisory Committee and a board member of the Maryland Association of Community Services.

Foreword

People with autism, especially severe autism, have not participated in the nation's labor force in any significant way. In recent years, even with the advent of supported employment, individuals with autism have had only marginal opportunities to work in competitive employment. The expectations of service providers, teachers, psychologists, physicians, and even family members about the working potential of persons with autism have been very low. There have been very limited vocational aspirations for people who have been labeled "autistic." One only has to review the existing research literature in the professional journals, as well as the commercially available curricula and textbooks in the area of autism, to see that vocational curricula and vocational training have played a minimal role. Marcee Smith, Ron Belcher, and Patricia Juhrs have for the first time introduced a comprehensive guide in the area of vocational curriculum and training for competitive employment that focuses specifically on persons with severe autism.

The authors have developed this curriculum from a deep base of clinical experiences and very intensive "hands-on" experiences with individuals with severe autism. I have had the opportunity to work with these authors and visit the job sites to see firsthand the vocational challenges that individuals referenced in this book overcame in order to be successful in competitive employment. Their clinical histories have by and large revealed long patterns of inappropriate social behavior, significant communication challenges, and, usually, histories of institutionalization. Their movement into competitive employment, after they have received the on-the-job training skills that are listed in this book, has played a major role in enhancing their lives.

The overriding strength of the vocational materials in this book is the fact that they have been field tested and empirically validated through years of direct instructional experience. Employers, co-workers, job coaches, and, of course, the authors have continually modified the descriptions of tasks and skills so that they would appropriately reflect the strengths or weaknesses of a given individual.

Another significant strength of this material is that it cuts across a wide range of businesses and industries and is not focused exclusively on food service or cleaning, two areas that have been traditionally stereotyped for people with severe intellectual disabilities or behavior problems. There is a significant breadth of jobs that will be of value to the employment specialist as he or she develops jobs in the community and searches for different vocational opportunities.

A third strength of this curriculum is that it can be utilized in vocational planning and assessment for individuals with autism and their families. The credibility of different vocational options will be greatly enhanced if families can review these materials and see the different types of jobs that their son or daughter may be able to complete successfully in competitive employment. All too often individuals are given only two or three job choices. For the first time, the materials in this volume will provide a much greater array of possibilities for individuals with autism to consider.

The individual job skill format within this guide is another asset, because good vocational instructional programs require objectives, a listing of materials, and a description of the work area. The strategic way that this curriculum is presented will facilitate teachers' efforts to be more effective. Universality is the major caveat for use of this curriculum, as well as other similar types of packaged curricula. Clearly, every student's needs and choices must be taken into account, and no one curriculum can meet all students' needs. However, the organization of the Smith, Belcher, and Juhrs curriculum is a very positive way of approaching the provision of vocational programs for students with significant challenges.

The time has well passed for individuals with autism to be sitting in segregated schools, residential facilities, or adult activity centers all day long, performing meaningless tasks. The time has passed for individuals with severe autism to be put into extended periods of time out, excessively drugged, and stigmatized. The time has passed for individuals with autism to be relegated to earning a dollar a day in a sheltered workshop or to be confined to a "day treatment" center. We live in an era when federal statutes call for the full inclusion of all people with disabilities into schools and the nation's work force. People with disabilities are affected by federal laws such as the Americans with Disabilities Act of 1990, the Developmental Disabilities Assistance and Bill of Rights Act of 1990, the Individuals with Disabilities Education Act of 1990, and the Rehabilitation Act Amendments of 1992. These laws do not endorse sheltered employment or segregated adult activity centers; they promote, through their language, inclusion into the work force. Similarly, this volume is a positive vehicle for helping direct service providers and families take advantage of this window of opportunity.

As of this writing, the U.S. economy is improving significantly, and every month large numbers of jobs are being created. Now is the time for people with autism to assert their right to obtain meaningful employment and for individuals in the field to help them reach a higher, more dignified level. For this to happen, individuals with autism will need to be trained in competitive employment skills, and the many job descriptions in this book provide a very good first step for this to happen. Smith and her colleagues are to be commended for developing and disseminating this important information.

Paul Wehman, Ph.D.
Professor
Departments of Physical Medicine and Rehabilitation
and Special Education
Medical College of Virginia
Virginia Commonwealth University
Richmond, Virginia

REFERENCES

Americans with Disabilities Act of 1990 (ADA), PL 101-336. (July 26, 1990). Title 42, U.S.C. 12101 et seq: *U.S. Statutes at Large, 104,* 327–378.

Developmental Disabilities Assistance and Bill of Rights Act of 1990, PL 101-496. (October 31, 1990). Title 42, U.S.C. 6000 et seq: *U.S. Statutes at Large, 104,* 1191.

Individuals with Disabilities Education Act of 1990 (IDEA), PL 101-476. (October 30, 1990). Title 20, U.S.C. 1400 et seq: *U.S. Statutes at Large, 104,* 1103–1151.

Rehabilitation Act Amendments of 1992, PL 102-569. (October 29, 1992). Title 29, U.S.C. 701 et seq: *U.S. Statutes at Large, 100,* 4344–4488.

Preface

Individuals with autism are underrepresented by supported employment efforts, considered by most supported employment agencies to be "too disabled" to work, requiring too much support to succeed, or failing to keep the job if they are served. Indeed, the effects of autism do appear incompatible with employment, in particular the severe language and social problems as well as the challenging behaviors that can include self-stimulation, aggression, self-injury, and property destruction.

However, despite outward appearances and historical reality, persons with autism have succeeded in the workplace, including those who are most severely affected by the disorder. During the last 15 years, we have personally observed more than 70 people with autism in their supported employment work experiences. Many of these workers have held jobs for 4 years or more and in some cases have earned more than their job coaches.

This book provides information on supports and methods that have been successful in helping persons with autism hold jobs. General guidelines on assessment, job development, and problem solving are provided. Specific information is provided on a number of vocational areas in which persons with autism have succeeded. This book was written primarily to share what we have learned about the many jobs held by individuals with autism, in the hopes that teachers, supported employment personnel, and employment specialists can use this information to seek and maintain employment for other individuals with autism. Details are provided on each job so that the reader can become familiar with the many kinds of tasks that individuals with autism have been hired to do. Additionally, supports provided at each job site are described, again, in recognition of the fact that a good match is necessary but not always sufficient for successful employment.

Each job that is described in this manual includes information on the workers with autism who held that job, including their cognitive level, language abilities, and problem behaviors. The authors recognize in many situations it is preferable to discuss an individual in terms of support needs rather than in terms of his or her weaknesses. However, the fact remains that individuals with autism have specific behavioral and cognitive challenges that the practical job coach or teacher must evaluate and take into account if a successful job match is to be made. It is not enough to know that a worker is behaviorally challenged and needs the support of a behavior plan in order to find the right job. Rather, the employment specialist must be acutely aware of the fact that the worker screams, head bangs, or destroys property, and must then take care to find a job in which those behaviors, should they persist, are not job threatening. Therefore, worker characteristics are provided for each job, so that the reader can become aware of the kinds of jobs that individuals with specific disabilities associated with autism have held. So, for example, the employment specialist for a young man with profound mental retardation, inability to speak in sentences, and problems with head banging can read about scores of jobs that other individuals with autism and those associated problems have held.

It is our hope that this book will be used to encourage the employment of persons with autism who in the past may have appeared to be unemployable and unsupportable.

Acknowledgments

The authors thank Karla Nabors for her review of the manuscript and for her excellent suggestions. Pamela Haas and Kathleen Wilde deserve special credit for collecting the data for this book and for compiling the job descriptions. The authors also thank Ellen Scott, Martha Summerville, Susan Ingram, Cynthia Meredith, David Bergmann, Harriett Cooper, and Shelley Wooten for assisting with data collection; John Solyst for sharing his experiences on job development; and Joseph Bartell for assisting with the tables and assembling the final manuscript. Special acknowledgment is extended to Paul Wehman for his ongoing advice.

Work on which this book is based was funded in part by Grant #HO23C10149 from the U.S. Department of Education. However, the opinions expressed herein do not necessarily reflect the position or policy of the U.S. Department of Education.

Note to the Reader

Although aware of the new definition of mental retardation put forward by the American Association on Mental Retardation (AAMR), we chose to use the conventional categories to designate levels of mental retardation—mild, moderate, severe, and profound. We have two reasons for this decision.

The first reason is that we believe that information communicated by the traditional categories is important in terms of the job match. A person whose intelligence measures in the profound range of mental retardation will most likely be suited for different kinds of jobs than a person whose intelligence measures in the moderate range of mental retardation. And whereas the new definition is helpful in terms of determining the kinds of supports the person needs, it has not been widely used to make job matches in the employment field. At some future point in time, after more experience has been gained with the new definition, it might be possible to readily translate that definition into specific job recommendations. However, to date, we do not have data that allow us to do so, and so we have proceeded with the former system, which remains useful in the job search.

The second reason for using the conventional categories is that persons with severe and profound mental retardation, as diagnosed by the traditional system, are underrepresented in supported employment. We want our job information to clearly communicate the fact that persons whose intelligence levels fall in the severe and profound ranges of mental retardation are employable. Furthermore, we want the reader to know what jobs people have held as encouragement to their own job development efforts for individuals with autism.

To Karla Nabors, Susan Ingram, and Cathy Fowler

A Guide to
Successful Employment
for Individuals with Autism

CHAPTER 1

Autism and Vocational Fitness

An Overview

Every competent employee brings to the job a combination of skills, educational background, and interests that make that worker a valued employee. The value of an employee is determined by how well his or her skills and interests fill a void for the employer. This is also true for employees with autism. Despite the problems of learning, communication, and behavior that are often associated with autism, each individual with autism has a unique combination of skills, interests, and potential. These factors can transform a person from being solely a person with autism to being a valued worker who happens to have autism. To assist an individual with autism to become a competent worker first requires a knowledge of the disorder and its implications for vocational fitness.

DEFINITION OF AUTISM

Autism is a developmental disability that is characterized by several behavior disorders (American Psychiatric Association, 1987; Rutter & Schopler, 1988; Schreibman, 1988). People with autism display three basic groups of characteristics. These principal characteristics are explained below with an emphasis on how they may present themselves in the work environment.

Principal Characteristics

Impaired Verbal and Nonverbal Communication All persons with autism have deficits in language and communication. These impairments range from being completely nonverbal to having an age-appropriate vocabulary with limitations in the ability to use speech functionally.

Most people with autism who develop speech have limited comprehension and expression. Typically, they have difficulty following instructions, understanding lengthy communications, and understanding abstract concepts or speech with emotional content. This difficulty understanding speech often leads to problems in following complex instructions from supervisors. A supervisor who provides an unbroken string of new instructions to an employee with autism might find that the employee could repeat the instructions, but be unable to act on them.

Individuals with autism often have trouble with abstract concepts and tend to interpret communications literally. It is not unusual for a person with autism to follow instructions literally. This tendency can lead to unanticipated misunderstandings; for example, instructing a stock clerk with autism to move a shelf full of glasses may result in disaster as the clerk attempts to move the entire shelf rather than each glass. Furthermore, people with autism often have trouble understanding the meaning of nonverbal communications, including voice intonation, facial expression, and body postures. Therefore, they may fail to pick up subtle, nonverbal cues that are part of all communications. Inadequate comprehension of verbal and nonverbal communications makes job performance problematic if a busy supervisor quickly gives instructions to employees with autism in the same manner that instructions are given to nondisabled employees.

The speech of people with autism is often literal and concrete. Individuals with autism may be capable of speaking of facts at great length; however, expressions of abstract notions are often rare. Additionally, they often restrict their conversations to a limited number of topics. For example, Allen is a worker with autism in an electronics assembly plant. If asked why he likes his job, Allen offers the most basic of responses, such as "I am a good worker" or "I like to solder." However, Allen spends a great deal of time discussing countless trivial facts about dead rock stars, one of his primary interests.

Individuals with autism often have a marked inability to use language functionally. Many do not seem to understand how to use speech to influence the environment in order to get what they want or need. For example, Margaret, a woman with autism, occasionally needs help completing a task at work. Without specific training, Margaret would yell and scratch herself rather than ask for help. Another employee with autism may spend hours in a cool bathroom and resist coming out to work because he is unable to tell his job coach that his work area is too hot for him.

People with autism are often unable to relate basic information about themselves, their environment, and what they just did. They may have particular trouble answering open-ended questions such as why, what, where, how, and when. For instance, a worker with autism may become agitated when a shopper asks him where a particular item is stocked in the store, despite having stocked the item himself. Another worker with autism may be unable to tell his supervisor that he was late because the public bus broke down.

People with autism also have difficulty participating in the back and forth exchanges necessary in conversations. They may walk away from a supervisor who is giving them important instructions, fail to ask for clarification on instructions, or abruptly interrupt the supervisor to make an irrelevant comment. Some people with autism talk excessively and may bother supervisors and co-workers by repeatedly and persistently speaking about the same topic or asking the same question.

Finally, people with autism may have characteristic speech abnormalities. These include abnormal speech rhythm (i.e., talking too fast or too slow), echolalia (i.e., repeating verbatim what was heard), lack of varied voice inflection (i.e., having monotone speech), and pronominal reversal (e.g., saying "you" instead of "I"). Each of these speech abnormalities makes functional communication at work difficult.

Deficits in Socialization One of the core characteristics of autism is an inability to engage in typical social relationships. Because of this inability, children and adults with autism appear to have a decided lack of interest in other people in their environment.

Social deficits are present throughout the life span; in adulthood they are evident in a failure to make friends and to engage in social interactions at work. Adults with autism can be extremely withdrawn and appear to prefer to spend hours by themselves pursuing solitary activities rather than engage in even brief social interactions. They may walk away or become agitated and even belligerent when someone talks to them. They often have trouble filling the time at lunch and breaks at work because they rarely initiate and engage in conversations. Typically, they have difficulty learning how and when to use specific social skills. They may fail to greet co-workers and supervisors in the morning, not look at a supervisor who is giving them directions, not request leave for vacations or medical appointments, and not chat with customers.

In addition, some adults with autism engage in inappropriate social behaviors. It is as though they are unaware of the rules of social interactions. They may touch co-workers improperly, blow on or sniff people who are talking to them, or refuse to share work space with co-workers. Often their social initiations seem intrusive and immature to co-workers. They may stand too close to other peoples' faces when speaking with them or ask embarrassing personal questions with an apparent unawareness of having violated social norms. Untreated, these behaviors can annoy co-workers and customers and make continued employment problematic.

Atypical Responses to Sensory Stimulation Persons with autism often display unusual responses to sensory stimulation. On the one hand they react in an exaggerated manner to preferred stimuli, and on the other hand they ignore important environmental events. They may be fascinated by unusual, specific sensory stimuli such as things that spin, shiny objects, certain textures such as hair or fur, and rotating water in flushing toilets. Often, they seek out objects and activities that provide desired stimulation to the exclusion of other activities. In addition, people with autism engage in a variety of stereotyped behaviors that provide them with sensory stimulation. These behaviors include repetitive noise making, hand flapping, rocking, twirling in circles, and jumping up and down. At work, engaging in such self-stimulatory behaviors and being preoccupied with certain stimuli interfere with task-oriented behaviors and impede work quality and production.

Although people with autism may desire certain sensory stimuli, they may also have a strong aversion to other particular sensory stimuli. They may be averse to certain noises, particular food textures, and fluctuations in lighting. They may seem acutely aware of certain sounds, sometimes responding to sounds that are barely audible. Some people with autism also attempt to block sensory stimulation by covering their eyes or ears. Furthermore, they sometimes fail to respond to painful or uncomfortable stimuli; for instance, they may fail to respond to changes in temperature by removing or putting on a sweater or coat. Some people with autism also engage in self-injurious behaviors, such as skin scratching and head banging, with no apparent perceptions of pain. Self-injurious behavior may be the most disturbing behavior for co-workers, supervisors, and the public to witness and may lead quickly to job termination.

Associated Characteristics

Autism is a pervasive disorder and can have numerous effects on the individual. In addition to the basic characteristics discussed above, autism is associated with several secondary features. These secondary features may or may not be present; if they are present, they can vary widely in degree from one person to the next. These features are described in terms of how they typically occur.

Difficulty Handling Change   Changes in routine and schedule are particularly troublesome to people with autism. For instance, individuals with autism may become destructive to property following minor changes in work schedules or activities. They may frequently try to avoid environmental changes by attempting to maintain sameness in the environment following changes and by always performing tasks in the same way. Environmental changes are so distressing to people with autism that they attempt to avoid them to the best of their ability. At work, people with autism may actively resist necessary changes in the environment. For example, a retail employee with autism may persistently put stocked merchandise in its original location rather than the new location specified by the floor supervisor. Another employee may insist on doing a task in the manner originally learned despite instructions to do it in a more efficient way. One young man with autism was so distressed at a change in his weekly routine that he asked if he could "repeat the week" to include the expected activities.

Visual-Motor Skills   Most people with autism possess visual-motor skills that surpass their general intelligence and their verbal skills. It is not unusual for a person with autism to have severe deficits in language and social skills but be able to accurately solder electronic components, for example. Such visual-motor skills represent a real asset for a person who is seeking competitive employment.

Mental Retardation   Although estimates vary from study to study, approximately 70%–80% of people with autism also have mental retardation (Sigman, Ungerer, Mundy, & Sherman, 1987). The presence of mental retardation means that job training is necessary not only to overcome the challenges of autism but also to overcome the cognitive and adaptive skills deficits associated with mental retardation. Persons with mental retardation and autism need more intensive instruction to learn work tasks and job-related skills than do people with autism who have no global cognitive deficits.

Behavior Problems   Individuals with autism often have single or multiple maladaptive behaviors. A partial list of maladaptive and sometimes dangerous behaviors includes aggression (e.g., hitting, kicking, biting, scratching, pushing, pulling hair, head butting others); property destruction (e.g., kicking or hitting walls, throwing objects, tearing clothing, breaking windows); vocal habits (e.g., noise making, yelling, laughing); verbal abuse (e.g., making threats, name calling, cursing and yelling at others); self-injury (e.g., head banging, self-hitting, self-biting, self-scratching, pulling own hair, self-induced vomiting); off-task and noncompliant behaviors (e.g., poor attention to task, refusal to work, frequent distractibility, prompt dependency); hyperactivity (e.g., pacing, difficulty sitting still, talking excessively, being in constant movement); tantrums (e.g., crying, stamping feet, jumping up and down, throwing self to floor); toileting difficulties (e.g., playing in urine and feces, stuffing the toilet to overflow); undressing in public; and bolting from staff. At first glance, these behaviors seem to preclude employment for a person who displays them; however, with proper supports, training, and intervention, experience shows that these and other maladaptive behaviors can be decreased or eliminated on the job, thereby ensuring continued employment.

Savant Skills   Individuals with autism sometimes have savant skills, that is, skills in specific areas of cognitive functioning that are present at a level above what one would expect given overall intelligence. In many cases it appears that a portion of their abilities are unimpaired despite deficits in other areas. Typically, these skills tend to be in nonlanguage areas and may reflect idiosyncratic interests. For instance, individuals with autism may be remarkably adept at performing numeric or calendar calculations in their heads, at playing music after little or no formal instruction, or at drawing and painting. They also may have unusual hobbies such as celestial navigation, memorizing sports statistics, or memorizing numbers on train engines or license plates.

Rituals and Compulsions   Individuals with autism sometimes have ritualistic and compulsive behaviors that interfere with job performance. Ritualistic and compulsive behaviors include arranging objects in a precise order, walking or riding via a specific route, obsessively picking at lint and frayed strings on clothing, carrying certain items everywhere they go, and routinely touching certain objects while walking past them. Deviations from these rituals and compulsions can result in catastrophic reactions that involve aggression, property destruction, and self-injury. For example, attempts to stop compulsive lint picking on the job in a laundry may result in self-injury and screaming from an employee with autism.

Fluctuations in Attention and Off-Task Behaviors   Persons with autism are often inconsistent in doing job tasks due to inattention and off-task behaviors. They may attend to work for only a brief period of time because they become easily distracted by favorite sensory stimulation, self-stimulatory behaviors, and rituals. Without intervention, off-task behaviors can severely impede productivity.

HISTORY OF LIMITED OPPORTUNITIES FOR PEOPLE WITH AUTISM

Historically, individuals with autism and their families have had trouble accessing appropriate educational, residential, and vocational services. Typically, services for people with autism have been either nonexistent or inadequate. For many years, schools and adult programs were not equipped to teach individuals with autism. At best, they were placed in schools designed for children with mental retardation or for children with emotional impairment or mental illness. Because of the lack of specialized treatment and services, these students were often suspended or expelled. In addition, when they finished their educations, there were no specialized vocational programs for them. They then remained at home or in the day rooms of institutions.

Dearth of Technology

The lengthy institutionalization of people with autism meant that techniques for educating them and for managing difficult behaviors were slow to develop. Early interventions that emphasized traditional psychotherapy to overcome the emotional detachment failed. The advent of punishment to control maladaptive behaviors had limited success provided that the punishing stimuli were severe, and it produced unwanted side effects of increased withdrawal and aggression toward others. In addition, punishment procedures could be implemented only in segregated environments and precluded community placement. Only within the last 2 decades have treatment procedures developed and been refined to educate people with autism and to modify their challenging behaviors using positive techniques that are compatible with community placements.

Segregated Environments

In the 1970s, segregated training centers such as day activity centers, prevocational centers, and sheltered workshops emerged to provide training in recreational, adaptive, and vocational skills to people with developmental disabilities, some of whom have autism. These centers provide an alternative to staying at home or to institutionalization and continue to be major centers of training throughout the country.

The philosophy of many training centers was that people with disabilities were not ready to assume the responsibilities of competitive employment and needed additional training before entering the work force. Vocational training centers provided the opportunity to learn job skills before seeking employment. Many of these centers had either contract work or created vocational tasks to mirror actual jobs. The notion was that employment would be the natural progression following a period of training. Training would occur until the individual displayed the skills that were assumed to be prerequisite for job placement.

The reality of vocational training centers was that most workers were never transitioned into actual jobs. Rather, sheltered work experience became a dead end for most people with disabilities. Individuals with autism in particular never displayed behaviors and skills considered necessary for job placement. They had a variety of maladaptive behaviors and displayed poor on-task skills and low productivity at the vocational center. It was unclear how they could work in competitive employment when they could not succeed in a more sheltered, less demanding environment.

Supported Employment and Continued Exclusion

In recent years, supported employment emerged as an alternative to segregated training centers. Federal legislation defined supported employment as paid employment where people with developmental disabilities are provided with supportive activities such as supervision and training that enable them to work in settings where people without disabilities are employed. As such, supported employment offers people with developmental disabilities the opportunity and the means to find and retain employment with the assistance of professional staff. For the first time, a technology evolved that made integrated, paid employment a viable alternative for many people with developmental disabilities. Since the mid-1980s, individuals with developmental disabilities have held a variety of jobs in a variety of industries. However, research has demonstrated that the beneficiaries of the supported employment movement have been predominantly people with mild or moderate disabilities. Individuals with severe or profound disabilities, including autism, have typically not been included in supported employment initiatives.

IMPLICATIONS OF THE SERVICE DELIVERY SYSTEM FOR WORKERS WITH AUTISM

Historically, the service delivery system has been less than amenable to providing supports for the employment of people with autism. Although the service delivery system is gradually evolving to provide incentives for supported employment, previous disincentives in the service system have had an impact on the employment of people with autism.

When a student with autism reaches 21 years of age, his or her entitlement to services as provided in the education system ends. Transition to adult services is often dependent on the availability of funds for the services needed to support the student's needs as an adult. The lack of a stable source of funding is a primary barrier to supported employment for adults with autism.

Adults with autism, when served in the community, are most often placed in sheltered environments such as day activity centers or training programs. This practice is encouraged by the federal Medicaid waiver program, which only funds supported employment placements for individuals who were formerly institutionalized.

Yet, the service system has benefited supported workers with autism with the Social Security Work Incentives programs. By using these programs—Plans for Achieving Self Support (PASS) or Impairment Related Work Expense (IRWE)—employees with autism contribute toward the supports and services they need to maintain employment and are then able to keep their supplemental security income (SSI) benefits and Medicaid insurance. For example, workers with autism can pay for psychological and behavior management services and related attendant care costs that are necessary to achieve or maintain employment. By doing so, they can maintain SSI and Medicaid benefits.

People with autism have historically been unable to benefit from federal and state rehabilitation funding administered through the federal Rehabilitation Services Administration and the department of rehabilitation in each state. Funding from these sources was earmarked for people who, because of disability, needed time-limited support and assistance. People with autism were generally excluded from job placement and coaching because there was a presumption that they were not employable. The primary services provided to people with autism by state rehabilitation departments were vocational assessment and psychological evaluation, and those assessments were often used to make the determination that the person was unable to benefit from rehabilitation services.

IMPLICATIONS OF CHARACTERISTICS OF AUTISM FOR VOCATIONAL CHOICE AND DEVELOPMENT

Despite a history of unemployment and the absence of stable funding sources for supported employment, people with autism have demonstrated the capacity to work. They often display characteristic strengths and weaknesses that have clear implications for vocational choice and development. When reviewing these characteristics and their implications, it is important to keep in perspective that each person with autism is an individual and has a unique pattern of strengths and weaknesses. However, there are certain characteristics that are part of the definition of the syndrome; these will be reviewed in terms of their implications for vocational choice and vocational development (i.e., teaching people with autism how to perform their jobs and supporting them in retaining employment). Any individual's traits may mitigate or exacerbate the effects of these implications. Table 1.1 lists the characteristics associated with autism and how they have an impact on vocational choice and development.

Communication Skills

The communication deficits of people with autism often have an impact on vocational choice and development. Jobs that do not require language or sophisti-

Table 1.1. Characteristics of autism and their impact on vocational choice and development

Characteristics of autism	Impact on vocational choice and vocational development
Impaired verbal and nonverbal communication	Select jobs with few communication requirements. Provide job coach support to assist with communication needs and provide training in communication skills.
Deficits in socialization	Select jobs with limited social skills requirements, limited contact with public, and solitary job duties. Provide job coach support to assist worker with socialization and provide training in specific social skills.
Abnormal response to sensory stimulation	Select jobs that either provide preferred stimulation or avoid nonpreferred stimulation.
Difficulty handling change	Select jobs that present few daily changes. Provide supervision and behavior management to handle changes.
Visual-motor skills	Select jobs that require good visual-motor skills.
Mental retardation	Select jobs that mirror cognitive ability. Provide supervision and job skill training as necessary.
Behavior problems	Select jobs that present few antecedents and at which behavior problems do not pose a danger to co-workers and are not job threatening. Provide job coach supervision to run behavior program and to manage difficult behaviors.
Savant and splinter skills	Select jobs that capitalize upon savant or splinter skills.
Rituals and compulsions	Select jobs that require attention to detail and exactness.
Fluctuations in attention and off-task behaviors	Provide supervision and behavior programs to increase on-task behaviors.

cated use of language are generally more suitable than jobs that do. For example, retail positions such as cashier or customer service person that require verbal communication would not be appropriate for individuals with autism. However, in the same retail environment, jobs such as warehouse worker, stock clerk, and merchandise pricer, which do not require extensive language skills, would be good choices for workers with autism. Likewise, in a library, an employee with autism may have difficulty functioning in an information resource position, but may excel at book sorting and shelving.

Although jobs should be sought that minimize the need for language and communication skills, all jobs require some level of communication with other people such as supervisors, co-workers, and customers. In some cases, it is possible to find a job match in which the worker with autism can successfully work, without support, despite difficulty with communication skills. However, many workers with autism need ongoing support and instruction in communication to hold jobs.

Workers with autism often need instruction or ongoing support to hold jobs that involve no interaction with the public. For example, Louise had a job soldering electronic components. She would perform well until she ran out of one of the components and would need to ask her supervisor for more. She required specific instruction in how to ask the supervisor for more work materials.

Shane is a man with autism who can use language fairly well and who can answer simple, concrete questions. To work independently stocking shelves in a hardware store, Shane needed initial instruction in how to communicate with customers asking for assistance. Shane was able to learn these skills and work with only occasional assistance from co-workers.

Nonverbal employees with autism are particularly challenged in the area of communication and require specific adaptations (e.g., picture books) and intervention as well as ongoing support to communicate with co-workers and supervisors. For example, Ralph has no verbal skills at all; this impairment has life-long implications for his vocational development. Although his job stocking shelves in a toy store does not require language, he is often approached by customers asking for assistance. Because of his lack of language skills, Ralph needs ongoing supervision and support to handle those situations.

Social Skills

Because autism is characterized by difficulty in establishing and maintaining relationships, jobs that rely heavily on good social skills are difficult for most people with autism. Job choices are typically limited to work that requires only basic social skills. For example, most people with autism would have difficulty succeeding as a telephone receptionist or secretary; however, this same person may succeed at a clerical job that involves filing, sorting, stapling, and paper shredding, tasks that do not require extensive social skills. Therefore, whereas a lack of social skills may restrict job choice, there are many jobs to choose from that do not require advanced social skills. In fact, an unwillingness to engage in social interactions may be viewed as a benefit by supervisors and company owners because these employees are not likely to waste time engaging in unnecessary social interaction with co-workers.

However, a lack of social skills can make retaining employment extremely problematic and it is not unusual for a person with autism to be terminated because of socially inappropriate behaviors. Co-workers and supervisors are not likely to tolerate inappropriate touching, intrusive questions, or the inability to share work space. Frequently, specific social skills training is required for a worker with autism to be able to retain employment for any period of time. Persons with autism may need to be taught how to greet co-workers, what conversational topics are acceptable, how to initiate and terminate conversations, and how to relate to customers. Many workers can be taught how to perform these skills independently. Other workers need the ongoing assistance of job coaches or other support personnel to serve as on-site interpreters who help negotiate the social demands of the environment.

Sensory Characteristics

The sensory characteristics associated with autism make some job environments more suitable than others for these workers. Yet, people with autism differ markedly in their sensory characteristics. Some people with autism are extremely sensitive to sensory stimulation and others seem oblivious to it. In considering jobs for these workers, attention should be paid to the sensory characteristics of the job. Some jobs provide sensory stimulation that the employee with autism may find enjoyable. For example, a worker with autism may enjoy hanging clothing for retail store displays because of the tactile stimulation involved. Another worker may thrive at washing dishes or cars because of contact with water and soap. In contrast, other jobs have specific sensory stimulation that some workers with autism might have difficulty tolerating. For example, a job in a noisy warehouse would be an unsuitable choice for a person with autism who is sensitive to loud noises.

Difficulty Handling Change

Autism can be associated with resistance to change—a characteristic that might be a limiting factor in job choice for some workers. Some work environments require daily or hourly changes in task, schedule, or location, whereas other work environments remain the same for years. Many people with autism perform better in jobs that are relatively stable in terms of tasks, routines, and scheduling.

Visual-Motor Abilities

Many people with autism have relatively good visual-motor abilities and do well in jobs that capitalize upon this area of strength. Some people with autism excel at jobs that require fine motor skills, such as small component manufacturing and printing, whereas others excel at jobs that require gross motor skills, such as warehouse stock management.

Mental Retardation

Since individuals with autism may have any degree of mental retardation, for these people jobs need to be selected that mirror their adaptive and cognitive skill levels. Individuals with mild or moderate levels of mental retardation may be able to perform jobs that are unrealistic for persons with severe or profound levels of mental retardation. For example, a person with autism and mild mental retardation may be able to shelve books in a library by call number, whereas a person with autism and severe mental retardation may be limited to gluing the call numbers onto the book spines. The cognitive level of the worker must be taken into account to ensure that tasks are appropriately challenging without being unrealistic.

Behavior Problems

Behavior management plans can often significantly reduce or eliminate the behavior problems that are sometimes associated with autism. However, some problems may continue to occur at a low level, and, if so, these problems may dictate job choice. Clearly, if a person with autism displays behaviors that would be destructive to a particular business, or to the business's product or customers, the person would not be compatible in that environment. For example, if a worker has a long history of rectal digging and toileting problems, then restaurant work should be ruled out. If a worker has a history of smashing glass, then jobs that involve working with fragile merchandise and breakables should not be considered. Instead, job choices should center on environments in which the worker's behavioral repertoire will not prove dangerous or job threatening.

Even after considering individuals' behavioral characteristics when choosing jobs, their serious, sometimes dangerous maladaptive behaviors can surface and present serious risks to employment, including frequent job turnover. However, with sufficient supports and behavior programs, people with autism and challenging behaviors can retain their jobs.

In recent years, positive behavior strategies have been developed that can eliminate or at least reduce the frequency of these behaviors and decrease the threat they pose toward employment. Therefore, a major component of vocational development for individuals with autism is the need for proven behavior strategies consistently implemented by trained staff for an indeterminate period of time. In addition, employers need to be assured that behavior problems will be handled efficiently by job coaches and not pose a danger to customers and other employees.

Splinter Skills and Hidden Strengths

Individuals with autism sometimes have splinter skills that are superior to their overall functioning level and that can be capitalized on for employment purposes. Examples of splinter skills include excellent reading skills despite poor spoken language; the ability to match to sample; good rote memory, especially for visual information; and arithmetic skills. Some businesses may benefit from an employee with these skills. For example, jobs in managing wholesale or retail stock require matching stock numbers to packing lists, a task some people with autism are capable of doing.

Often splinter skills present themselves as hidden strengths that are related to the symptoms of autism but that have some utility in the work environment. Professionals and parents are often struck by the excellent attentional skills displayed by people with autism when pursuing activities that interest them. A person with autism may spend uninterrupted hours assembling puzzles, drawing intricate designs, arranging objects in specific order, pulling threads from fabric, or memorizing advertisement jingles. Although the task itself may have limited functional utility, many people with autism are capable of attending to activities for relatively long periods of time. It is possible to develop this ability to enhance job performance. Workers with autism often do better than their nondisabled counterparts because of their willingness to spend hours, days, and years performing the same repetitive tasks.

Many of the activities pursued by people with autism require attention to minute details, which is a valued skill for many jobs. For example, some individuals have a compulsion to arrange papers in a certain order. This compulsive behavior could be useful in an office job or a printing company where the person would sort, collate, and align papers for use in books and manuals. Likewise, ritualistic tendencies mean that people with autism are likely to do the same task in the same way each time. Many jobs in manufacturing, printing, and retail require exacting levels of precision. Furthermore, although people with autism may be slow to learn new tasks, they display an excellent ability to remember the steps of a task and repetitively perform them. This attention to minute detail coupled with a tendency to do tasks the same way every time means that, with the proper supports, people with autism are capable of maintaining high levels of productivity and work quality. These skills and abilities often allow the worker with autism to perform at superior levels during longer periods of time than workers without autism. Employers who seek to reduce job turnover often appreciate these characteristics.

IMPACT OF AUTISM ON EMPLOYABILITY

Individuals with autism present many challenging characteristics and behaviors that make them appear to be unsuitable candidates for competitive employment. Severe problems with social deficits inhibit normal relationships with co-workers and supervisors, and bizarre social behaviors annoy co-workers, supervisors, and the public. The language deficits often associated with autism can limit comprehension of instructions from supervisors and impinge on the ability to communicate pertinent needs to others. Poor attentional skills and off-task behaviors such as self-stimulation can make it unlikely that employees with autism will meet their employers' goals for productivity and quality. Furthermore, people with autism have difficulty learning tasks quickly and attending to tasks in a consistent manner, which often results in low-quality work and poor productivity, particularly in the early phases of employment. In addition, behavior problems can occur that pose a serious danger to others. In summary, the characteristics of autism make it difficult to obtain job positions, learn new job tasks, respond to the social demands of the workplace, and maintain employment.

On the surface, the employment prospects for people with autism appear bleak; however, experience has proven that with proper intervention and supports, individuals with autism can work in a variety of businesses and industries. Workers with autism have held such jobs as stock clerks in retail stores, electronic component assemblers, printers' assistants, clerical workers, bulk mailing clerks, tee-shirt manufacturers, advertisement flyer distributors, greeting card manufacturers, warehouse workers, catalog order fillers, computer cable assemblers, and recycling workers. They have been employed by small businesses, large national corporations, and government agencies. They have retained employment for as long as 10 years in one job. Their wages have ranged from 50% of minimum wage based on productivity to three times the current minimum wage with the majority of employees earning at least minimum wage.

Workers with autism have observable strengths that can be capitalized on to make them attractive prospects to employers. These include attention to detail and a willingness to do repetitive tasks with an apparent tolerance for boredom. For certain activities, people with autism have good on-task skills.

Specialized intervention and support services have mitigated the impact of the disorder on employability by enabling people with even severe autism to use their strengths in competitive employment. Specialized treatment includes positive behavioral interventions; job task training; social skills training; and assistance in communicating with supervisors, co-workers, and the public.

Ongoing support services may need to be provided to employees with autism from job coaches. In turn, job coaches need support from supported employment supervisors and instructional and behavioral specialists. It is important to remember that employees with autism may require intervention and support throughout the day for an indefinite period of time to succeed at work. In contrast, other individuals with autism may be able to work relatively independently with only drop-in supervision and self-managed behavior programs.

SUMMARY

The principal characteristics of autism are impaired language and nonverbal communication, deficits in socialization, and unusual responses to sensory stimulation. In addition, autism is associated with several other characteristics including mental retardation (70%–80% of people with autism also have some degree of mental retardation); rituals and compulsions; difficulty handling changes; and a variety of difficult, sometimes dangerous, behavior problems. People with autism generally have well-developed visual-motor skills and sometimes have savant skills.

Historically, people with autism have not had appropriate educational, residential, and vocational services. Many were institutionalized for long periods of time or expelled from the few available programs. Even when appropriate educational services were provided, they were unable to participate in their communities once they completed their educations. Typically, they did not succeed at vocational training centers for people with mental retardation and physical disabilities, and rarely were they considered for competitive employment. For the most part, people with autism have been excluded from recent supported employment initiatives as well.

Rehabilitation funding has historically excluded persons with autism because of their presumed lack of vocational fitness. Recent federal legislation, including changes in the designation of autism, changes in the rehabilitation law, the Americans with Disabilities Act of 1990, and changes in federal education laws have encouraging implications for people with autism. These changes make it easier to include people with autism in the vocationally oriented service system. However, a stable source of funding for supported employment services for adults is still lacking.

Experience has demonstrated that having autism does not mean a person is unemployable; rather, people with even severe autism have had successful job histories. When vocational choice is tempered by the characteristics of the individual worker and when adequate supports are provided, employability becomes a reality. Workers with autism have enjoyed paid, integrated, competitive employment in a variety of environments given realistic job choices and sufficient on-the-job training and support.

REFERENCES

American Psychiatric Association. (1987). *Diagnostic and statistical manual of mental disorders* (third edition—revised). Washington, DC: Author.

Americans with Disabilities Act of 1990 (PL 101-336, July 26, 1990), *U.S. Statutes at Large* 104 (Title 42 USC 12101) pp. 327–378.

Rutter, M., & Schopler, E. (1988). Autism and pervasive developmental disorders: Concepts and diagnostic issues. In E. Schopler & G.B. Mesibov (Eds.), *Diagnosis and assessment in autism* (pp. 15–36). New York: Plenum Press.

Schreibman, L. (1988). *Autism.* Beverly Hills, CA: Sage Publications.

Sigman, M., Ungerer, J.A., Mundy, P., & Sherman, T. (1987). Cognition in autistic children. In D.J. Cohen, A.M. Donnellan, & R. Paul (Eds.), *Handbook of autism and pervasive developmental disorders* (pp. 103–120). New York: John Wiley & Sons.

CHAPTER 2

Vocational Planning for Workers with Autism

Although workers with autism have many strengths and skills that make them valuable employees, they need more vocational planning than their co-workers without disabilities. Vocational planning for workers with autism includes a vocational assessment of the worker, an assessment of the supports that the worker may need, and methods for implementing the supports at work. This chapter discusses the process of vocational planning for workers with autism.

METHODS OF VOCATIONAL ASSESSMENT

Vocational planning for people with autism begins with an assessment of their vocational skills. The first goal of the vocational assessment is to determine the worker's strengths, weaknesses, and interests, and to evaluate the person's ability to perform jobs tasks. The second goal of the assessment is to determine the suitability of a particular job. The initial goal of vocational assessment can usually be accomplished in less than 1 month, at which point informed job choices can be made. Once the person has started a job, vocational assessment continues and provides information for making intervention decisions and, possibly, future employment decisions.

Traditionally, the abilities of people with autism have been underrated on vocational assessments, resulting in the conclusion that they were not ready for employment. Valid vocational assessments of people with autism must include a variety of techniques, including standardized tests and evaluations, criterion-based assessments, and more informal assessment techniques. These methods have advantages and disadvantages; yet, each contributes in some way to the vocational assessment process.

Standardized Assessments

Standardized assessments refer to any test or evaluation that is norm-referenced; that is, it takes the individual's raw test performance and converts it to a standard score that rates performance relative to some norm group. As such, standardized tests compare the performance of the person being assessed to the performance of a number of people who underwent the same assessment.

Standardized tests include tests of intelligence, academic skills, language abilities, social skills, and specific vocational abilities (e.g., the ability to do fine motor tasks). Standardized tests are particularly useful when the individual is not well known to supported employment staff and when other sources of information are not available. Information across a range of areas can be gleaned relatively quickly with these measures.

Information derived from standardized tests can be valuable in developing a list of the person's strengths and weaknesses, both of which have implications for job selection and job placement. Many people with autism have splinter skills that are not easily observable, but that can be detected by standardized testing. People with autism, because of their poor language skills, often seem less competent than they are. Standardized tests that measure nonverbal skills, such as visual-motor coordination, fine motor control, and nonverbal reasoning, often reveal that the person has marketable skills that were not readily apparent during informal observations. Additionally, some people with autism have relatively good language skills, a fact that obscures weaknesses in reasoning, judgment, and comprehension. Standardized tests can be instrumental in detecting these weaknesses.

Strengths and weaknesses detected by standardized tests can often help determine whether an individual should be considered for a certain job. Alma, for example, demonstrated superior skills in visual-motor coordination, visual discrimination, and fine motor coordination on a standardized intelligence test. This performance made her a good candidate for a job opening in a manufacturing firm that required assembly of small electronic parts.

Nonetheless, standardized tests have some limitations that must be considered. They are usually done in a manner that may underrate the vocational skills of someone with autism. Typically, standardized assessments are done in unfamiliar surroundings by people who are strangers to the person with autism. Because people with autism often do not behave well or perform optimally in novel situations, standardized assessments can underestimate their abilities and functioning levels. As an example, Larry, who now works as a retail stock clerk, was initially evaluated at a vocational assessment center. He had a difficult time in this unfamiliar environment, and, as a result, his vocational evaluation noted numerous and frequent behavior problems and difficulties with attention and task performance. The vocational evaluation recommended that Larry attend a vocational center before seeking employment, thereby underrating his potential. In fact, Larry went on to become a successful employee in a retail warehouse, using well-developed gross motor abilities that he had not revealed in the testing situation.

Typically, people with autism are compared to norm groups of people without autism. Usually, these norm groups are made up of people with average intelligence or mental retardation. Those with autism often do not score well compared to these norm groups. For example, Larry scored in the more severely disabled range on vocational tests, but his subsequent employment history as a retail stock clerk bore out his work skills.

Standardized vocational assessments are time-limited, static evaluations; that is, they evaluate either what individuals know or what they can do at the time of the testing. Although static evaluations have some utility in terms of what a worker can do, they fail to capture what the person with autism is capable of learning or doing over time. The fact that Meredith falls far below average on a small component assembly task that she does for an hour during a vocational evaluation does not mean she cannot meet expected productivity rates for an electronic assembly task after she does it at an actual job for several weeks. This last point means that standardized assessments may be lacking in terms of predictive validity; that is, performance on these assessments does not accurately predict performance on an actual job task.

Standardized assessments are often oriented toward uncovering deficits in functioning in that they focus on what the person is supposedly incapable of doing. This information can limit the job search. For example, Larry's evaluation noted his obvious deficits but it failed to discover that he has good on-task skills in structured environments. Information on what workers can do is more valuable than what they cannot do when considering jobs in competitive industries.

Criterion-Referenced Assessments

Criterion-referenced assessments measure the individual's ability to do a specified task by collecting performance data on the steps of that task. These assessments can be used to evaluate the person's vocational abilities by taking data on some specific vocational skill. As such, criterion-referenced assessments provide the most direct measure of what an individual can actually do. Ongoing criterion-referenced assessments can be done by taking baseline data on job tasks, setting goal criteria, and then collecting ongoing data to determine whether goal criteria are achieved.

Criterion-referenced assessments can be done prior to employment on sample tasks from jobs that the employee might be seeking. For example, if the employee is considering working at a poster manufacturing firm, criterion-referenced assessment might be done on rolling posters prior to job placement. The task of rolling posters is then broken down into its component steps, and the individual's ability to do each step of the task is measured. In some cases, it is possible to have the individual with autism actually do a real job for a period of time to evaluate performance. Some employers may have temporary work that allows for sampling of job performance. In addition, community training sites can be established at some businesses. These sites typically allow the individual with autism the opportunity to work in a job for a period of time without pay.

It is highly desirable that most criterion-referenced assessments occur on the job. Such on-the-job assessments occur by placing the worker with autism in the best-matched job and then performing an ongoing criterion-referenced assessment process. For example, Meredith, a woman with severe autism, did not undergo extensive vocational evaluations. Instead, a review of her records and her psychological evaluation suggested that she had better visual-motor skills than language abilities. Therefore, she was placed in a job as an electronic component assembler shortly after she entered the supported employment program. Her criterion-based vocational assessment included taking data on her productivity rate and the accuracy of her work output. In addition, data was taken on important social skills such as asking for help and greeting co-workers.

In general, criterion-referenced assessments should be used to measure productivity rates, production accuracy, and the ability to check for and correct errors. These three skills can serve as a basis for reliable job performance in virtually any job position. A productivity rate is assessed by simply measuring the rate of product output. This may be the number of boxes packed, posters rolled, plastic bags filled and sealed, or clothing placed on hangers. Accuracy can be assessed by recording whether or not the worker correctly and independently performed the steps of the task. Checking and correcting for errors is done by recording whether or not the employee identified and corrected errors. Meredith received criterion-referenced assessment on productivity and accuracy, and because her accuracy was excellent she did not need to check or correct her errors.

Criterion-referenced assessments are useful for people with autism for a number of reasons. First, they can be done by people who are known to the individual, such as a job trainer or a job coach. Second, because criterion-referenced assessments can be done by familiar people in familiar surroundings, such as the supported employment agency or on the job, they create circumstances that tend to optimize the performance of the workers.

Third, criterion-referenced assessments are not norm-referenced. An individual's performance is compared to a set goal or criterion, not to the performance of some norm group. As such, they offer greater utility than norm-referenced assessments. For example, an ongoing criterion-referenced assessment of Meredith's productivity in assembling electronic components let both support staff and her employer know exactly what her rate of productivity was. In contrast, Meredith's score on a norm-referenced assessment, such as an intelligence test, might have little or no relationship to her productivity rates at work.

Fourth, criterion-referenced assessments are oriented toward uncovering the individual's vocational strengths and toward providing effective instruction to meet vocational goals. A competency orientation initially helps support staff make decisions concerning whether or not an individual with autism would succeed at a specific job. Once the worker begins the new job, criterion-referenced assessments provide frequent measures of how well vocational goals are being attained.

Fifth, criterion-referenced assessments are dynamic, not static, because they provide an ongoing assessment of the worker's vocational skills; that is, assessment of skills does not stop until set criteria are achieved. Even after criteria are achieved, assessment probes may be necessary to ensure that learned skills are remembered and used when necessary. In addition, as the requirements of the job change, the nature of the skills being assessed also changes. For example, when Meredith mastered the task of soldering wires, a criterion-referenced assessment was done on a probe basis once per month. When her job was changed to include a new assembly task, a criterion-referenced assessment was started immediately to determine baseline skill level and the effectiveness of training strategies.

Finally, unlike standardized assessments, criterion-referenced assessments allow for evaluating the generalization of learned skills; that is, they can be used to evaluate whether learned skills are used in new environments. For example, Wesley was trained to say "good morning" to his supervisor. A criterion-referenced assessment was then used to determine whether he also said "good morning" to co-workers. The assessment of generalization is particularly important for workers with autism who are not likely to generalize spontaneously.

Informal Assessments

Informal assessment refers to evaluations that are done by support personnel without giving formal tests. These assessments rely primarily upon gathering information on the individual's vocational skills, language abilities, and behavioral competencies from a variety of sources. Informal assessments share many of the advantages of criterion-referenced assessments. To begin with, there is no need for the person with autism to be separated from familiar people and familiar environments because the assessments are done by interview, record review, and observation. Informal assessments are also not norm-referenced; they consist solely of gathering information on the individual's vocational competencies and needs without regard to the performance of other people. Informal assessments are also dynamic in that they collect information on the person's vocational skills as observed over a period of time by previous caregivers. Information on vocational strengths, interventions that work, learning styles, and generalization of learned skills can all be collected using informal assessments. Informal assessments include a review of records, interviews with previous caregivers, behavioral observations, and trial and error.

Review of Records Reviewing records provides useful information concerning what the individual is capable of doing, the individual's work experience, and training strategies that have been effective or ineffective. For people with autism, record reviews are particularly useful to catalog behavior problems that can interfere with vocational performance. For example, a review of Meredith's records suggested that she had excellent fine motor skills and attention to detail. This information was included in her vocational assessment and led to recommendations for pursuing manufacturing jobs. In addition, although she had these valuable work skills, she also had periods of aggression, self-injury, and property destruction, all of which were likely to impinge on her vocational success if left untreated. Uncovering this information in her records allowed Meredith's support personnel to take preventive measures in the vocational planning process.

Interviews with Caregivers   Caregivers can be interviewed for more information about a person with autism. Caregivers may include parents, previous teachers if the individual was in school, and program staff who have been responsible for the care of the individual. Usually, people who have worked closely with a person with autism have in-depth knowledge of his or her strengths and weaknesses, likes and dislikes. They can also assist in evaluating whether certain job positions would be suitable for the individual. Caregivers tend to relate more information about the individuals' weaknesses and training and intervention needs than about their strengths; therefore, it is important to encourage them to comment on the individuals' abilities as well as disabilities.

Observation   Observing the person performing vocational or prevocational tasks in his or her job placement provides the most direct source of information regarding what the individual is capable of doing. Direct observation also gives clear implications for intervention needs. For example, Larry's ability to attend to task in structured situations was not reported in his norm-referenced vocational evaluation or by previous caregivers; it only became apparent as staff observed him doing different tasks in structured situations. Similarly, supported employment staff observed that Joe paced excessively, but that he had a good sense of direction. Therefore, they thought Joe would enjoy a job delivering advertisement flyers to homes in his neighborhood.

Trial and Error Assessments   Individuals who receive supported employment often hold several jobs before settling into a stable job position. For example, Ike had jobs as a bulk mailing clerk and printing company employee before finding long-term employment in a warehouse position. Such job turnover should not be viewed as a failure of the individual, but as a failure to find a suitable job match. As such, information gleaned from job turnover has valuable implications for vocational development and should be included in any ongoing vocational assessment. It is likely that a person with autism will not succeed at a particular job if similar jobs resulted in failure. Joe's continual difficulty at sitting still for even brief periods of time made it unlikely he would succeed at jobs similar to the bulk mailing or printing company jobs.

AREAS OF VOCATIONAL ASSESSMENT

A thorough vocational assessment on a worker with autism entails using a variety of assessment methods to evaluate vocational functioning in several different areas. Areas of vocational assessment include basic work skills, communication skills, social skills, ability to follow instructions, skills required to do certain jobs, functional academic skills, learning style assessment, vocational preferences, and behavior challenges. The lack of specific skills is not used to exclude a worker from competitive employment; rather, the results of an assessment are used to make decisions about the job match, support needs, and intervention needs of the worker with autism.

Basic Work Skills

Basic work skills refer to the skills needed in virtually any job position. In many instances, the absence of these skills has been used to exclude persons with autism from the work force. Basic work skills that need to be evaluated include personal grooming, toileting, attendance and punctuality, transportation skills to and from work, and attention to task.

Communication Skills

An evaluation of communication skills is an important component of the vocational evaluation process. The focus of the evaluation needs to be on functional communication as it might relate to employment. Ideally, communication skills are evaluated in a norm-referenced fashion, as well as informally to assess relevance to potential jobs.

Communication skills to assess include the ability to communicate basic wants and needs and to relate personal information about oneself such as name and address. For people with expressive language, it is necessary to evaluate their comprehension of language. Evaluation of written communication skills may also be helpful, since for some people with autism, the ability to use written language is a strength. In addition, efforts must be made to evaluate work-related communication skills such as asking for assistance when necessary, requesting work materials when needed, and asking for clarification on instructions. Finally, information is needed on communication-related idiosyncracies, such as repetitive questioning, echolalia, verbal perseverations, and verbal rituals.

The communication evaluation must be done in a realistic and functional manner so that informed decisions can be made about the job match. The absence of spoken language does not preclude employment, but it must be taken into account in the job match process. Similarly, good expressive language coupled with comprehension problems does not rule out employment, but it does have implications for the job match.

Social Skills

Assessment of social skills is a necessary area for vocational assessment. Although the absence of rudimentary social skills does not rule out employment, it certainly will have an impact on the job match process. The assessment of social behaviors should include an evaluation of essential social skills, such as greeting and conversing with others, as well as attention to aberrant behaviors, such as touching others inappropriately and repetitively asking personal questions.

Response to Verbal Instruction

It is important to evaluate a worker's ability to understand and respond to verbal instructions. This assessment should focus on the number of steps that a worker is able to follow in sequence. For instance, Joe has difficulty following even single-step instructions, whereas Meredith can remember and independently follow multiple-step instructions. The ability to follow instructions has implications for job selection. Workers who have difficulty following lengthy instructions are more likely to succeed at jobs with simple tasks, whereas workers who are adept at following and remembering several steps can perform more complicated job tasks.

Requisite Skills

Each job has requisite skills and it is important to assess if a worker with autism has or can learn them. Requisite skills to be assessed may include work rate, work accuracy, strength, endurance, gross or fine motor skills, mobility, and attention to task. In some instances, the need for requisite skills may preclude employment. For example, a job that requires high levels of visual discrimination would be improbable for a worker with a visual impairment. Likewise, a job that requires physical strength would be improbable for a worker with poor muscle development.

The need for requisite skills might not rule out a particular job, but it may be considered an intervention need. For example, Dylan may initially have difficulty meeting the accuracy requirements of rolling posters straight, but he can be taught to improve his accuracy. It is essential to distinguish between workers who can and cannot learn requisite skills in order to avoid excluding workers with autism from good employment opportunities. When the vocational assessment is inconclusive, the best alternative is to place the worker with autism in the job and allow him or her the chance to succeed.

In assessing requisite skills, it is necessary to evaluate the worker only for those skills that are required at the particular job. For instance, Meredith's vocational assessment revealed that she could probably work as an electronic assembler doing one task repeatedly at a table and working at her own pace. It was determined that she had the requisite skills, including a moderate but steady work pace, reasonable on-task attention, and fine motor skills. In contrast, Meredith would probably not do well at a fast-paced assembly line job.

Functional Academic Skills

It is generally useful to assess the worker's functional academic skills to assist in job selection. Some people with autism have superior reading, writing, and arithmetic skills, whereas others have no academic abilities. High level academic abilities are essential in many jobs such as clerical filing positions—only workers with necessary academic skills should be considered for these jobs. However, for any worker with autism, the absence of academic skills should not be used to exclude him or her from other jobs that require low levels of academic skills. For example, Larry has a job as a retail merchandise pricer despite being unable to read the price list or adjust the pricing gun. His job coach or other support personnel provide assistance while these skills are being taught, including long-term support if necessary. Some workers can use good match-to-sample skills to compensate for an inability to read. For example, Charles cannot read, but he works in a library where he sorts books into bins. He does this task by matching the letter codes on the spines of the books with the letters on the bins.

Learning Style Assessment

Knowing how an individual with autism best learns a task can be a valuable piece of information to learn during the assessment process. Some people with autism, such as Meredith, learn well with modeling and verbal instruction alone, whereas others require more physical assistance to learn. When a worker with autism also has mental retardation, more intensive instructional strategies such as prompt hierarchies may be necessary. The style of learning for an individual with autism can be determined by interviewing past instructors and by trying different techniques to see which work best.

Vocational Preferences

The assessment of vocational preferences can be particularly difficult with people with autism. However, some people with autism may be able to express their vocational preferences and all verbal people with autism should be interviewed to discern their preferences. Unfortunately, many verbal people with autism may be unable to adequately express their personal vocational preferences due to language impairments and a lack of knowledge about vocational options. In addition, interviewing on personal preferences is impossible for nonverbal individuals. In general, the personal preferences of these workers must be gleaned from an intimate knowledge of the individuals' likes and dislikes. For example, working at a job that results in soiled hands and clothing would not be a preference for a woman with autism who is meticulous about her physical appearance. Similarly, a man who has demonstrated a long-term aversion to water would not be happy washing cars for a living.

Behavior Challenges

As discussed in Chapter 1, disruptive or even destructive behaviors that are challenges to employment can be associated with autism. Problems with aggression, self-injury, pica, elopement, stereotypy, motor rituals, screaming, and unusual vocalizations should be identified. The history and frequency of these behaviors should also be ascertained if possible. The vocational assessment should include a description of these challenges and, if possible, the functions of the problematic behaviors and the strategies that have been successful in their amelioration. Assessment of behavior challenges can be done through observation, a review of records, and interviews with people familiar with the person with autism.

ASSESSMENT OF SUPPORTS

One of the principal ways to ensure the vocational success of individuals with autism is to make good decisions about the level of support required for competitive employment. One of the most frequent errors is not planning for adequate support upon initial acceptance into the supported employment program. Decisions that ensure that appropriate levels of support are provided from the beginning of employment can greatly increase the likelihood of vocational success.

Information Gathering

Assessing the level of support necessary to ensure vocational success requires collecting comprehensive information about the worker from a variety of sources. As discussed earlier in this chapter, information on the worker can be gathered from a review of records, interviews with caregivers, direct observations of the individual, and an evaluation from a psychologist.

Areas of Assessment

When considering the level of support to be provided to a person with autism, special consideration needs to be given to behavior problems, language skills, social skills, toileting skills, transportation skills, and responses to change.

Behavior Problems The presence of behavior problems is the single most important factor in considering the level of support to be provided. As discussed earlier, people with autism sometimes engage in behaviors that are decidedly dangerous to themselves or others, such as aggression, self-injury, pica, property destruction, and running away from staff. These behaviors need to be given special consideration in determining the level of support. Other behaviors such as self-stimulation and rituals may not be dangerous, but they still have an impact on decisions concerning the level of support needed.

A thorough assessment of behavior problems is recommended before making any commitments to the level of support to be provided. Factors to consider include the nature of the behavior problems (i.e., what the person does), the number of behavior problems, the frequency, the severity, the duration, and the predictability (i.e., how easy it is to predict that a problem behavior will occur). In addition, staff should assess the person's ability to respond to redirection when engaging in a problem behavior. Finally, attention should be paid to the social acceptability of the problem behavior. Behaviors such as loud humming while working are more acceptable on the job than are aggression, property destruction, and feces smearing.

For each person with autism, all of the above behavior factors should be considered when determining support needs. Individuals with autism who engage in dangerous behaviors should always be provided with direct supervision from a job coach who is trained to prevent injury. Provided that these behaviors are sporadic and manageable, the job coach may be able to supervise other workers at the same time. For example, Meredith can be aggressive, self-injurious, and destructive to property; however, these behaviors occur sporadically, are often predictable, and are relatively short in duration. Thus, Meredith's job coach supervises one other worker with autism who has no other dangerous behaviors.

For a few workers with autism, the nature, number, frequency, and severity of behaviors is such that one-to-one supervision and treatment from a job coach is necessary to ensure their safety. Fred displays a variety of self-injurious behaviors, such as head banging against walls, arm biting, skin picking, and hitting himself in the head with objects. These behaviors occur many times an hour and are severe enough to cause physical damage. Fred requires constant monitoring and intervention to prevent injury, as well as one-to-one supervision from a job coach. It is important to note that Fred would require this high level of supervision to ensure his safety regardless of whether he was in an institution, a vocational center, or a competitive job.

Often, it is possible to decrease the level of support provided as behavior problems decrease and more appropriate behaviors are learned. However, a conservative approach is to always provide continual supervision if a dangerous behavior has occurred within the past year.

Some people with autism do not have any dangerous behaviors but still display behaviors that are job threatening. These include verbal outbursts, noncompliance, noise making, and hyperactivity. The continual presence of a job coach may be necessary to provide behavioral treatment for these problems and reduce their threat to employment.

Language Skills   The language abilities of a person with autism also have implications for the level of support needed. In general, people who are nonverbal or have extremely limited language will need more support than persons with better developed language skills. People who cannot speak are unable to express their needs to supervisors and co-workers; therefore, they require the support of a job coach to anticipate their needs and function as their communicator. Workers who can talk but do not use language functionally require the assistance of a job coach to teach necessary language skills and to support the employees in evolving efforts to use language. The job coach is also necessary to act as a language mediator between the individual and others in the work environment. In contrast, someone with autism and good functional language abilities may be a good candidate for part-time support from a job coach or independence on the job.

Social Skills In assessing social skills to help determine support needs, it is important to attend to both social skill deficits and to the presence of maladaptive social behaviors. People with autism who have fairly well-developed social skills and no disruptive, job-threatening social behaviors may be able to work with a low level of support or work independently. In contrast, workers with few social skills probably need the full- or part-time support of a job coach to assist them in social interactions and to assist with integration.

The presence of inappropriate social behaviors is reason for full-time support from a job coach. Intrusive, inappropriate social skills, such as asking repetitive questions, speaking too closely to others, and touching others inappropriately, can be annoying to supervisors, co-workers, and the public. Workers with such behaviors often require continual supervision from the job coach to manage the behaviors and teach appropriate social behaviors. If inappropriate social behaviors are not disruptive, or happen infrequently, and if the worker is competent in job performance, full-time job coaching might not be necessary. If available, support from a co-worker might suffice.

Toileting Skills Most workers with autism have adequate toileting skills; however, some workers with autism have difficulty using the bathroom independently and may engage in feces smearing if left unattended. In fact, for some persons with autism, problems with toileting will be their most job-threatening behavior. For workers with toileting problems, it is important that they receive continual supervision from a job coach when they use the bathroom. Employers and co-workers are not likely to tolerate messy bathrooms and typically will not volunteer to perform toileting-related supervision.

Transportation Skills The need for instruction or assistance in traveling to and from work should always be included in assessing the level of support needed. Many people with autism display a good sense of direction and an excellent memory for bus routes; they require minimal instruction before traveling to and from work independently. However, in assessing the transportation needs of workers with autism, safety should always be the primary concern. If someone with autism is going to take public transportation independently, it is important to consider how behavior problems may have an impact on other people using the same transportation. Some individuals with autism may have the skills required to travel independently, but may also display behaviors such as aggression, self-injury, property destruction, or touching strangers—all of which preclude independent travel. Workers with dangerous behaviors or inappropriate social behaviors that may draw adverse reactions from strangers should not be allowed to travel independently. Instead, they should be provided with long-term supervision and instruction on how to use and behave on public transportation. After there have been no problem behaviors for a specified period of time, such as 1 year, supervision can be faded out. Occasional covert observations of workers using public transportation helps ensure that behavioral gains are maintained. However, some people with autism will probably always need supervision on public transportation because of their functioning level and behavior problems.

Responses to Change Catastrophic responses to change can be the most problematic aspect of teaching people with autism in the community. It is not unusual for a minor change to precipitate violent or self-injurious behaviors. How an individual with autism responds to change should always be assessed as part of determining support needs. People with autism who have few behavior problems but have adverse reactions to change may require low levels of support during times of stability and increased levels of support during times of change.

NECESSARY SUPPORTS

Workers with autism have typically been excluded from integrated, competitive employment because of the learning, social, and behavior challenges they present. Although workers with autism have been successful in working in a variety of jobs, this success has not been achieved independent of support. A variety of supports are necessary if more individuals with autism are to succeed in the workplace. Supports include job coaching, behavior management, instructional technology, and natural supports. Table 2.1 provides guidelines for establishing necessary supports based upon an assessment of the worker's behavior problems, language abilities, social skills, and cognitive functioning level. Table 2.2 includes some sample cases for determining supports.

Job Coach

Many individuals with autism can work only with the assistance of a job coach. The job coach may be needed full-time, part-time, or on a drop-in basis. There are a variety of roles that the job coach might need to fill to adequately support the worker with autism. These roles include providing assistance with adapting to the culture of the workplace, integration, learning the task, communication, and behavior management. The job coach might need to remain with the worker throughout the workday to provide instruction, supervision, monitoring, and behavior management. In some cases, less-than-continuous job coaching is needed and drop-in supervision may be sufficient.

Adaptation Any worker who starts a new job must become familiar with the rules and culture of the workplace. Rules and culture include such details as dress code, amount of talking or noise making that is tolerated, and time and place of breaks. Location and access to the employee lounge, cafeteria, lockers, vending machines, and other relevant areas must also be learned. Because many workers with autism have no verbal language or limited verbal language,

Table 2.1. Guidelines for establishing supports

Behavior problem	Language abilities	Social skills	Cognitive functioning level	Necessary supports
Dangerous behaviors, such as aggression, self-injury, property destruction, pica, or running away	Nonverbal to speaks in sentences	Extremely deficient to limited	Normal to profound mental retardation	Continuous job coach support to manage dangerous behavior Behavior management program Social skills training Back-up emergency support available
Disruptive, possible job-threatening behavior, such as noise making, hyperactivity, inattention to work, and self-stimulation	Nonverbal to speaks in sentences	Extremely deficient to limited	Normal to profound mental retardation	Continuous job coach support to manage job-threatening behavior Behavior management program Perhaps social skills training
No dangerous or job-threatening behavior within last year	Nonverbal to speaks in few words	Deficient to limited	Moderate to profound mental retardation	Continuous job coach support to teach work tasks and bridge social skills and language gap Social skills training

| No dangerous or job-threatening behavior within last year | Speaks in sentences but does not use language functionally | Limited but generally appropriate | Normal to mild mental retardation | Intermittent job coach support to teach work tasks and assist with social skills
Self-managed behavior program to maintain gains
Social skills training |
| No dangerous or job-threatening behavior within last year | Speaks in sentences and can use language functionally | Limited but appropriate | Normal to moderate mental retardation | Natural supports
Drop-in assistance and checks to help implement natural supports
Self-managed behavior plan to maintain behavior gains |

Table 2.2. Sample cases for determining supports

Behavior problems	Language abilities	Social skills	Cognitive functioning level	Necessary supports
Running away Pica	Nonverbal	Extremely deficient	Severe mental retardation	Continuous job coach supervision to prevent injury Behavior management program run by job coach Instructional programs
Severe, frequent self-injury Aggression Self-stimulation	Speaks in a few words	Extremely deficient	Moderate mental retardation	Continuous one-to-one job coach supervision to prevent injury Behavior management program run by job coach Instructional programs
Infrequent periods of agitation Inappropriate sexual behavior	Speaks in sentences on a few topics	Very limited	Moderate mental retardation	Continuous job coach supervision to manage infrequent, but job-threatening behaviors Behavior management program run by job coach Social skills training
Aggression Self-injury Property destruction	Speaks in full sentences	Limited and inappropriate	Moderate mental retardation	Continuous job coach supervision to manage dangerous behavior and prevent injury Behavior management program run by job coach Social skills training

				Intermittent supervision from job coach who works with another person at the same company Ability to provide one-to-one supervision during a crisis Social skills training Self-managed behavior program
Rare head banging but can be dangerous	Speaks in full sentences but has difficulty using language functionally	Limited but appropriate social skills	Moderate mental retardation	
Aggression Self-scratching Clothes tearing Cursing Yelling	Speaks in full sentences but has difficulty using language functionally	Limited social skills	Mild mental retardation	Continuous supervision from job coach to manage dangerous behaviors Self-managed behavior program Social skills training
No current dangerous behaviors, but history of aggression and property destruction	Speaks in full sentences and uses language functionally	Withdrawn but adequate, appropriate social skills	Mild mental retardation	Natural supports Weekly drop-in supervision from support personnel Self-managed rating system

(continued)

33

Table 2.2. (continued)

Behavior problems	Language abilities	Social skills	Cognitive functioning level	Necessary supports
No dangerous or job-threatening behaviors	Speaks in full sentences and uses language functionally	Withdrawn but adequate, appropriate social skills	Borderline cognitive functioning	Natural supports Telephone contacts by support personnel to employer
Self-injury Rituals Noncompliance	Speaks in full sentences	Withdrawn but adequate, appropriate social skills	Normal cognitive functioning	Continuous job coach supervision to manage injurious behaviors and encourage working Behavior management programs
No dangerous or job-threatening behaviors	Speaks in full sentences	Withdrawn but adequate, appropriate social skills	Normal cognitive functioning	Natural supports

the job coach may need to teach the employee how to adapt to the rules and culture of the workplace. This teaching can be done informally or formally (e.g., incorporating workplace rules and amenities into a behavior management plan or formal instruction plan).

Integration The job coach may need to play a key role in integrating the worker with autism into the workplace. Individuals with autism often have severe social difficulties that may result in withdrawal from others. In these cases, the job coach will need to draw the worker out and help incorporate him or her into the social culture of the workplace. In other cases, the worker with autism may be outgoing, but so socially inappropriate that integration is not achieved. In these cases, the job coach needs to help the worker develop appropriate social skills to maximize integration. Finally, some workers with autism have no verbal language and the job coach can serve as a mediator between the worker and environment. For example, the job coach of a nonverbal worker with autism taught her to approach each co-worker in the morning and wave a greeting. Workers with autism who are invited to eat lunch with co-workers and attend company picnics, Christmas parties, and other gatherings often need the job coach to go along to ensure cooperative participation.

Socialization Workers with autism may need specific, formal training in the social skills necessary to adapt to the workplace, and the job coach can provide daily or weekly social skills training. Although in some cases it is possible to phase out the job coach once the skills are learned and demonstrated, in other cases the job coach may be required to provide necessary cues and reinforcers to ensure the continued use of those social skills.

Instructional Assistance Often, workers with autism who are nonverbal and have profound mental retardation can learn job tasks rapidly and can then work at rates comparable to co-workers who do not have disabilities. However, workers with autism who are challenged by language deficits and learning problems might find it impossible to learn directly from a co-worker or supervisor. Even workers with autism who have relatively good language skills might need concrete instruction and teaching methods that ensure maintenance and generalization. In these cases, a job coach is needed who has the skills to communicate and teach workers with autism.

Maintenance of Job Performance For many workers with autism, simply learning the job task is not sufficient to guarantee maintenance of job skills or adequate levels of productivity. Often, a job coach is needed to assist the worker in these areas.

Communication Communication deficits associated with autism can be devastating. A worker with autism who is nonverbal or has severe deficits in expression and comprehension needs a job coach to serve as a communication bridge between him or her and the employer. Instructions, changes in routine, and feedback might need to be communicated by the job coach in a precise manner so that they can be understood and tolerated by the worker with autism.

Behavior Management Although destructive behaviors such as self-injury and aggression have traditionally been considered incompatible with employment, many workers with autism who display these behaviors have successfully held jobs. However, in all cases of successful employment, workers with autism and destructive behaviors had behavior management plans. Behavior management plans are implemented by job coaches who receive intensive on-site training and monitoring. Although it is often possible to teach self-management to a worker with autism, for those individuals who exhibit aggression, self-injury, or property destruction, successful behavior management should include ongoing job coaching. Once difficult behaviors have been brought under control, or even eliminated, it might be necessary for the job coach to continue implementation of a behavior management plan to prevent recurrence of destructive behavior. The role of the job coach in behavior management of individuals with no verbal skills or limited verbal skills is especially critical and it is difficult to fade.

Safety Individuals with destructive behaviors of aggression and self-injury can pose a threat to the safety of themselves and others. Individuals who have problems with property destruction or misuse of property pose a threat to the property of co-workers and the employer. Although severe aggression, self-injury, and property destruction do not preclude employment, it is imperative to ensure the safety of the worker with autism, as well as co-workers, customers, and property. In cases where dangerous behavior is a risk, the job coach needs to be competent to intervene to prevent injury.

Behavior Management Plan

Some workers with autism have deficits in social skills that can be corrected by time-limited social skills training. However, there are individuals with autism who have severe behavior problems and who can hold jobs only with the support of a behavior management plan. Behavior management plans can be implemented directly at work by the job coach, and they can be effective in managing even the most severe behavior problems, including aggression, self-injury, and property destruction. Behavior management plans work through a variety of strategies and have multiple purposes, including instruction, contingency management, and prevention.

Instruction Behavior management plans can be instrumental in teaching social and behavioral skills at work. Often, problem behaviors can be found to have a definite purpose or function for the individual, and a behavior management plan with an instructional component is needed to teach the worker with autism a more acceptable behavior. For example, Joey often screamed and flapped his arms at his job at a printing company. A functional assessment revealed that the purpose of this behavior was to obtain assistance with his task. His behavior plan included social skills training to teach him how to ask for assistance when having difficulty with a task.

Motivation   At times, it is necessary to use a formal behavior management plan to provide motivation for the worker with autism to do the job or to conform to social expectations. Motivation can be provided through a variety of schedules of positive reinforcement. Numerous reinforcers are naturally available at the workplace, such as praise, social attention, handshakes, soft drinks, vending machines, the opportunity to visit with other workers, and the opportunity to take breaks from work. Positive reinforcement might be needed to increase productivity and to strengthen acceptable social behaviors. In the example of Joey, mentioned above, not only was he taught how to ask for assistance, he was also provided with reinforcers for working quietly without screaming, as well as for asking for assistance.

Decrease Problem Behaviors   Behavior management plans might be necessary to decrease the frequency of problem behaviors at work. Many workers with autism have behaviors that, if unchecked, could result in termination. Screaming, loud noise making, excessive self-stimulation, motor or verbal rituals, property destruction, pica, self-injury, and aggression are examples of behaviors that could jeopardize employment. If these behaviors are present, a behavior management plan is necessary to decrease their frequency. Reducing the frequency of problem behaviors can often be achieved by providing the workers with other means for achieving their purposes, by providing positive reinforcement for more acceptable behaviors, and by placing the problem behaviors on extinction.

Avoid Problem Behaviors   The behavior management plan often includes strategies for preventing the occurrence of problem behaviors. Prevention can often be accomplished if the functional assessment has identified antecedents and setting events that trigger misbehavior, and the environment can then be rearranged to eliminate or mitigate the effects of those events. For example, Albert often was self-injurious upon arrival at work. A functional assessment revealed that a setting event leading to self-injury was a small breakfast. This setting event was eliminated by making sure he had a large breakfast before leaving for work. In another example, Linda often screamed during thunderstorms. Although thunderstorms could not be eliminated, their effects could be mitigated by providing Linda with additional attention and assistance during the thunderstorms, and drawing the curtains so that she was not as distracted by the rain as she performed her job tasks.

Maintain Gains   Dramatic reductions in problem behaviors can be seen within several weeks of implementing a behavior management plan at work. However, withdrawal or even fading of the plan can result in a recurrence of problem behaviors. Often the continuing implementation of the behavior plan is needed to maintain gains at work.

Instructional Procedures

Workers with autism can often learn complex tasks, but they do not necessarily learn them as easily or as quickly as workers without autism. Instructional procedures are often needed as a support to learn the job task and to achieve acceptable levels of productivity and accuracy. Instructional procedures may be informal, such as demonstration or verbal instruction. Or, they may be formal, such as prompt systems, graduated guidance, stimulus fading, shaping, or other procedures to enhance generalization and maintenance.

Natural Supports

Many individuals with autism need more support than is naturally occurring in the workplace. For individuals with severe autism, successful employment can only be maintained with intensive support. In many cases, support entails constant monitoring to ensure that work is done and that cooperative behavior is maintained. Workers with pica must be closely observed during all waking hours to prevent ingestion of inedibles. Workers with high frequency self-injury require close supervision and implementation of time-consuming behavior programs to maintain safe behavior. Workers with histories of property destruction often cannot be left unmonitored for even a few minutes. The time and training necessary to support these workers is not naturally occurring in the workplace and must be provided for these workers so that they may succeed vocationally.

There are workers with autism who are minimally affected by the disorder. These individuals have relatively strong communication skills, no challenging behaviors, and do not have profound mental retardation. Although these individuals are awkward socially and may need adapted instruction when beginning the job, they are often capable of working with naturally occurring supports. These workers can often maintain successful employment with the help of involved co-workers or supervisors who are willing to expend additional time on providing instructions and assistance.

Some individuals with autism may need intensive support at the beginning of employment. At this time, a job coach is needed to teach the rules of the workplace as well as the job tasks. Once the worker adapts to the workplace and the task, outside support can be faded and co-workers and supervisors can take over the supervision and assistance. A job coach or other outside support personnel might need to do drop-in visits to provide monitoring and supplemental instruction as needed.

Some workers with autism need no outside support. These workers tend to be much less disabled by autism and do not have serious behavior problems in their repertoire. These workers may be able to maintain employment solely with the assistance of co-workers and supervisors who may or may not need to provide extra assistance.

Other workers with autism may function best with a combination of natural supports and job coaching. Natural supports may be used to provide some instruction, monitoring, and assistance with integration. In addition to the natural supports, job coaching can provide specialized instruction, intensive behavior management, and emergency support should dangerous behavior problems occur.

Co-workers and company supervisors can provide supports to the worker with autism in a variety of ways.

1. Co-workers can provide additional instructional assistance following initial training by a supervisor.
2. Co-workers or supervisors can provide support in the form of motivation by providing attention, feedback, and even praise throughout the week.
3. Co-workers or supervisors can assist the worker to become integrated into the work environment by eating lunch with the worker, taking breaks with the worker, inviting the worker to company social events, or assisting the worker in engaging in social activities with other workers.
4. Co-workers can provide instructions and feedback to the worker with autism on how to behave at social events, group meetings, or when interpersonal activities are necessary. For example, one young man with autism needed to be gently told by co-workers that it was impolite to eat the entire birthday cake at a co-worker's birthday party. Another young man with autism was questioning a supervisor and was so intent on getting a response that he followed her into the women's bathroom to continue the conversation. The supervisor needed to educate this young man on workplace etiquette.

When determining the amount of support needed for the worker with autism, it is important to consider the fact that individuals with autism have traditionally been excluded from the workplace, and even today they are vastly underrepresented in supported employment efforts. Successful employment cannot be achieved without adequate supports, and often those supports are not naturally occurring. The danger in the premature push for natural supports is that if the supports are insufficient and the worker fails, the worker might be considered generally unfit for any employment. Failure to succeed without natural supports should not be taken as failure to succeed at work. Rather, natural supports might be used to augment job coaching for those workers with autism who cannot succeed with natural supports alone.

IMPLEMENTING SUPPORTS AT WORK

Administrative Structure

An administrative structure must be developed that provides the supports necessary for the worker with autism. A workable system includes an overall director of the supported employment program who supervises coordinators. The coordinators are then responsible for the support and supervision of several supported employment sites. A coordinator ensures that necessary supports for each job are in place, including trained job coaches, behavior management plans, instructional plans, and development of natural supports. The coordinator also is responsible for providing emergency back-up should destructive behaviors occur that require additional personnel. The coordinator makes weekly, and sometimes more frequent, visits to each worksite to monitor the performance of the worker, the job coach, and the concerns of the employer. If the workplace is dependent on natural supports, the coordinator makes visits to evaluate the progress of the worker and the effectiveness of the supports.

Implementation of Job Coaching

Coaching workers with autism often requires specialized expertise in autism and in the support of workers with autism. Prior to serving as a job coach, the individual must be instructed in policies, procedures, and strategies for serving the worker with autism. Prior to placement on the job, the job coach needs formal training in behavior management, language issues, instructional procedures, normalization, and integration procedures. The job coach must also be given specific training in instructional plans and behavior plans that will be implemented at the assigned job site.

Once the job coach is placed at a worksite, he or she must be taught the actual job task as well as the rules and regulations of the workplace. Follow-up training must also be provided on actual implementation of instruction and behavior plans. Initially, it might be necessary for the coordinator or another experienced job coach to overlap with the new job coach until he or she becomes competent enough to provide support at the assigned site. Weekly monitoring conducted by the coordinator ensures that the job coach is providing adequate support. Failure of the job coach to properly support the worker with autism can result in termination of the worker's employment.

Implementation of Behavior Management and Instructional Support

The worker with autism typically has an individualized habilitation plan (IHP) that designates vocational, social, community integration, and behavioral goals for the coming year. These goals are specific to the worker's job. Strategies for achieving these goals are put in written form and the job coach is trained by the coordinator or by a training specialist to implement the strategies at work. Training initially takes place in an office environment with role play and rehearsal to ensure that the job coach can perform the procedures. The follow-up training and monitoring that are done at the worksite ensure that the job coach is implementing the strategies as scheduled and with precision.

Formal monitoring of the implementation of the behavior plan can be done through procedural reliability checks. A specialist visits the workplace and observes the job coach to determine the percentage of steps of the behavior plan that are followed accurately. Job coaches are expected to obtain a procedural reliability rating of at least 90%. Failure to attain at least 90% results in retraining or personnel action, whichever is warranted.

The job coach takes data on instructional and behavioral progress, as designed in the IHP. Review of the data provides information on whether the worker with autism is making progress on instructional and behavioral goals. For example, if the worker has difficulty with screaming at work, and the data reveal that during the first 2 months of employment and behavior plan implementation screaming decreased from an average of 10 incidents per day to less than one per day, it would appear that the behavior plan is effective and the worker is making progress.

Direct observation of the worker with autism is also done periodically by the coordinator or an instructional or behavioral specialist to assess behavioral and instructional progress. The observer determines whether worker performance is consistent with data collected by the job coach. The observation provides a sample of worker performance that can be used to evaluate progress and effectiveness of instruction and behavior plans.

Employer feedback is also obtained to ensure that progress and performance are satisfactory. In addition to customary performance reviews, the coordinator might make weekly or monthly contact with the supervisor to assess worker performance.

As a result of information obtained from data, direct observation, and employer feedback, it may be necessary to modify instruction or behavior plans. These modifications are done periodically to maximize worker performance.

Implementation of Natural Supports

Natural supports involve reliance on company employees to provide support to the worker with autism. These supports may be provided in conjunction with job coach support or they may occur alone. The implementation of natural supports for workers with autism involves determining the kind of support needed and who will provide the support, and then enlisting the cooperation of the employer. This arrangement can be worked out by the job development specialist, the supported employment supervisor, the job coach, an advocate, or in some cases by the worker with autism. The support system and worker performance are evaluated periodically to ensure that the arrangement remains satisfactory.

The employer may decide that the job coach is no longer needed and initiate the use of natural supports him- or herself. In these cases, the employer typically provides support within the company, determines that it is sufficient, and then informs the supported employment agency that the job coach is no longer needed.

In some cases, although the worker with autism appears capable of independent employment, natural supports have actually evolved over time, enabling that worker to maintain employment. Unfortunately, there are cases in which the support is not formally recognized and if the source of support leaves the company, the performance of the worker deteriorates and termination is likely. For example, one worker with autism was working independently at a restaurant job with drop-in supervision once per week. He was doing exceedingly well at a variety of tasks. Abruptly, his performance deteriorated and his job was threatened. A behavior specialist who was called in to assess the situation discovered that the supervisor had been providing a great deal of support, including specialized instruction, frequent feedback, daily social attention, and occasionally taking the worker out to lunch. When that supervisor was transferred, no such support was provided by the new supervisor. The result was a deterioration in worker performance. The former supervisor was contacted and supports that he had provided were formalized and implemented by his successor. This case illustrates the problems with supports that evolve without formal recognition. If informal supports do evolve, it is important that they be recognized so that if the individual providing the support leaves, a replacement can be found.

Backup for Instructional and Behavioral Crises

Workers with severe autism may maintain some level of acceptable behavioral adjustment, but then may on occasion display potentially dangerous behaviors at work, such as aggression, running away, uncontrolled screaming, and property destruction. Often, it is possible for the job coach to control the situation; however, there may be times when the job coach needs back-up emergency assistance to ensure the safety of the worker, co-workers, and property. If this possibility exists, it is imperative that a support system be in place so that the job coach can access emergency assistance quickly.

The back-up system involves several key factors. First, there must be someone available at all times who can respond quickly to the crisis. This is often the worksite coordinator or the director of the vocational program. Second, the job coach must know the criteria and method for obtaining such assistance. Finally, the emergency back-up personnel must be instructed on how to intervene effectively to assist the job coach and bring the situation under control. With an efficient back-up system, it is possible for individuals with aggressive or otherwise destructive behavior to maintain employment for many years.

SUMMARY

Vocational planning for adults with autism requires assessing the worker's vocational competencies and needs, and then providing the necessary level of support to ensure employment success. Standardized assessments typically underrate the abilities of workers with autism and greater use of nonstandardized assessments is recommended. Nonstandardized assessments include ongoing criterion-referenced assessments to evaluate how well a worker with autism is meeting the vocational requirements of the job. As such, they have direct implications for job training. Areas of vocational assessment include evaluations of basic work skills, responses to verbal instruction, requisite work skills, functional academic skills, learning style assessment, and vocational preferences. It is also important to assess the support needs of the worker with autism. This includes an assessment of behavior problems, language abilities, social skills and behaviors, transportation skills, and responses to change.

Following a vocational assessment and assessment of support needs, adequate support should be provided to increase the likelihood of successful employment. Most workers with autism require the assistance of a job coach. The job coach assists the worker in meeting the requirements of the job, encourages integration, teaches social skills, and bridges the communication gap. The job coach also runs behavior management programs, manages problem behaviors when they occur, and implements instructional strategies. Natural supports can also be used to provide support to the worker with autism.

The high level of support required by workers with autism means that an administrative structure needs to be developed that is capable of providing the support. Key elements in the administrative support are coordinators to provide training and emergency back-up to job coaches, extensive training for the job coaches, and formal observation of behavior management and instructional program implementation.

CHAPTER 3

Finding and Keeping a Job

Helping people with autism find and keep jobs can be a challenging task for support personnel. They must attend to factors related to employment as well as the characteristics of the disability. People with autism are significantly different from people with other disabilities in terms of their strengths and weaknesses and their special requirements and supports. These requirements must be systematically applied to finding appropriate jobs, establishing employment in competitive business, and maintaining employment. This chapter examines how the nature of autism has an impact on finding, securing, and maintaining employment.

THE JOB SEARCH

Although individuals with autism often share certain patterns of strengths and weaknesses, they are as unique as individuals without autism. For a person with autism to succeed at work, it is necessary to find a job that matches not only the characteristics of autism, but also the characteristics of the individual. Finding a job refers not just to locating any job for a person with autism, but to making thoughtful decisions concerning the type of employment opportunities available. Good decisions at the level of job hunting promote long-term employment for people with autism.

Workers with autism can utilize the same methods of finding employment as workers without disabilities. Locating a job begins with searching for available jobs in the local area. Job searches require that the employment or job placement specialist explore employment opportunities in local industries, businesses, retail stores, and companies. Because regions vary considerably in the kinds of jobs that are available, it is essential that the employment specialist specifically evaluate the local area for jobs. For instance, although opportunities for manufacturing positions are limited in Washington, D.C., jobs in the printing industry are numerous. To explore job availability, the employment specialist must gather and process information on jobs from several different sources.

Printed Materials and Job Fairs

Local newspapers provide an ongoing source of information on current openings in a variety of fields in the area. The want ads give information on specific companies that are seeking workers, as well as provide an opportunity to see what kinds of jobs exist in the work force.

The Yellow Pages can also be helpful. They provide a comprehensive list of companies, any of which may be seeking new employees. The Yellow Pages are particularly useful when trying to find a specific job for an individual with a proven record of success in a certain job. For example, if Ryan did well at a printing company that recently went out of business, the Yellow Pages would offer a list of other printing companies in the area.

Some organizations and businesses also publish newsletters, bulletins, and trade journals that list potential jobs in specific fields such as manufacturing or printing. Furthermore, local government agencies, such as the chamber of commerce, sometimes sponsor job fairs that offer face-to-face contact with potential employers.

The Job Canvas

In the job canvas, the employment specialist walks around targeted areas and meets potential employers. In most locales, businesses are grouped according to their type of work. For instance, retail stores and restaurants tend to be grouped in one area, whereas manufacturing industries and warehouses are grouped in another area. This means that the canvassing employment specialist can often go to an area and visit several businesses within a few hours.

Canvassing enables the employment specialist to meet owners face-to-face and encourage them to talk about the nature of their businesses, including specific job tasks that are performed. Many owners and supervisors are pleased with the interest displayed by the employment specialist and are willing to disclose details concerning their businesses. In many instances, an impromptu tour of the business can be arranged. A tour gives the employment specialist a chance to observe the work environment and the kinds of jobs being performed by the employees. The employment specialist can then point out the job tasks that could be done by workers with autism. Finally, canvassing also helps the employment specialist to remain alert to new businesses opening in the area. New companies and businesses sometimes need numerous employees and may be willing to give workers with autism an opportunity.

Networking

Networking means utilizing existing or evolving relationships with others to find jobs. Family, friends, business acquaintances, and organizations such as clubs and churches are all valuable sources of potential jobs. Simply talking to acquaintances about a search for employment can result in valuable leads or even a job opening. In addition, employers and owners often know other business professionals who may be hiring in the same or closely related fields.

When jobs are found in national or local chains or franchises, it is likely that the same job may be available in another company in the chain. For example, two workers with autism were employed at a local retail chain store. The store manager was pleased with their performance and within 6 months two other stores in the chain hired workers with autism. Similar jobs have been found in other retail establishments, in the restaurant industry, and in the delivery industry. Jobs may also be found by asking prospective or current employers if they know anyone else who is hiring.

Seasonal Opportunities

Job availability varies seasonally and the employment specialist can take advantage of this natural trend. Often late summer and early fall are the best times to find jobs because many entry level positions are being vacated by students returning to school. Employers may be anxious to fill these jobs quickly with workers who will stay for longer periods of time. In addition, the approach of winter holidays means that retail stores will be looking for new employees to fill a variety of jobs. Although these jobs may be labeled temporary in nature, many of these positions become permanent after the holidays. Finally, specific locales may have seasonal industries such as tourism and horticulture that can offer short-term employment that may evolve into long-term employment.

INITIAL CONTACT

The initial contact with a potential employer might occur face-to-face through canvassing or over the telephone from leads in the want ads, the Yellow Pages, or from networking. The first goal of this initial contact is to find out whether the job would be appropriate for the worker seeking employment. The employment specialist learns certain basic facts about the job, then makes an initial decision about its appropriateness for the individual seeking employment. At this point, it is better to err on the side of optimism rather than prematurely reject a potentially good job.

The second goal of the initial contact is to convince the employer or owner to consider hiring individuals with autism. The employment specialist explains that hiring workers with autism is desirable and valuable to the business, not an act of charity.

Typically, employers have no knowledge of autism or supported employment. The employment specialist briefly explains the nature of the supported employment program, the strengths that workers with autism have, and the advantages to the employer in hiring these workers.

Initial employer reactions to this first contact vary markedly—some employers openly consider the possibility of hiring a worker with autism and other employers quickly reject the idea. If the employer seems interested, the job specialist schedules a face-to-face meeting to explain the supported employment program and the nature of autism in greater detail.

The meeting gives the employment specialist the opportunity to observe the work environment and the tasks performed. The first meeting is a good opportunity to leave the employer with an information packet concerning the supported employment program. This packet of information should include a brochure that explains the nature of supported employment, stresses the advantages of hiring workers with autism, and contains a list of companies employing workers with autism. The package should also include a general description of the nature of autism that emphasizes what workers with autism can do and their potential contribution to the business. The purpose of the package of information is to expand the employer's knowledge of supported employment and autism and to point out the employment successes of people with autism. This knowledge can help pique the employer's interest in the possibility of hiring people with autism and dispel any possible misconceptions.

FOLLOW-UP

Often the initial contact will not result in a job position. Follow-up contacts are usually necessary to answer the employer's remaining questions and to advance the consideration process. The goal of follow-up contacts is to gradually move toward employment. It is hoped that the employer has considered hiring someone with autism and only needs some further clarification before making a decision. Some employers may have been too busy to read the information packet or to seriously consider hiring a person with autism. A gentle reminder from the employment specialist helps to refocus the employer to the possibility of hiring someone with autism.

Because employment specialists typically have ongoing contact with several potential employers, it is helpful for them to keep a log of contacts. The log should list the date of the contact, the name of the person contacted, what was discussed, and what conclusions were made. The contact log assists the employment specialist in following up with employers in a timely fashion before they lose interest or hire someone else. The contact log also helps the employment specialist avoid inadvertently discussing the same issue with the same employer. Finally, managers in large companies change jobs often and the log is a valuable tool for remembering to whom the employment specialist spoke. It is not uncommon for the initial contact person to no longer work for the company and for the new manager to be more receptive toward hiring individuals with autism.

INITIAL JOB ANALYSIS

Once a potential job is found, an initial job analysis should be done. The job analysis serves two basic purposes. First, it helps determine whether the job is generally suitable for a person with autism. Second, it assists in determining the suitability of the job for a specific worker with autism.

Performing a job analysis requires identifying and assessing several different facets of the job. It consists of several components, including an examination of basic tasks; a vocational skills inventory; an assessment of environmental factors; and an examination of job requirements, behavior management issues, and integration issues.

Catalog of Basic Job Tasks

A job analysis begins by making a thorough list of the various tasks to be done as part of the job. These include tasks that are done daily as well as tasks that are done only occasionally. This list includes set-up activities and break-down activities, if they are part of the worker's responsibility. Failure to do a thorough catalog of tasks can jeopardize employment. If not all tasks are identified, there is a risk that the worker could accept a job and then find that there are tasks involved that he or she is not capable of performing.

Vocational Skills Inventory

The next step in the job analysis is to assess the basic skills necessary to complete job tasks. The vocational skills inventory can be completed by observing employees of the business do their required jobs and by identifying the skills necessary to do them. Specific consideration should be given to the need for fine or gross motor skills; speed; accuracy; cleanliness; strength; and functional academic skills, such as reading, writing, or arithmetic. In addition, given the social and language deficits displayed by people with autism, special attention needs to be paid to the social and language requirements of the job.

Environmental Factors Assessment

A thorough job analysis must also include an assessment of important environmental factors, particularly those related to potential behavior problems. Environmental factors to consider include the physical layout of the company, proximity of co-workers, noise level in the work area, safety issues, temperature, and weather for outdoor jobs. These factors interact with worker characteristics or interests to make some jobs more favorable than others. For example, it is unlikely that a worker with autism who makes loud, repetitive noises will succeed in a library sorting books despite his ability to do the task. However, this same worker may succeed in a job sorting bottles by color in a large, noisy recycling warehouse. A worker who has a preference for walking and pacing would probably not enjoy a job that provides a small, constricted work area and demands long hours of table work in that work area.

Job Requirements

Job requirements refer to aspects of the job that are not directly related to the tasks to be performed. These include rules, regulations, and other employer expectations. Specific job requirements to be assessed in the job analysis are arrival and departure times, break and lunch times, dress code, and time card regulations.

Behavior Management Issues

A thorough job analysis for people with autism is not complete without due consideration to challenging behaviors and how they will be managed. For example, if a job is being sought for a young man with autism and problems with pica, the initial job analysis must take into account the opportunities for pica in that environment and the possibilities of managing pica successfully.

Integration Issues

Opportunities for contact with people without disabilities should be assessed as part of any job analysis. Some work environments are decidedly more hospitable than others. The employment specialist should evaluate the social climate of the workplace and formulate an opinion as to whether the person with autism will fit into the existing environment. Attention should be paid to social interactions that occur during work and during breaks as well as outside of work.

JOB MATCHING

Job matching refers to matching the skills and interests of a particular worker to the requirements of a certain job. A comparison is made between the requirements of the job and the vocational capacity of the individual to determine the suitability of the individual for the job. The goal of job matching is to take advantage of the inherent strengths of the individual to heighten the chances for success on the job. Job matching assumes a particularly important role in supported employment for workers with autism due to their typical behavioral characteristics, patterns of strengths and weaknesses, and idiosyncratic preferences, all of which have clear implications for job placement.

The process of job matching is complex and assumes that the employment specialist has detailed knowledge about both the characteristics of the individual being placed and the requirements of the job. Because this may not be the case, it is recommended that job matching decisions not be made solely by any one individual; instead, an interdisciplinary approach is recommended. Following a detailed job analysis and a vocational assessment of the person with autism, involved professionals and advocates should meet and discuss the pros and cons of the potential job. The focus of this discussion should be on identifying the strengths of the individual that make success in that job likely, the weaknesses that might make employment problematic, and how any weaknesses can be overcome. In matching people with autism to job requirements, special attention should be paid to the nature of the job tasks, job complexity, number of tasks, need for flexibility, need for good judgment, and environmental factors.

Nature of Job Tasks

The employment specialist must evaluate the nature of the job tasks in relation to the individual's strengths, weaknesses, and interests. Given that people with autism, by definition, have deficits in language and interpersonal skills, jobs that are heavily dependent on skills in these areas are generally ruled out. Jobs that entail creating documents or that require a great deal of interaction with customers, visitors, or the public are often not within the ability levels or interests of workers with autism.

In general, people with autism do better at tasks that require visual-motor skills, fine motor skills, visual discrimination, or gross motor skills. These workers often do well at jobs that require movement, assembly, attention to detail in the performance of a task, and precise routines. Some workers with autism display an uncanny ability to do precise fine motor work, such as assemble small electronic components. Others may not possess the dexterity to do fine motor tasks, but they may be proficient at tasks that require gross motor skills. For example, a man with poor fine motor skills may be unable to work doing assembly tasks, but he may be able to work in a warehouse lifting heavy boxes. A job's strength requirements also need to be considered. For example, a worker with autism may not be strong enough to do a heavy lifting job in a warehouse, but he may have enough strength to sort bottles to be recycled.

Job Complexity

There are no set rules about job complexity when seeking employment for people with autism. Individuals with autism have cognitive abilities that range from the profound range of mental retardation to the superior range of intelligence. Furthermore, an individual with autism might have some skills that measure in the superior range and other skills that measure in the range of mental retardation. Therefore, the job seeker must match the complexity of the job to the individual's cognitive capacities. Albert, for example, has autism, is nonverbal, and has profound mental retardation. He has a great deal of difficulty learning new tasks and performing tasks that exceed two or three steps. Albert needed a job that lacked complexity. A good job match for Albert was stripping the plastic from clothing in preparation for its display on the sales floor. This is a simple task and Albert performs it well. Gina, however, has autism, average intelligence, uses verbal language, and has above average fine motor skills. She is capable of performing complex tasks; a good match for her is a job that requires her to solder tiny wires as part of an electronics assembly task.

Number of Job Tasks

The job specialist must assess the number of tasks involved in the job and make a determination about the tolerance and capacity of the job seeker for handling these tasks. People with autism vary considerably in terms of the number of different tasks they can learn or tolerate in their job. Many of them work best when their job entails a few tasks that must be done precisely the same way each time. For others, having to learn too many tasks too soon can be problematic. Some workers with autism enjoy change and can learn a variety of tasks quickly. In fact, some of these workers *prefer* jobs that provide variety.

Need for Flexibility

Related to the number of tasks performed is the frequency of change and the predictability of change. Most people with autism have difficulty handling change and work better in consistent, structured environments with few changes. Employment opportunities must be evaluated in terms of the need for flexibility on the part of the worker. Companies that are disorganized and require abrupt changes in jobs and schedule can create problems for some employees with autism.

Need for Good Judgment

Jobs must also be evaluated in terms of requiring employee judgment and, therefore, the ability of the job seeker to make judgments. Some jobs have tasks that are done the same way each time and require little judgment. These include manufacturing assembly tasks and printing tasks such as collating and binding. Other jobs require that the employee make judgments during the performance of the task. Some jobs that have typically been considered good for people with mental retardation actually require judgments that can often be difficult for people with autism. Examples of such jobs are janitorial positions, cooking, and housekeeping. These jobs often require the employee to make decisions during the course of the work. For instance, a short order cook may have several dishes to prepare and must make judgments about the order or even the method of preparation. A janitor may have to make judgments about what to clean and whether or not something is clean.

Many people with autism have difficulty making judgments concerning tasks and do better in jobs in which tasks are done the same way each time. Martha, for example, is a young woman with severe autism and average intelligence. She has great difficulty with problem solving and making judgments. She was terminated from her job at a pizza restaurant because she lacked both the flexibility and judgment that food preparation required; however, she excelled at her job in a fuse assembly plant. She was able to learn to perform numerous electronic tasks, all of which required precise fine motor movements and good visual-motor coordination, but did not require good judgment, problem-solving skills, or flexibility.

Environmental Factors

When matching people with autism to jobs, it is important to consider environmental factors that may impinge on work performance or behavior and social problems. Social and behavioral issues can be the greatest obstacles to job success, and there are environmental factors that can exacerbate or highlight difficulties in these areas. These possibilities must be carefully evaluated in light of the job seeker's social and behavioral functioning. Environments should be sought that do not have the potential for magnifying existing social deficits and that can make them less noticeable or less likely to occur.

Leonard provides a good example of the importance of environment. Leonard worked in a warehouse where his ritualistic spinning was an obstacle to co-workers and equipment. The warehouse environment was a poor one for him because it magnified the effects of his problems with mobility. After he was terminated from that employment, he went on to enjoy success in a tee-shirt factory where he had his own work space and where his spinning did not hamper co-workers or equipment.

Marianne provides another example of the importance of environment. She is a worker with a history of loud vocalizations. Her first job was in a quiet office environment. Although she was capable of doing the tasks, her noise making was obvious and disruptive. Marianne later found success at a job in a large stockroom with a background noise level that was considerably higher than that of the quiet office. In that environment, her noise making was obscured by the background noise and was well tolerated by co-workers.

JOB DEVELOPMENT

In addition to finding jobs that are suitable for workers with autism, it is also possible to develop jobs specifically for people with autism. Job development refers to designing jobs to suit workers with autism by selecting a specific subset of tasks in a job position and using that subset to create a job.

Many job positions require employees to perform a variety of tasks. Often, some, but not all, of these tasks within a given job position would be difficult for the employee with autism to perform. Some of the tasks might require social or cognitive skills that are beyond the worker's capacity. For instance, retail stock clerks unload trucks, manage inventory, stack boxes, unpack boxes, price merchandise, and put merchandise on display. Because the job seeker with autism might not be able to perform all of these varied jobs, a subset of the jobs might be more reasonable. For example, the worker could be hired to stack and unpack boxes.

Mildred and Ernie are two workers with autism who benefited from job development in a restaurant. At a popular neighborhood restaurant, kitchen staff were responsible for a variety of cooking and cleaning tasks that included wrapping potatoes in aluminum foil to be baked and rolling up silverware in napkins to be put on the tables. After negotiating with the supervisor, Mildred and Ernie were hired to do the potato wrapping and to roll the silverware.

CONDITIONS OF EMPLOYMENT

Once a suitable job has been found or developed for a person with autism, some final factors need to be considered before securing employment. The employment specialist needs to evaluate the conditions of employment and ensure that these are acceptable. Conditions of employment include starting pay; number of hours of work per week; schedule; potential for increased pay and hours; travel distance to and from work; general safety of the work environment; and benefits available, including paid vacation, sick leave, and medical and dental care.

SECUREMENT OF THE JOB

After the job specialist has found a job, performed an initial job analysis, and determined that the job is a good match for the job seeker, the job must be secured. If the employer has not made an offer of employment, the job specialist might need to dispel any lingering doubts and explain the advantages of hiring the worker with autism for the specific position.

Dispersion of Doubts

In many instances, an employer's doubts can be eased by explaining and offering evidence for the proven success of workers with autism and the supported employment agency. This can be accomplished by having the employer contact other companies that successfully employ people with autism; by providing written references from other employers; and, if feasible and desirable, by having them observe other workers with autism on the job. Sometimes it is helpful to show the employer any awards or accreditation that the agency has received or local newspaper articles about the agency's supported employment program. Finally, a videotape featuring employees with autism at work and interviews with co-workers and supervisors can be a powerful tool to dispel remaining doubts.

Emphasis of Advantages to Employers

Although they may not be immediately apparent to the employer, there are numerous advantages in hiring workers with autism. These need to be explained to the employer using terms that can be understood by a lay person. The primary goal of an employer or supervisor is to hire dependable workers who can complete a job independently after a short training period. In a positive manner, the employment specialist should focus on the strengths of the workers with autism that would help an employer achieve this goal. Some of the advantages of hiring workers with autism are outlined below.

Work Skills Workers with autism often have strong visual-motor skills and the ability to do a repetitive, exacting task without becoming bored. Some employers experience high turnover in positions that require repetitive work and would appreciate an employee who does not get bored with the job. The specialist may want to explain that it may take the workers with autism longer to learn a task, but that once a task is learned they will remember how to do it and achieve the employer's productivity goals. In some instances, the applicant with autism may have had similar work experience that also needs to be pointed out to the employer.

Work Habits   An employment specialist can guarantee the good work habits of employees with autism. These include coming to work on time, taking lunch and breaks at the scheduled time, and rarely missing work due to illness. In addition, the employment specialist can point out how an apparent weakness in social and language abilities may be an asset on the job. Employees with autism are not prone to taking unscheduled breaks to chat with co-workers or use the telephone to call friends or family.

Agency Support Services   Often, a primary concern of an employer is how much time and effort will have to be devoted to employees with autism. Although most employers are willing to make an extra effort to assist employees with autism, they will not do so if it interferes with their other job duties. The employment specialist can assure the employer that the agency will provide the additional training and support necessary for employees with autism. The employment specialist can explain that support will be available for as long as the worker with autism needs it.

In addition, the role of the job coach in providing training and support needs to be fully explained to the employer. In many instances, the job coach acts as a bridge between the employer and the worker with autism. The job coach teaches the worker with autism to meet the supervisor's goals, and he or she implements strategies to eliminate problem behaviors and assists the worker in communicating with supervisors and co-workers. Job coaches also help ensure that productivity levels will be kept high in the initial phases of employment by assisting with production.

Because some workers with autism have serious social and behavior problems, these need to be discussed with the employer. The employer needs to be assured that the job coach is trained to handle any problem behaviors that may occur. The employment specialist can explain what problem behaviors may occur and how they will be handled. It is important for employers to know that neither they nor the co-workers will be expected to intervene during behavior problems.

Targeted Jobs Tax Credit   An important employer incentive for hiring people with disabilities is the targeted jobs tax credit (TJTC), a federal program that has been extended by Congress numerous times. Although the tax credit is less than it once was, it is still an incentive that many employers choose to take advantage of. TJTC is issued in each state through the Department of Labor and vocational rehabilitation agencies. Tax credit vouchers can be obtained for the employer from the state employment office. The voucher is presented to the employer on the day of hire and employers earn tax credits based on a portion of wages paid.

Employer Recognition Employers in both the public and private sector have received recognition as a result of having employees with autism. Recognition can range from awards presented by the supported employment or placement agency to awards presented by national organizations and politicians. Local newspaper or television stories are sometimes done on the employer's experience in hiring people with autism, which can be good publicity for the employer. The prospective employer can be made aware of the possibilities of recognition and awards by being given copies of press releases, newspaper articles, or other materials that describe the recognition that workers with autism have brought to their employers.

Clarification of Job Responsibilities

It is essential that the employer and employment specialist clarify exactly what responsibilities the employee with autism will have. In addition, these two individuals should discuss the productivity and quality requirements of the job. The employment specialist must also clarify how many workers with autism will be employed, how many hours they will work each week, and when the employer wants to start the new employee(s).

THE JOB SET-UP

Once a job has been found and secured, the necessary preparations must be made for the worker with autism to begin. Adequate attention to preparing the job helps ensure an efficient start-up and that the employer's initial perceptions are favorable. Adequate preparation can also help avoid problems in the future and enhance the productivity of workers with autism. Preparation time varies from job to job and is dependent mostly on the complexity of the job. A minimum of 1 week is usually required for set-up.

During the initial set-up, it may be unreasonable to expect the job coach to do all the necessary preparations. Job coaches may lack the expertise necessary to prepare and make initial decisions concerning the job position. Thus, the involvement of other agency staff is essential in establishing employment. Involved agency staff should include people with experience in setting up job positions, supervisors responsible for overseeing the job placement, and experts in behavior management strategies and instructional techniques who can teach job skills to workers with autism. Once the support staff are in a position to provide necessary input, the set-up can begin.

The Job Coach's Knowledge of the Job

The first step in establishing the job is for the job coach to thoroughly learn the job. The job coach is usually taught by a supervisor or other company employees. It is often instructive to observe an experienced worker doing the job, particularly if the job is complicated. The job coach should then spend some time actually doing the job while noting the necessary skills and the sequence of steps and tasks.

Completion of Job Task Analyses

For most new positions, task analyses need to be written for the major job duties. These will help clarify the steps required in doing tasks and provide a framework for teaching the employee with autism. Typically, writing task analyses requires two individuals. The job coach should do the job task while the coordinator or instructional specialist records the steps in sequence. Sometimes the job coach can write the task analysis while observing a company employee do the task. Required skills should also be noted during this step. Some jobs require specific skills such as reading, writing, and weighing or measuring materials. These specific work skills need to be targeted by the job coach because they may require special instructional strategies.

Although an initial job analysis was done, the job coach might find that it needs some revision after experiencing the job him- or herself. The job coach should revise this initial analysis by adding and deleting duties based on observations and instructions from supervisors.

Determination of Productivity Rates of Workers without Disabilities

During the set-up phase, the job coach and agency staff should measure the productivity rate of workers without disabilities. These productivity rates provide a standard against which the productivity rates of the employees with autism can be measured. In addition, they provides a clear goal toward which the employee with autism should strive. Typically, rates of productivity of workers without disabilities are obtained by measuring the productivity of either the job coach doing the job or a co-worker who agrees to the procedure.

Evaluation of Environmental Factors that May Relate to Behavior Problems

During the job set-up, staff should look for any environmental factors that may lead to behavior problems or that may pose a danger to the worker with autism. Once these factors are identified, adaptations or supports can be arranged to mitigate their effects. For example, the physical layout of the work area may present some potential hazards for individuals with autism who run away or who eat inedibles. With the permission of the supervisor, it may be possible to rearrange the work area so that exits are not immediately accessible or in view of a worker who tends to run away. Similarly, agency staff can arrange to regularly clean up a work area to remove potentially hazardous small objects if the worker has pica.

The Job Coach's Observation of the Work Environment

The job coach needs to closely observe the work environment and talk to supervisors and co-workers to evaluate other aspects of the work environment that may affect the new employee with autism. Agency staff must learn the rules, regulations, routines, and schedule of the company. Knowing what is expected of an employee will help the job coach structure the behaviors and schedule of the worker with autism to conform to these expectations.

During these initial observations, the job coach must pay special attention to assessing the social milieu of the company. It is important to identify needed social skills so that the employee with autism can be taught them if necessary. Agency staff should observe the frequency and nature of social interactions among co-workers, and among co-workers, the public, and the supervisory staff. The following questions should be answered: Do co-workers talk while working or only during breaks? What do they talk about? Is the social atmosphere friendly and informal or more reserved and formal? How important are language skills in getting along with co-workers? This information will help the job coach assess how well the worker with autism will relate to co-workers and identify social skills that may need improvement.

Natalie's case provides a good example of the benefits of social skills assessment during the set-up stage. Natalie is a woman with average intelligence and autism. She does not readily initiate conversations with others and often does not respond when others initiate conversations with her. Natalie secured a job in a retail store stocking and straightening shelves. It was apparent during set-up that because Natalie was working on the sales floor she might need to answer inquiries from customers. A social skills program was designed to teach her to respond to customer inquiries by orienting toward them and providing them with requested information. The social skills training was implemented and Natalie was able to learn the skill to her employer's satisfaction.

The set-up phase also gives the job coach an opportunity to establish a working relationship with co-workers and the supervisor. Good working relationships may be invaluable if problems arise in the future.

Meeting of Support Staff with Supervisors and Co-workers

During the set-up phase, it is sometimes valuable for support staff to meet with supervisors and co-workers to explain the nature of autism and supported employment. Specific topics to be covered include characteristics of people with autism and how they may be displayed at work, the job coach's role in assisting the worker with autism, and the co-workers' and supervisors' involvement with the new employee. Company employees are often interested in how they should interact with the employee and how to handle problems should they arise. This information can help company employees feel more comfortable and be more effective in working with their new co-worker with autism.

THE BEGINNING OF WORK FOR THE EMPLOYEE

After completing set-up procedures, the worker with autism can begin his or her job. If more than one worker with autism was hired, it is advisable to start only one person at a time. Often this should be the worker who agency staff perceive to be most likely to succeed on the job and least likely to have job-threatening behaviors. After the first employee with autism adjusts to the demands of a new job, additional employees can begin working according to the agreement made with the employer.

It is desirable that in general no more than two workers with autism work in the same area at any given company. In some instances, if work is available and if the employer agrees, more than two, but never more than four, workers may be employed. If too many workers with autism are employed in one area, there is a greater likelihood that social or behavior problems will occur. In addition, a subgroup of workers with autism is less desirable because it tends to further segregate these workers from integrated work experiences.

The Worker's Knowledge of Job Tasks and Work Routine

The primary role of the job coach or other support person is to instruct the new employee on how to do required job tasks and to explain the work routine. Much of this instruction takes place informally with the job coach walking the new employee through the activities of the day. Experience with employees with autism in a range of jobs has shown that with adequate motivation job tasks can usually be taught using modeling and verbal instruction alone. The job coach should provide adequate verbal instruction and explanation so the new employee knows exactly what is expected. In addition, the job coach should model how to do the tasks while providing verbal explanations.

The job coach can refer to the job task analyses to teach steps in an orderly sequence. When modeling and giving instruction, it is important that the job coach provide instruction before the new employee makes errors and has to be corrected. Correcting workers with autism can be problematic and may lead to behavior problems. Additionally, it is important that the job be taught correctly the first time. If the worker with flexibility problems learns to do the job one way, it can be extremely difficult to teach a new method.

Occasionally, the worker with autism requires more formal, systematic instruction to learn how to do new job tasks. This is particularly true if the employee is more severely disabled, if job tasks are complicated, or if several different job tasks need to be learned.

Assessment of Accuracy and Productivity

Experience has shown that teaching employees with autism the sequence for doing job tasks can be readily accomplished. A more prevalent difficulty is ensuring that the items produced by these workers meet the quality and productivity standards. The job coach or support personnel must regularly inspect the work output of employees with autism for accuracy and rate. Inaccurate work or low productivity might require that staff develop and implement more formal, systematic instruction or take other measures to improve accuracy.

Behavior Management and Social Skills Training

It is critical during set-up that possible job-threatening behaviors or social problems be targeted and addressed with a behavior management plan. Job coaches and their agency supervisors need to meet, define the problem behaviors, assess functions of these behaviors, and develop behavior management procedures. The job coach needs to be trained in implementing these procedures and be prepared to begin the behavior plan on the first day of employment.

Lonnie is a man with autism, profound mental retardation, and high rates of self-injury. His self-injury is in the form of head banging. A behavior plan was developed for him based on a functional assessment. The plan included alternate sensory stimuli, positive reinforcement for cooperative behavior, and frequent access to desired reinforcers either through the reinforcement program or through noncontingent scheduling. Additionally, his self-injury was put on extinction and emergency procedures for preventing injury from head banging were included in his plan. This plan was implemented concurrently with the start of his new job. Lonnie, despite his severe autism, mental retardation, and history of high frequency head banging, has been able to maintain employment for the past 10 years. Additionally, his head banging is significantly reduced from hundreds of times per day to less than one incident per month.

ONGOING SUPPORT OF THE JOB COACH

Because of their involvement with workers with extensive problem behaviors, job coaches often require ongoing support from agency staff to do their jobs effectively. Following their training, it is recommended that job coach staff go through performance-based evaluations on targeted job skills. Performance-based evaluation refers to evaluating the job coach's work performance. Typically, evaluations should occur frequently in the initial phase of employment so that the job coach quickly learns exactly what is expected. The frequency of evaluations can then be gradually decreased.

In general, two types of performance evaluations are necessary. First, a checklist evaluation requires agency supervisory staff to visit the job coach at the company and check to see that targeted aspects of the job have been done. Suggested targeted job duties include data collection for behavioral and instructional interventions, having necessary supplies to run programs such as written schedules and reinforcers, and following prescribed intervention programs. Although these checklists provide an indication of what the job coach is doing, they do not assess how well the job coach is performing.

Second, a proficiency-based evaluation is used to assess how well a job coach is performing his or her job. Proficiency-based evaluations require that agency supervisory or support staff observe the job coach actually performing the job duties, then rate the performance and provide feedback. For example, to rate proficiency on behavior plan implementation, the supervisor observes the job coach implement the plan and rates whether or not each step of the behavior plan was implemented. Low ratings result in either retraining or personnel action or both. Follow-up proficiency evaluations can then be done to assess improvement.

EMPLOYMENT MAINTENANCE

The goal of job maintenance is to assist employees with autism in retaining employment for long periods of time. To ensure long-term employment, it is often necessary to ensure long-term support and attend continuously to a variety of critical issues, including behavior management and social skills development, which have been discussed in detail in previous chapters. Relationships with co-workers and supervisors, integration in the workplace, and employee evaluations are also important topics and are discussed below.

The Handling of Problems with Supervisors and Co-workers

The social deficits inherent in autism place workers with autism at risk for problematic relationships with co-workers and supervisors. One of the principal ongoing roles of the job coach is to handle problems that arise between the employee with autism and supervisors or co-workers. Having a job coach available ensures that potentially job-threatening problems and behaviors can be managed quickly and effectively. In many instances, a good job coach can identify potential or evolving problems and intervene before they threaten employment.

Annalee's case provides a good example of the role of the job coach in handling problems with supervisors and co-workers. Annalee is a woman with mild mental retardation and autism. She had problems with taking property, including money. Unfortunately, she began to take money from the purses of her co-workers. The job coach assisted Annalee in making retributions to co-workers and her behavior plan was amended to cover this problem. However, because of the job-threatening nature of the problem and the fact that the behavior was also criminal in nature, it became the job coach's responsibility to monitor Annalee closely to prevent a recurrence of the problem.

Encouragement and Support of Integration

Given the social withdrawal that workers with autism display, it is important for the job coach to actively encourage and support interactions with co-workers. This is done by modeling appropriate interactions, assisting and instructing the employee with autism in social interactions, and arranging social activities both during and after work. In addition, the job coach can be a valuable source of information for an employee who is interested in befriending a co-worker with autism. Employees with autism who have severe mental retardation and no verbal skills have been able to participate in numerous social activities at work, including parties, company picnics, and company banquets, as a result of the support of their job coaches.

Employee Evaluations

One of the best ways to retain a job is to ensure that employees with autism are making adequate progress on their vocational and behavioral goals. This is best accomplished through examining ongoing data and summarizing progress over a period of time. Employees who show continual increases in quality and productivity and decreases in problem behaviors are not likely to be terminated. In addition, regular assessments of progress alert agency staff to developing problems so that, if necessary, rapid interventions can be made.

The satisfaction of the employer must also be assessed as part of the employee evaluation process. The most efficient way to determine how employers and supervisors feel about the performance of employees with autism is to periodically ask them. This can be done informally or formally by requesting that the supervisor fill out an evaluation of the employee. This evaluation may also include questions designed to assess the supervisor's thoughts concerning the job coach's and the agency's performance. Finally, if employers evaluate their employees, it is important that workers with autism be included in this process.

ENHANCEMENT OF INDEPENDENCE

Increasing opportunities for independence on the job should be a goal for all employees with autism. Although most employees will always need some level of supervision and support on the job, independence can be enhanced through effective programming.

Necessary Target Skills for Independence

The first step toward increasing independence on the job is to target exactly what skills are required for independence. In many instances, employers will have strong feelings about making workers with autism independent and their need to be involved in the decision-making process. Typically, skills necessary for moving toward independence are high quality work with productivity at rates of workers without disabilities. In addition, workers with autism typically cannot display any behaviors that are dangerous to themselves or others for a specified period of time or any other job-threatening behaviors as targeted by agency staff and employers.

Self-Management Teaching

In recent years, self-management has evolved as a means to teach people with developmental disabilities how to manage their own behaviors. Teaching self-management involves turning responsibility for implementing behavioral control procedures away from agency staff and to the individual him- or herself. Typically, the employee with autism is trained in self-monitoring and possibly even self-reinforcement.

For example, Martin is a man with average intelligence and autism. He had problems with task completion and working quietly (he often talked to himself while he worked). Martin was taught to rate himself hourly on task completion and working quietly. If he was successful in all of his ratings, he rewarded himself with an extra dollar of spending money at the end of the day. Martin was able to successfully manage his behavior and maintain employment through his self-management plan. His job coach was faded back from daily to weekly drop-in visits.

Fade Behavior Program

After a period of time, behavior programs may no longer be necessary. If behavioral improvement has been maintained for an extended amount of time, behavior programs can be gradually faded or withdrawn completely. Social skills training can be reduced from several times per week to weekly, biweekly, monthly, or even terminated once the skill is reliably demonstrated. Reinforcement schedules can be thinned or changed to self-reinforcement. Obvious cues, such as pictures or written schedules, can be transferred to self-management or gradually faded.

Supervision Transfer to Nonprogram Staff

It is sometimes possible to transfer supervision to company staff. Although largely unproven as an intervention with autism, using such natural supports has gained popularity in recent years. The use of natural supports seems particularly appropriate for employees with autism who have verbal language and few behavior problems. These employees often require little, if any, extra attention from company supervisors, and supervisors may be willing to take over sole supervision. It is sometimes possible to recruit a co-worker who is willing to serve as a support and advocate for the employee with autism. This person can provide extra instruction and socialization, mediate between the supervisor and employee with autism, and contact agency staff if necessary.

SUMMARY

Workers with autism often need assistance in finding a job and keeping that job. Jobs can be located in the same way that people without disabilities find jobs (e.g., the newspaper, Yellow Pages, networking). However, jobs must be secured that match the worker's strengths, weaknesses, and interests with the characteristics of the job. Employers often need to be educated on autism and the nature of supported employment, as well as given an appraisal of the advantages of hiring people with autism. Once the job is secured, the work environment needs to be prepared for the worker's beginning. Support personnel might need to learn the job, and job training, behavior management, and social skills programming might need to be developed and put into place. Systems of evaluation and monitoring must be developed and implemented to ensure continued job adjustment. If the worker needs the support of behavior management or job coaching, then efforts should be made to maximize independence to the greatest extent possible.

CHAPTER 4

Socialization on the Job

A serious issue in assisting people with autism to find employment is their sometimes severe social deficits. If not managed adequately, socialization problems can become job threatening or make employment virtually impossible. Some people with autism have serious behavior problems such as poor social skills, aggression, self-injury, property destruction, pica, screaming, misuse of others' possessions, and self-stimulation. These can present challenges to employment, but they do not preclude employment.

Individuals who have a history of these behavior problems have worked successfully in a variety of jobs. Often, these individuals have maintained jobs despite the continuing presence of these behavior challenges. In many cases, severe social problems have been ameliorated in the workplace through social skills instruction and behavior management.

When individuals with autism were primarily confined to institutions, it was easy to blame the presence of aggression, self-injury, self-stimulation, withdrawal, and other behavior challenges on their confinement and segregation. Unfortunately, work, even integrated, competitive work, is not a cure for these problems. Individuals with autism who have a history of challenging behaviors are likely to engage in those behaviors in the work environment as well. The purpose of this chapter is to examine methods for meeting the challenges of socialization in the workplace.

INTERVENTION IN THE WORKPLACE

Traditionally, service providers and educators assumed that behavior problems needed to be eliminated prior to job placement. Students with autism were consigned to segregated classrooms and segregated schools and were not considered candidates for work-study programs because of their severe behavior problems. Their school programming was geared toward solving these problems in the classroom prior to placement in a job. For many students, solutions did not come before graduation; therefore, school experiences did not include vocational experiences. Many adults with autism are placed in vocational training centers or day activity centers where staff spend years preparing them for work by attempting to solve behavior problems prior to considering supported employment or integrated employment.

Time has demonstrated that "pre means never" for individuals with autism. Their social deficits can be so pervasive that they are never satisfactorily eliminated and job placement and employment are never attempted. These individuals spend their lives preparing for something that will never materialize.

Despite the bleak statistics on employment of individuals with severe disabilities, students and adults with autism have had successful job experiences. A major thrust of these experiences has been socialization directly in the job environment. There are several compelling reasons for solving social problems directly at the job rather than in pre-employment environments.

Targets Are Precise

An individual with autism can have a myriad of socialization problems. These can range from social skills deficits, such as failure to greet others, to severe destructive behaviors, such as aggression. When attempting to solve these problems outside of the work environment, targeting behaviors for change can be problematic and the establishment of priorities becomes arbitrary. However, in the workplace, it becomes obvious very quickly which behaviors are job threatening and which are not. Priorities are easily established that conform with the demands of the job.

Arnold provides a good example of this situation. Arnold, who had severe deficits in social skills, such as talking to himself, incessantly talking to others, finger flicking, rocking, and occasionally scratching himself, was placed in a job training center. Targeting behaviors for change became arbitrary—there was no rationale for choosing one over another. When Arnold secured a job at a printing company with the support of a job coach, prioritization of social goals became obvious. The self-talk did not matter because it was not heard over the noise of the printing machinery. Finger flicking and self-scratching were obviously problematic because they were incompatible with productivity. Increased productivity was targeted as a goal, along with associated goals of decreasing the frequency of self-scratching and finger flicking.

Eddie is another young man with autism who had severe deficits in social skills that were precisely targeted once he began a job stocking shelves in a toy store. Eddie was occasionally approached by customers and asked where certain toys could be found. Eddie would continue to stock the shelf as if customers were not talking to him. He would not orient toward them nor would he respond to their questions. Teaching Eddie to face customers when they spoke to him and answer their questions became a priority social behavior for him.

Problem or Not?

Some behaviors might be problems in one environment, but not in another. The demands of the work environment dictate whether or not the behavior is a problem. In many cases, attempting to change a behavior outside of the workplace is an exercise in irrelevance. Clint provides a good example of this situation. Clint often paced in his classroom and teachers targeted this behavior over several years with varied success. When Clint was placed in a job at a newspaper recycling plant, pacing ceased to be seen as a problem. His job entailed walking, essentially pacing, throughout a large warehouse area picking up piles of newspapers. As a result, there was no need to target pacing for behavior change.

Role Models

A major advantage of dealing with socialization at work is the abundance of good role models. People with autism learn a great deal from watching other people. When individuals with autism are placed solely with people who have social and language deficits, there is limited opportunity for good modeling to take place. However, when working in jobs alongside co-workers without disabilities, there are more opportunities to observe positive role models. Here, the individual with autism is able to observe other adults greeting each other, chatting, helping, sharing, cooperating, and interacting in socially positive ways. These co-workers can be an important social influence on the individual with autism. Lenny, a young man with autism, quickly learned to greet others in emulation of co-workers several weeks after starting his job.

Cues

Behavior is often determined by cues in the environment. In segregated environments, cues for acceptable behavior often must be contrived. In a day activity center, to encourage conversation, an instructor might have the participants with autism form a circle and then prompt each person to say "hello" and give the day and date. The prompts for socialization are staged and the result appears stilted and forced. However, cues for conversation occur naturally at work, as co-workers stop to greet the worker with autism upon arrival, as they chat with that worker and each other in the break room, and as they congregate at the coffee machine or lockers throughout the day. These cues for conversation occur naturally and repeatedly throughout the day, and as they do, they serve to promote conversation skills for the worker with autism.

Generalization

Generalization, the ability to transfer what has been learned in one situation to a new and different situation, is often difficult for people with autism. An individual with autism might learn to order a pizza in a mock classroom situation, but may need to learn the skill again at the local pizzeria. Similarly, a student with autism might learn to ask for assistance instead of head banging in the classroom, but may need to learn this skill again at his job at the convenience store. Teaching the student a skill in one environment does not eliminate the need to teach it again in a new environment. One way of overcoming problems with generalization is to teach the skills in the target environment. If an individual with autism needs to learn to order pizza, this skill is best taught at the pizzeria. If the person with autism needs to learn to greet co-workers, this skill is best taught at a job with co-workers, instead of in a contrived classroom environment. Providing socialization directly in the job environment avoids problems with transfer.

Abundance of Tasks

Often, absence of constructive activity can serve as a setting event for challenging behavior. Left to his or her own unoccupied devices, an individual with autism is more likely to engage in self-stimulation, self-injury, property destruction, and even aggression than if provided with constructive, structured activity. The abundance of structured tasks found in the workplace is often a natural antidote to these behaviors. Consequently, the decline in frequency of these behaviors may occur more rapidly in the workplace than in segregated training settings that often lack an ongoing supply of structured tasks.

Natural Reinforcers at Work

Good social behavior typically does not come easily or naturally to individuals with autism. Often, reinforcers are necessary to establish and maintain these behaviors. In classroom and training settings, reinforcers must often be contrived and artificial because naturally occurring reinforcers may be limited. The work environment is potentially rich in natural reinforcers, which can strengthen social skills. Natural reinforcers at work include the snack room; a coffee counter; a break room; work and work materials; machinery; work products; and, most importantly, the attention of co-workers and supervisors.

Stuart, a young man with autism, provides a good example of naturally occurring reinforcers at work. Stuart was fascinated with trains and his job at the bookstore provided him with frequent opportunities to read and purchase books on trains. Edward, a student with autism, was fascinated with Batman; his job at the toy store provided him with multiple opportunities to look at, handle, and purchase Batman products.

MANAGEMENT OF PROBLEM BEHAVIORS

Management of destructive behaviors at work begins with the job match, closely followed by a systematic process for developing interventions at work. This process is based on determining the purpose that the problem behaviors serve in the workplace and providing the worker with more acceptable alternatives.

The job match may serve to prevent or mitigate the effects of behavior problems at work. As detailed in Chapter 3, the ideal job match involves a job at which unusual behavior is not considered problematic. For example, Melvin often tears paper, and his job destroying unused bus transfers rewards him for performing this behavior. As another example, Linda occasionally shrieks and squeals, and she enjoys a good job match at a recycling center where the noise level requires her co-workers to wear headphones and to be unaware of her shrieking.

Pinpoint the Problem

Once the worker with autism is placed in a job, any problems that arise must be pinpointed precisely. In some cases, the problems are obvious, such as aggression or self-injury. In other cases, the problems are difficulties with social skills that are specific to the job environment. Lenny, for example, occasionally needed to take a message to the floor supervisor and then wait for a response; however, he often walked away as the supervisor was speaking. Lenny's problem needed to be pinpointed precisely. To attempt to "improve his social skills" would be too broad to be a goal. To teach him to wait for his supervisor to finish talking before he walked away would be a more manageable goal.

It is important to prioritize behaviors and to avoid attempting to pinpoint behaviors for change if they are not creating problems. Albert presents a good example of this tendency. Albert had some self-stimulation behaviors and his work productivity appeared to be low (i.e., he worked at 45% the rate of workers without disabilities). His job coach wanted to increase his productivity; however, the management were very happy with his productivity and his job was secure. Therefore, rather than change a behavior that did not need changing, it was decided to target more pressing problems, such as his occasional self-injury and aggression.

Functional Assessment of Targeted Behavior

Once a behavior is targeted for change, it is necessary to do a functional assessment in the workplace. A functional assessment involves determining the function that the behavior serves in that environment through data collection, observation, and interviews. Behaviors often serve basic functions such as obtaining assistance or attention; escaping from or avoiding certain tasks; obtaining desired items, such as food or coffee; or having the opportunity to engage in preferred activities, such as going for a walk. Some behaviors might serve the purpose of sensory stimulation, such as finger flicking or rocking. Some forms of self-injury, such as self-scratching or even head banging, may serve the function of self-stimulation.

Strategy Selection

Once a functional assessment is complete, strategies can be selected based on the functional assessment. New behaviors can be selected and taught that can serve the functions that maladaptive behaviors used to serve. Strategies can be chosen that can best teach those acceptable alternatives or that can be used to build social skills that are essential for the work environment. There are several categories from which strategies can be selected. Table 4.1 lists recommended strategies according to the function that the problem behavior serves for the worker. In using Table 4.1, it is important to remember that any one behavior may serve more than one function; therefore, multiple strategies may be necessary to decrease a problem behavior. Although Table 4.1 includes common functions for workers with autism, it does not include all possible functions; therefore, strategies may be necessary to address unlisted functions as well.

Antecedent Manipulations Antecedent manipulations are those strategies that involve changing or rearranging antecedents (or events that immediately precede a problem behavior) as a way of decreasing the likelihood that the behavior will occur. Antecedent manipulations can also involve manipulating setting events. Antecedent manipulations occur when the antecedents to misbehavior are identified and then rearranged, eliminated, or mitigated. For example, Jane's job coach noted that if she spoke to Jane in a harsh or critical tone, Jane was likely to scream. She eliminated this antecedent to screaming by only speaking to Jane in calm, even tones, and by avoiding a critical manner. Benny's job coach noted that transitions from one task to another were antecedents to self-injury. These antecedents were mitigated by presenting Benny's schedule to him in written form at the beginning of the day, then having him refer to it throughout the day, prior to transitions. When Benny knew what his schedule was ahead of time and saw it in written form prior to transitions, he was less likely to injure himself.

Workers with autism who cannot read and who have a history of task avoidance may be more likely to cooperate when tasks are presented through the use of picture schedules—pictures of the worker doing the assigned tasks throughout the day. Picture schedules can be used with workers with autism who cannot read as a way of mitigating the effects of transitions and task presentation.

Setting events are events that precede the problem behavior by several hours or longer, which make it more likely that the behavior will occur. Setting events can be eliminated or mitigated to reduce the likelihood of problem behaviors at work. Or, the individual may need to be taught a more acceptable way to respond to the setting event. One type of setting event is a physiological event; that is, physical conditions that can have an impact on behavior, such as illness, caffeine effects, hunger, and fatigue. Physiological setting events can often be eliminated or mitigated by scheduling snacks, drinks, coffee, or even medical care. If the worker has physiological problems that cannot be eliminated, he or she might need to be taught a more acceptable way to handle them. Jane, for example, would typically cry and refuse to work when she was ill. She was taught to tell her staff when she was sick, rather than to simply cry and refuse to work.

Table 4.1. Problem behaviors and recommended strategies

Problem behavior and functions	Recommended strategy	
	For nonverbal workers	For verbal workers
Destructive behaviors		
To avoid or escape tasks	Picture schedule to encourage compliance Contingent reinforcement for doing tasks	Written schedule to encourage compliance Self-rated behavior checklist for doing tasks
To obtain attention	Contingent or noncontingent attention Extinction	Noncontingent attention Extinction
To obtain desired consequence, such as food or drink	Contingent or noncontingent reinforcement Extinction	Noncontingent reinforcement Extinction
To obtain assistance	Anticipate and provide assistance	Social skills training
To obtain sensory stimulation	Provide alternate sensory stimulation	Provide alternate sensory stimulation
In reaction to environmental change	Picture schedule	Written schedule or calendar
In reaction to setting event	Avoid setting event Mitigate effects of setting event	Teach ways to handle setting events
Disruptive behaviors		
In reaction to instructions to do tasks	Picture schedule to encourage compliance Contingent reinforcement for desired behaviors	Written schedule to encourage compliance Self-rated behavior checklist
To gain attention	Contingent or noncontingent attention Extinction	Noncontingent attention Extinction

(continued)

Table 4.1. (continued)

Problem behavior and functions	Recommended strategy	
	For nonverbal workers	For verbal workers
In reaction to change	Avoid unnecessary changes Contingent reinforcement for handling change	Social skills training to handle changes
In reaction to criticism and corrections	Avoid critical approach	Social skills training to handle criticisms and corrections
To gain desired outcome or object	Contingent reinforcement Extinction	Noncontingent reinforcement Social skills training in appropriate ways to get outcome or object Extinction
Social skills		
Skill difficulty	Social skills training	Social skills training
To get attention	Social skills training Contingency management Extinction	Social skills training Noncontingent reinforcement Extinction
To gain assistance	Social skills training Avoid antecedent by anticipating and providing assistance	Social skills training
Low productivity		
Low motivation	Differential reinforcement of high rates of behavior	Self-monitoring of productivity Self-reinforcement for high rates of productivity

Environmental Manipulations   Setting events can also refer to environmental events or characteristics, such as work space, number of people in the area, noise level, temperature of the work environment, and other working conditions. Certain setting events may be associated with certain social or behavior problems, and, if possible, those setting events can be eliminated or mitigated. If not, the worker might need to be taught a more appropriate way to respond. For example, Ellen is likely to engage in self-scratching if there are too many people or too much noise in her work area. Fortunately, she works in a large warehouse and it was possible to move her work area away from foot traffic to a section of the building where other employees tend not to congregate. Jack works in a factory that can become noisy, which is disturbing to Jack. The effects of the noise were mitigated by providing Jack with headphones and favorite tapes. Elma would begin to curse when other workers came to share her work space. It was not possible to eliminate this setting event; therefore, Elma was taught a more acceptable way to respond. She was provided with social skills training so that if a co-worker came to share her work area, she provided a greeting and welcomed him or her to her table.

Setting events also include the amount of attention provided to the worker, the amount of work, and other instructional or work factors that can have an impact on the worker's behavior. Environmental manipulations might be necessary to eliminate or mitigate the effects of these types of setting events. For example, Peter's social problems at work emerged when the work load was too low. This problem was eliminated by making sure that Peter had enough work to keep him busy throughout the day.

Angie provides another example. She often cried at work, which was associated with being taught new tasks. It was determined that the instructional methods were not appropriate and more systematic instruction was used. Angie's crying was also associated with going long periods of time without attention from her supervisor; therefore, Angie's supervisor began to check in on her at least hourly.

Rearrangement of tasks or scheduling considerations can also help promote socialization at work. Martin was a young man with profound mental retardation and autism who was nonverbal. He worked in a stockroom hanging pants and pricing clothing. After working for about 45 minutes, he would sit on the floor and refuse to get up. Allowing Martin a short break about every 30 minutes or alternating a preferred activity (e.g., pricing) with a less preferred activity (e.g., hanging pants) helped eliminate his refusals.

Contingency Management   Although a worker with autism receives a salary or other financial compensation for work done on the job, it might be necessary to supplement this salary with other more immediate forms of reinforcement. Wages are typically paid weekly or biweekly, and this schedule of reinforcement might be too infrequent for an individual with autism who has severe social or behavior problems. More frequent schedules of reinforcement with more social or concrete reinforcers may be necessary. To assist them to display acceptable social behavior at work, people with autism who are nonverbal may require food reinforcers; sensory reinforcers, such as lotion or scents; activity reinforcers; or social reinforcers, such as praise. If social attention is powerful enough to maintain acceptable behavior, then only social attention should be used. However, if stronger, more concrete reinforcers are needed for job retention, then they should be used. Timing is also a consideration—depending on the individual worker, it might be necessary to schedule reinforcers as frequently as every 15 minutes or as infrequently as weekly or biweekly.

Reinforcers might be scheduled on a surprise basis—the worker is provided with a reinforcer for cooperative behavior on a variable schedule, such as approximately every hour. Or, reinforcers can be scheduled for completing a set amount of work. For example, the worker may receive a short break for every 50 units of work completed. Workers might also be provided with reinforcers at set time intervals, such as every 2 hours, provided that certain social and work rules have been followed during that time.

Generally, reinforcers are provided for specific behaviors that are incompatible with targeted misbehavior. For example, if Joan occasionally screams at work, reinforcers might be necessary for quiet working. If Albert spends most of his day finger flicking instead of stocking shelves, he might need to be provided with reinforcers for stocking shelves. If Martha engages in self-injury at work, she might need to be provided with reinforcers for keeping her hands on her work. Linda has problems with self-scratching and often draws blood; she is provided with reinforcers at set intervals for having clear skin.

One schedule of positive reinforcement that has proven valuable at work is the differential reinforcement of high rates of behavior (DRH). This schedule involves providing positive reinforcers for high rates of behavior to encourage the worker to work faster. Occasionally, workers with autism will engage in off-task behaviors, such as self-stimulatory behaviors, and the result is poor productivity. Bill's case provides a good example of the use of a DRH in a work environment. Bill is a man with moderate mental retardation and severe autism who worked in the stockroom of a department store. He spent a great deal of time off-task while he engaged in finger flicking and other self-stimulatory behaviors. His employer was dissatisfied with his slow work pace; therefore, a DRH schedule was implemented. With this schedule, Bill was allowed to go to the popcorn stand in the store in which he worked if he completed a certain amount of work by the end of the day. This schedule required that he work at a specified high rate to receive his reinforcer. The DRH schedule was effective in increasing Bill's productivity.

Noncontingent Reinforcers   Rather than provide reinforcers contingent on acceptable behavior, it is sometimes more effective to provide reinforcers on a regularly scheduled basis to prevent misbehavior. If a functional assessment reveals that Johnny is often aggressive in order to obtain food, the best intervention method may be to provide small, nutritious snacks hourly. If Jane's functional assessment reveals that she often approaches co-workers and asks a series of perseverative questions, she might be provided with scheduled times during the day when she can chat with co-workers. At other times, she is directed back to work if she attempts to chat with a co-worker.

Alternate Sensory Stimuli Some disruptive or interfering behaviors serve the function of self-stimulation. For example, Lucy often picks at her skin and causes bleeding that damages the merchandise in the store in which she is employed. Bert has problems with pica and will try to eat pins and tacks he finds on the warehouse floor. Marvin enjoys tearing the corners off of pieces of paper he finds. Unfortunately, his employer's invoices are not spared. All of these workers are engaging in behaviors that appear to serve the functions of self-stimulation. An effective strategy for managing these behaviors is to provide alternate, more acceptable sensory stimuli. Lucy is provided with lotion to rub on her arms several times per day. Rubbing lotion is an alternate sensory stimuli that replaces the sensory feedback provided by skin picking. Bert is provided with crunchy snacks throughout the day to replace the sensory stimulation provided by tacks and pins. Marvin is allowed to keep a stack of papers near his work area and during breaks he can use the stack for paper tearing.

Extinction Extinction is the process of decreasing the frequency of a behavior by severing the connection between the behavior and those events that are reinforcing it. If a behavior is followed by a reinforcer, the behavior will remain useful to the individual. To eliminate a problem behavior, it is important to eliminate sources of reinforcement for that behavior.

The functional assessment reveals sources of reinforcement for the undesired targeted behavior. For example, the functional assessment may suggest that Michael's head banging is often followed by attempts to calm him down by giving him coffee. The functions of his head banging, therefore, might include obtaining coffee and attention. An imperative strategy is to ensure that his head banging is no longer followed by coffee. In another example, Melinda often cries at work. A functional assessment reveals that when she cries, she is provided with comfort and assistance. Melinda uses crying as a means of obtaining these two forms of attention. Her crying must be put on extinction by making sure it is no longer followed by comfort and assistance.

Extinction must never operate alone. If a behavior is serving a purpose for an individual, it is important to attempt to provide the individual with another means of achieving that purpose in addition to simply putting the behavior on extinction. If Michael, in the earlier example, is head banging to obtain coffee, then coffee should be provided on a scheduled basis throughout the day, or it can be used as a reinforcer for acceptable social behavior at work. In either case, Michael should be provided with an acceptable means of obtaining coffee. In Melinda's case, she must be taught a more socially acceptable means of asking for assistance and comfort and her crying should be placed on extinction.

Social Skills Training   Some workers with autism who engage in unacceptable or even destructive behaviors at work benefit from structured social skills training to replace the destructive behaviors with more socially acceptable ones. Other workers with autism have no destructive behaviors and do not require complex behavior management strategies; however, these workers may have deficits in social skills that specific social skills training can alleviate.

Social skills training is a structured package of procedures designed to teach an individual a specific social skill. In many cases, it is sufficient to merely tell the individual to engage in the social behavior. For example, if Bill can simply be told he needs to greet his co-workers upon arrival, and if telling him is sufficient, then he does not need social skills training. However, if mere verbal instructions do not suffice, then a more structured approach might be necessary. A social skills training package that includes demonstration and the opportunity to practice is often effective when teaching social skills to workers with autism. The opportunity to see the skill performed and then to practice the skill makes it more likely that when the need arises, the individual will respond correctly. The focus is on action, rather than explanation.

An effective social skills training package for a worker with autism begins with a short explanation. It is noteworthy that social skills training does not focus on long, abstract explanations about why the social behavior is desirable. Often individuals with autism have difficulty processing abstract notions, such as the rationale for social skills. They respond well, however, to being taught how to do the skill. A short, concrete explanation can be included, but the focus should be on how to do the skill, rather than why. For example: "John, it is important to ask for help when the copy machine jams. If you ask for help, then someone can help you fix it so you can start copying again right away."

Following the explanation, the trainer provides specific instructions, describing exactly how to perform the targeted social skill. For example, John is told, "If the copy machine jams, you need to go get the supervisor and tell her that you need help because the copy machine is jammed." The explanation is followed by a demonstration in which the trainer shows how to respond if the copy machine jams. Following the demonstration, the worker is asked to pretend that the machine is jammed and to role-play telling the supervisor and asking for help. The worker is then given feedback on the performance and asked to role-play again. Typically, three role plays should be done, practicing the same skill all three times.

Following the demonstration and role plays, the worker is given instructions for generalization. This instruction typically takes the form of a reminder that if the copy machine jams during the workday, the worker should ask for help, as in the role play. Finally, when the worker is observed performing the skill correctly at work, occasional praise can be provided.

Social skills training can initially be scheduled once or twice daily, then quickly faded to twice per week, then once per week, then biweekly. When the skill has been reliably demonstrated, the social skills training may be terminated. In some cases, if termination of the role play results in failure to perform the skill, it may be necessary to schedule occasional booster sessions, such as once every 2 weeks.

SELF-MANAGEMENT

Self-management refers to the application of behavioral control procedures to one's own behavior. Ideally, any individual who is on a behavior management plan can be eventually transferred to a self-management plan in which behavior is under self-control rather than another person's control. There are several self-management procedures that have been used successfully by workers with autism to manage their own behavior at work.

Self-Rating

Some workers with autism require frequent reminders of the rules of behavior to act and perform acceptably at work. Allowing workers with autism the opportunity to review those rules at regular intervals and to rate themselves on compliance with those rules has been a successful self-management tool. Workers with autism who can read can often engage in self-ratings without assistance. Daniel provides a good example of a young man with autism who used self-rating to manage his behavior at work. Daniel was employed at a retail store where he often talked aloud to himself. He had a self-rating program that required that he rate himself hourly on whether he had worked quietly during the past hour. Daniel rated himself hourly and if he earned all of his checks for working quietly, he was provided with a special snack at the end of the day. Daniel worked without a job coach, but drop-in monitoring revealed that he accurately and honestly complied with his self-ratings.

Olin, a man with average intelligence and autism, was on a more complicated self-rating system. Olin had a history of screaming, hitting others, and throwing property. At the end of each workday at his job at a manufacturing firm, Olin rated himself on the following rules: 1) worked quietly, 2) kept hands and feet to self, and 3) used property for its intended use. Even though there were no reinforcers provided for compliance, Olin's self-rating system was sufficient to eliminate aggression, property destruction, and screaming at work.

Workers with autism can participate in rating themselves even if they cannot read. These workers need a job coach or other support person to read the rated items to them at prescribed time intervals, and then the workers place checks or minuses in designated boxes. Often, an additional item is added that reads "Rates Self Accurately" to encourage honesty.

Self-Reinforcement

Some workers with autism can learn to use the principles of reinforcement to self-manage their behavior. A worker with autism can be taught to achieve certain criteria and then to take a reinforcer. Ellie provides an example of a woman with autism and low average intelligence who combined self-rating with self-reinforcement to manage her own behavior. Ellie had a history of aggression, property destruction, and cursing at others. She rated herself twice daily on the following behaviors: 1) keeping her hands and feet to herself, 2) correctly using property, 3) speaking politely, and 4) rating herself accurately. At the end of each workday, she rated herself and if she followed each of the rules that day, she would walk to a nearby convenience store and buy herself a cup of coffee.

Vince is a man with autism and profound mental retardation who was taught to set a timer and take a chip for a reward when the timer rang after 30 minutes of remaining on task.

Schedules

Some workers with autism improve productivity and cooperation at work if they have written schedules to follow. These schedules typically need to include a listing of their assignments and the times of breaks, lunch, and dismissal. Workers with autism who are literate can often learn to write their own schedules and to follow those schedules with little or no staff support.

Workers without writing or language skills can be taught to follow their own picture schedules. They can be taught to refer to the picture schedule, perform the pictured task, return to the schedule, follow the next pictured task, and so forth throughout the day. Teaching workers to refer to picture schedules enables them to operate with less dependence on the job coach or other support personnel.

Accuracy Checklists

Some workers with autism have difficulty performing each step of a task carefully, or they may occasionally skip critical steps of a task. Providing written lists of required steps and then teaching the worker to refer to the list between steps is a self-management strategy that can help the worker with autism achieve higher levels of accuracy without continual prompting from a job coach or other supervisor. Burt is a man with average intelligence and autism who worked in a print shop. He often jammed the copy machine because of the hurried manner in which he performed the steps. Burt was taught to refer to a list that included each step and the word "stop" between steps. This list helped him to slow down to the point where he could operate the machine without jamming it.

Self-Monitoring

Workers with autism with some reading and math skills who have productivity problems can be taught to measure their production rates and then graph them. Workers will strive to achieve their goals so that their graphed productivity meets the goal line drawn across the top of the graph.

CASE STUDIES
• • • • • • •

Elizabeth

Elizabeth, 34 years old, is employed at a manufacturing firm where she is paid $6.35 per hour for making electronic parts. Elizabeth has good fine motor skills and does her work with precision. She exhibits social skills such as greeting co-workers, answering questions, and saying "good-bye" when leaving work. However, Elizabeth has been diagnosed as having autism, and her intelligence measures in the low-average range. She has some behavior problems, which if left unchecked could prove job threatening. Occasionally, Elizabeth throws her work materials and her work tools. Additionally, she has periodic outbursts of crying, screaming, and tearing her clothes. She also engages in mild self-injury in the form of scratching herself.

Behaviors that were targeted for change were crying, screaming, clothes tearing, throwing work materials, and self-injury. A functional assessment was done and setting events and functions were identified. Setting events included lack of sleep the night before, lack of an adequate breakfast, and trouble with allergies. Antecedents to crying, clothes tearing, and throwing work materials included having difficulty performing a new task. Often, these behaviors were followed by a sympathetic response from her work supervisor who would ask her what was wrong, offer assistance, and provide a short break from work. Functions of the problem behaviors of crying, throwing work materials, and clothes tearing appeared to be to obtain assistance, escape from difficult tasks, and obtain attention in the form of comfort and counseling. Her skin scratching appeared to serve the function of self-stimulation, as she often did this in the absence of other tasks.

The results of the functional assessment were used to select strategies for improving socialization at work. The setting event of lack of sleep was eliminated by ensuring that she went to bed at a reasonable hour. Elizabeth was in the habit of watching late-night movies and, as a result, would often only get 5 hours of sleep. She was encouraged to go to sleep by 11:00 P.M. and was taught to tape late-night movies with her VCR for viewing at another time. She also was taught to eat larger breakfasts before leaving for work. Furthermore, her physician was consulted about her allergies and medications were prescribed to minimize allergic reactions. Because she often had severe behavior problems when having difficulty with a new task, instructional procedures were evaluated and redesigned to provide more error-free learning. Additionally, social skills training was implemented to teach Elizabeth how to ask for assistance when having difficulty with a task. Social skills training was provided twice per week, just before starting work for the day. A schedule of positive reinforcement was designed that allowed Elizabeth to accumulate points each hour for working quietly, keeping her clothes and work materials in good order, completing assigned tasks, and keeping her skin clear. If she earned at least 90% of her points for the day, she was allowed to select either a favorite snack or a favorite activity as a reinforcer. Elizabeth was also offered hand lotion about once every 2 hours to provide a more acceptable means of self-stimulation than skin scratching. Finally, her misbehavior was put on extinction. Crying, clothes tearing, and throwing materials were responded to by simply directing Elizabeth back to task, with as little discussion as possible.

Elizabeth's intervention plan, which was based on a functional assessment and implemented at her workplace, was successful in reducing the frequency of her problem behaviors. Eventually, the rating system was changed to self-rating and Elizabeth learned to evaluate and rate her own behavior. Finally, more acceptable social skills increased in frequency, such as asking for assistance when she had difficulty with a task and working quietly.

Milton

Milton is 28 years old and is a productive worker who prepares trays of snacks for vending machines under the supervision of a job coach. Although Milton has autism and profound mental retardation as well as an inability to speak, he earns the same pay rate as his co-workers without disabilities. Milton had socialization problems, including loud yelling and head banging, which occurred about four times per day. A functional assessment was done and antecedents were noted. Antecedents included being corrected; being told, "No, don't do that"; and seeing snacks of other co-workers that he was not allowed to have. Occasionally, to calm him down, his job coach would offer him a snack or promise him a snack if he stopped hurting himself. If the job coach was correcting him, she would immediately back off if he began to self-injure. The functions of his self-injury appeared to be to terminate correction by the job coach and to obtain food.

Strategies for improving socialization were selected based on the functional assessment. The job coach avoided the use of the phrase "No, don't do that." Instead, she gave frequent praise—about every 30 minutes when Milton was working well—and if he was engaging in a misbehavior, she gave him specific verbal instructions to direct him back to task, without using the word "no." For example, if Milton began to finger flick, she would gently say, "Pick up the tray," rather than, "No, don't finger flick." Milton was also offered a small snack about every hour as a reinforcer for calm, on-task behavior, which eliminated the need for him to engage in self-injury to get food. Finally, his self-injury was placed on extinction. He was given no food during or immediately after head banging; instead he was simply directed back to work. Milton's self-injury decreased in frequency rapidly following implementation of his socialization strategies.

SUMMARY

Autism can be associated with severe deficits in social skills, including the presence of destructive behaviors. Although these behaviors may decline in frequency when an individual obtains a job, there is a possibility that they will persist at an unacceptable level even in integrated, competitive work environments. Socialization problems are best treated in work environments, rather than waiting to solve the socialization problems prior to job placement. Socialization on the job is enhanced by co-workers who can serve as role models, ample cues for acceptable behavior, structured work schedules, and the presence of natural reinforcers. Behavior problems can be solved directly at work by taking into account the behavior problem during the job match, by doing a functional assessment at work, and by choosing intervention strategies based on the functional assessment. Environmental manipulations, rearrangement of antecedents, elimination or mitigation of setting events, contingency management, provision of desired outcomes, alternate sensory stimuli, and social skills training can all be done directly in the work environment to achieve improved socialization.

CHAPTER 5

Strategies for Solving Problems at Work

Experiencing difficulties at work is common among people with and without autism. Most people experience problems at work at least once during their career. For many workers, problems are a permanent part of the job experience. Some of the problems that workers with autism experience are common to all workers; others are associated with their disability. This chapter surveys many of the difficulties that people with autism encounter at work, as well as strategies for prevention and correction.

The various problems are discussed in several categories. Although these categories are not necessarily mutually exclusive, they provide some order to the discussion. The categories include: administrative problems, employer-initiated problems, co-worker–initiated problems, and worker-initiated problems.

ADMINISTRATIVE PROBLEMS

If a worker is in a supported employment program, administrative problems may occur as a result of difficulties within the supporting agency. Administrative problems may also occur during the job procurement and employment process, which are independent of the worker and the employer.

Poor Job Match

A good job match is critical for any worker, not just workers with autism. Yet, a poor job match can be more devastating to a person with autism because it can exacerbate problems that already exist because of the disability. Job matches can be poor for many reasons. The primary reasons are that the job is too difficult, the worker is not interested in the task, or the worker's behavior or social problems are in some way exacerbated by the work environment.

Many workers with autism lack the language skills, social skills, and interpersonal skills to deal with stresses that result from a poor job match. For example, if the job duties are too difficult, a worker with autism might respond with severe self-degradation, possibly even self-injury. Or, if the sequence of duties or the actual performance of those duties is too unpredictable, some workers with autism might become extremely upset and behavior problems may ensue. A job can also be problematic if it is well outside the range of the worker's interests. For example, if a worker with autism has an aversion to water-related activities, it would be extremely difficult to encourage adaptation to a job at a car wash. An individual with autism who prefers to pace and walk about would be poorly matched to a job that requires seated desk work all day.

Failure to take into account existing behavior problems is the number one cause of a poor job match. Workers with autism and significant behavior problems can work in a variety of environments; however, there are some environments that would be problematic. For example, an individual with a history of screaming might do well in a large, noisy warehouse where his loud voice volume would go unnoticed; however, a poor job match would be the public library, where being quiet is mandatory. An individual with autism who has a history of clothes tearing and property destruction would be poorly matched to a job in the stockroom of a designer dress shop; however, property destruction would not be a job-threatening factor at a recycling center that involves sorting aluminum and plastic drink containers.

The best way to avoid poor job matching is to follow a careful procedure in job selection. As discussed in Chapter 3, finding a good job match involves evaluating the demands of the job; the nature of the environment; and the strengths, weaknesses, and interests of the worker. The process is not very different from that of finding jobs for people without disabilities. The difference may lie in the margin of error, which is certainly narrower for many individuals with severe or moderate autism.

A poor job match can result in the worker being fired. If the job is threatened, and it is apparent that a poor job match is the reason, a supporting agency can attempt to salvage the situation by increasing the level of support. For example, if the individual's social behaviors become job threatening, it might be possible to keep the job if social skills training is implemented or an effective behavior change plan is used, even though the environment is not ideal. In these cases, additional supervision or support may be needed temporarily. Or, it may be possible to negotiate changes in the job with the employer. For example, if the worker is having a great deal of difficulty performing the task, the employer might be amenable to the worker only doing part of the task.

Unclear Expectations

Sometimes workers with autism, similar to workers without autism, find themselves in jobs that require a higher level of productivity than they are capable of accomplishing. If a worker's production rate is not high enough, he or she is in danger of being fired. One way to avoid such a predicament is to have a clear understanding of the productivity requirements prior to starting work. If the requirements are too high, taking into account good training and even a good motivational program, then either sufficient support should be provided by a supported employment agency or the job should be rejected. To avoid unclear expectations, it is important that the worker or support personnel understand the production requirements of the job and that the employer understand the production level that can be expected from the worker.

It is also important to have clear expectations about the tasks involved in the job. For supported workers, it is necessary for support personnel or the job development specialist to actually try the task or observe the task being carried out so that a determination can be made of the worker's fitness to do the job. Having the job duties and production requirements specified in writing prior to employment is also helpful to ensure that the job is manageable for the worker.

Sometimes, despite efforts made to clarify these issues, a worker is unable to meet the production requirements of the job. It may be that the support personnel overestimated the worker's ability to perform the task. At that point, several steps can be taken to prevent job termination. For workers with autism who have job coaches, a behavior plan can be developed that is designed to increase productivity. Also, schedules of reinforcement that are designed to increase rate, such as differential reinforcement of high rates of behavior (DRH), can be implemented. Another possibility is to renegotiate the worker's pay to a level that is commensurate with the productivity level. The worker might even be amenable to obtaining a special worker's certificate from the Department of Labor that allows the employer to pay the worker with a disability based on the production level. In addition, the worker's level of support can be increased until he or she is able to meet production requirements.

Lack of Support

Although there are certainly workers with autism who can hold jobs independently, there are many who cannot work without support. For those workers, lack of support can lead to job failure. Support must be sufficient in several areas: support personnel to worker ratio; number of hours of support per day; and the number of days, weeks, or years that the support is available.

A lack of support can result in productivity problems or in behavior or social problems. These problems often occur not because of a lack of support personnel, but because personnel are not sufficiently trained or do not reliably implement instructional or behavior programs. Support personnel must be sufficiently trained to provide the needed instructional, behavioral, and social support to help the worker succeed. Also, the support personnel must implement such support with precision. Simply sending a job coach to work with an individual with autism is not necessarily sufficient support. If the worker has problems with self-injury, aggression, screaming, or noncompliance, an untrained job coach may exacerbate the problem. Many of the more destructive behavior outbursts that have occurred in work environments have occurred when workers were supported by poorly trained job coaches or by job coaches who did not correctly implement behavior and instruction programs.

Frequent changes in job coaches or support personnel can also represent a lack of support. Review of the data for numerous individuals with severe autism over several years revealed that periods of increased serious behavior problems often coincided with the presence of substitute support staff or staff turnover. Typically, workers do well when supported by their regular job coach; however, if the job coach is absent and is replaced by a substitute, some workers are likely to be uncooperative. In those cases, it is often prudent to have the worker miss work rather than go to work with a substitute job coach who is not able to provide sufficient support.

If the employer and supporting agency communicate early enough about job problems due to insufficient support, it is often possible to retain a job by increasing the level, expertise, or stability of the support. In some cases of individuals with severe autism and serious behavior problems, it may be necessary for them to miss work until support personnel are sufficiently trained.

Transportation Problems

Some workers with autism are able to travel independently to work; however, many workers must be provided with transportation by the supporting agency. Supported transportation can be provided by a company van, the job coach, or supervision on public transportation. Unreliable transportation schedules can result in a worker being late to work, which may put the job in jeopardy. It is important when accepting jobs that realistic starting times be negotiated, with consideration given to the fact that the worker must be given transportation by support personnel. Many employers are willing to negotiate flex time or starting times that are realistic for the transportation service. Transportation-related problems are best solved before beginning a job by working out realistic schedules that are compatible with the agency's ability to provide transportation.

Parent or Guardian Problems

Occasionally, jobs are jeopardized because of problems relating to parents or guardians. These problems generally involve the parent or guardian disapproving of the job or the parent or guardian going to the work site and interacting with the employer in a way that jeopardizes the job.

Parent/guardian problems are best handled by prevention. If the worker with autism is working under the auspices of an interdisciplinary team, then the parent as a member of the team can provide input on the acceptability of any proposed jobs. The support agency must then have procedures in place for dealing with parental opposition and the role of the parent at the workplace. If parental support and agency–employer relationships are not defined through established policies and procedures, then parent/guardian problems can escalate into job loss. If problems in this area occur, it suggests that adequate procedures are not in place that safeguard the best interests of the worker while taking into account the input and concerns of the parent or guardian.

EMPLOYER-INITIATED PROBLEMS

Occasionally a job is put into jeopardy because of problems that occur with the employer or that are initiated by the employer, but are not directly caused by the worker. Most employer-initiated problems are not unique to workers with autism, but in some cases they disproportionately affect them.

Bankruptcy

An employer-related problem of major consequence is bankruptcy and dissolution of the company. There is little that can be done about this problem, and if the company goes out of business, the worker is surely out of a job. Usually, the employer provides some warning to the worker or to the supporting agency so that other employment can be sought while the worker still has a job. Rarely, but on occasion, no notice is given and the worker may experience a period of unemployment.

Seasonal Slowdowns

Some work is seasonal and, therefore, subject to slow periods when demands for the company's product or service are low. For example, some retail stores are extremely busy between Thanksgiving and Christmas, but experience slowdowns during the 2 or 3 months that follow Christmas. During seasonal slowdowns, it is possible that workers will have a reduced work schedule or even a temporary layoff. Sometimes, the temporary layoff turns into a permanent separation.

One way to handle a seasonal slowdown is to be prepared for it. Often, employers do not explicitly warn job seekers about the seasonal nature of the work. A worker might begin a job in October and consider it permanent employment, only to be unexpectedly laid off in January. Sometimes these disappointments can be avoided by asking about such possibilities during the initial job interview.

The effects of seasonal slowdowns may be minimized by workers who do exceptionally good work. Employers often do all they can to maintain some level of employment for valued workers, including those with autism, during seasonal slowdowns. If the worker with autism is extremely slow or has a spate of disruptive behaviors at work, that worker might be at higher risk for a seasonal layoff than more proficient co-workers. Sufficient support can be a critical factor in avoiding the effects of seasonal layoffs by ensuring that the person works and behaves to his or her best ability.

Financial Problems

Related to seasonal slowdowns is the issue of financial difficulties. A company's work flow may slow down to the point that the payroll cannot be met. For example, a business that depends on government contracts may not have a contract renewed 1 year, which would result in a reduced work schedule. Periods of financial difficulty may be brief or they may endure for several years, providing an uncertain and abbreviated work schedule. The worker with autism and the supporting agency may be faced with having to decide whether to wait out the uncertain situation or seek employment elsewhere. Sometimes part-time, casual work can be found to fill in the gaps. For example, two workers with autism worked for an electronics firm that experienced temporary work reductions due to a lack of work. These two workers found part-time work with a flexible schedule at a mailing firm. On days when there was no work at the electronics firm, they would put in a full day at the mailing company.

Businesses with financial problems may decide to streamline operations to save money. Unfortunately, streamlining may mean terminating the employment of workers with autism, especially if those workers have low productivity. In such situations, providing the support necessary to maximize their performance may save their jobs.

Relocation

Occasionally, it may be necessary or to the benefit of the business to relocate. Typically, the employer gives employees considerable notice of an impending relocation. Furthermore, the relocating employer may offer the workers with autism a job at the new locale; however, that locale may be out of their traveling range. In some cases, the employees are informed up to 1 year in advance. Such notice provides them and the support agency with enough time to find another job.

Change in Management

Often, a worker's manager or supervisor develops a special, supporting relationship with that worker. Support can be in the form of extra assistance with the task, additional instruction, special treats, and special social attention. One manager of a large retail outlet often ate lunch with and assisted a worker who had severe autism and had difficulty cutting up his lunch. Another manager saw to it that his employee with autism always had snacks and drinks available to him throughout the workday. Because this worker had a history of severe self-injury when not provided with sufficient snack foods, the manager's treatment of him was instrumental in his success at the job.

When a supportive manager leaves, there exists the possibility that the new manager will not provide the same supports. Lack of support then leads to poor performance and, finally, to job loss. In cases where a supportive manager leaves, it is prudent to arrange to have another person, even if it is not the incoming manager, provide the same supports as the exiting manager.

When supportive managers leave, it may be that they are replaced by managers who do not have positive inclinations toward the workers with autism. In fact, they may even have the opposite reaction—they may see a worker with autism as a burden and not appreciate his or her service to the company. Obviously, such a change in management can be job threatening. The supporting agency must be sensitive to the attitude of the new manager and attempt to change it through education, good rapport, and adequate support to the worker to ensure that his or her performance is acceptable.

CO-WORKER–INITIATED PROBLEMS

Co-workers are often extremely supportive of workers with autism. Their support can range from being friendly to assisting the worker with social integration or to providing assistance with task performance. However, there are occasionally problems generated by co-workers that can make work difficult for an employee with autism.

Teasing

In some instances, co-workers have been known to tease workers with autism. Sometimes the worker does not recognize the malicious intent and interprets the teasing as social overtures. In other cases, the worker with autism understands the meaning behind the teasing and becomes upset. Teasing by co-workers can be handled by teaching the worker with autism acceptable responses or by having support personnel intervene on behalf of the worker. It might also be possible to teach the worker with autism more acceptable social skills or work habits so that he or she is less of a target for teasing. In extreme cases, where the teasing interferes with the worker's ability to do the job, it may be necessary to involve management; however, involving management is not a preferred approach, as it puts a burden on management and usually does not serve to end the teasing. In most cases where teasing persists, the worker with autism learns to disregard the teasing and it eventually stops.

Bossing and Harassment

Occasionally, co-workers boss or harass the worker with autism. They may provide instructions that are not necessary and continual critical feedback. If the worker with autism has support personnel, such as a job coach, that person can intervene and act as a buffer between critical co-workers and the worker with autism. In extreme cases, in which the bossing and harassment are interfering with the worker's ability to do the job, it might be necessary to involve management personnel.

Resentment

Co-workers may resent workers with autism. They may feel degraded that a person with an obvious intellectual disability is doing the same job that they do. They may also resent the low productivity of the worker and the disruptive or unusual behavior that occasionally occurs. Co-worker resentment is rarely job threatening, but it can cause uneasiness. Attitudes can possibly be changed through a short training session on autism or some other intervention that assists co-workers to view the worker with autism more positively. If the worker is assisted by a job coach, he or she can help co-workers overcome negative attitudes by being pleasant and helpful, rather than defensive and adversarial.

Uneasiness

Workers with autism sometimes display behaviors that make co-workers uneasy. Screaming, self-injury, pica, and disrobing are examples. Support personnel must be sensitive to the effects of these kinds of behaviors on co-workers and work actively to prevent them or mitigate their effects on the work environment. If the worker is being disruptive, it might be best to leave the work area temporarily, for the benefit of other workers. Although leaving might not be the best behavioral response (i.e., the worker might learn that by screaming he can avoid work), the attitudes of co-workers must be considered. Usually, after several months, co-workers become more accepting of workers with autism and lose their uneasiness.

WORKER-INITIATED PROBLEMS

Autism is a disorder of social behavior and language, and as such many of its characteristics can be job threatening. Worker-initiated problems include poor work performance, poor social skills, disruptive behavior, aberrant behavior, destructive behavior, and refusal to work. In many cases, it is possible to ameliorate their effects through prevention or intervention.

Low Productivity

Low productivity is a major component of poor work performance. Although many workers with autism work at or above the levels of their co-workers without disabilities, there are workers with autism for whom productivity is a problem. Several factors contribute to low productivity; they are discussed on the following pages.

Difficulty Learning New Tasks Some workers with autism have difficulty learning new tasks. During their learning period, productivity might be low. If initial low productivity is expected, the employer may be patient if informed that this might occur. The job coach might need to assist with task completion during the learning period to ensure productivity. Occasionally, it is possible to obtain samples of the work and provide a short, unpaid training period prior to actually beginning the job. This provides a nonstressful environment for the worker to learn the task. Then, when the worker begins work, the productivity rate is acceptable from the start.

Short Attention Span   Productivity may be low due to a short attention span. The worker with autism may work for only several minutes and then stop. Jason, a man with moderate mental retardation and autism, held a job in a printing company where he would work for several minutes, then stop and stare off into space. Liza was a woman with severe mental retardation and autism who had a job in a stockroom. She would hang several pairs of pants, then leave her work area to wander through the stockroom. Both workers needed behavior management plans to improve productivity. Jason's plan was simple—he was provided with cards that indicated "Work" and "Break." He was taught that while the "Work" card was posted, he was to keep his eyes on his work and do his job. Liza's plan consisted of providing positive reinforcers for progressively longer periods of attending to task.

Distractibility   High levels of distractibility can also interfere with productivity. A worker with autism might be easily distracted by even small changes in the environment. For example, an announcement over the loudspeaker, a siren in the street, or even a co-worker passing by can distract the worker and interfere with productivity. Ernie, a man with average intelligence and mild autism, worked in a computer manufacturing firm. Ernie had drop-in supervision from a job coach and was assisted at work by co-workers. Whenever a siren would sound, Ernie would jump up from his work area and rush to the door to watch the emergency vehicle drive by. Ernie needed specific feedback from his drop-in job coach and reminders from his co-workers about the need to remain in his work area when sirens sounded. He was put on a self-management plan that allowed him to rate his own behavior. One item on his self-rating included remaining in his work area. In another example, Darren, a worker in the stockroom of a retail store, was distracted by passing co-workers. Each time a co-worker passed him, Darren would greet him or her. Some co-workers passed by frequently so the greetings interfered with Darren's productivity. Darren was provided with social skills training to learn to greet co-workers only the first time he saw them each day.

Low Cognitive Skills   Autism can be associated with mental retardation; therefore, it is important that realistic assessments of the worker's productivity be made during the initial job negotiations. If the worker is simply not capable of meeting the production requirements, it might be necessary to provide additional support or seek employment elsewhere.

Interfering Behaviors   Workers with autism may engage in behaviors that interfere with work, for example, self-stimulation, such as finger flicking or rocking. Self-stimulation also includes nonproductive activity with the work material itself, such as excessive handling or flipping of the material or excessive visual inspection of an item. Productivity can often be increased through positive reinforcement schedules that target high production rates. The reinforcers provide an incentive for the worker to remain on task rather than engage in the competing behavior. Allen had a low production rate due to high levels of finger flicking. He was placed on a behavior modification plan that provided a reinforcer if he completed a set amount of work each hour. Finger flicking itself was placed on extinction. This plan successfully increased his productivity level with a concomitant decrease in finger flicking.

Rituals   Some workers develop rituals that interfere with productivity. For example, a young man who placed stock on the sales floor of a drug store would spin each item prior to setting it down. He needed a great deal of instruction and monitoring to teach him to perform the task without the ritual.

Lack of Motivation   Workers with autism might work slowly because of low motivation. If they lack language or counting skills, their paycheck may not be sufficient motivation to work at acceptable levels. Often, a behavior plan that provides more concrete and frequent reinforcers, such as breaks or favorite snacks, can provide sufficient motivation to increase productivity to acceptable levels.

Motivated to Work Slowly   Occasionally, well-meaning support staff inadvertently encourage the worker to work slowly. This unfortunate situation occurs when the job coach, instructor, or another support person praises the employee for working, even if the person is working slowly. For example, John, a man with profound mental retardation and severe autism, works in a stockroom hanging clothes. He takes the hanger, looks at it, flips it, stares off into space, and finally puts the pants on it and hangs them up. The entire sequence takes about 5 minutes. Upon completion, the job coach enthusiastically praises him for hanging the pants. He then takes the next hanger and repeats the sequence. From John's point of view, he has been praised for looking, flipping, waiting, and finally hanging. Based on the praise, he assumes his production level is just fine. The job coach is puzzled as to why he works so slowly. The job coach is unaware that by providing praise for the drawn-out task performance, he is actually encouraging low productivity.

If high productivity is the desired behavior, praise, reinforcers, and rewards should follow increased rates of behavior and should not be provided for slow performance. John's job coach remedied the problem by demonstrating how to hang the pants quickly, instructing John to do it fast the way he did, then praising him for working quickly when he actually worked quickly. This approach was effective in increasing his productivity.

Occasionally, despite all instructional and behavioral attempts and despite adequate support, a worker might lose the job because of low productivity. If this occurs, it is especially important when seeking a new job that the worker's productivity potential be seriously considered and the demands of the job be exactly specified.

Low Quality

Workers with autism, similar to other workers, can produce low quality work. There are numerous reasons for low quality work. Occasionally, the worker with autism is in a hurry to finish the job and makes careless errors in the process. Other times, interfering behaviors, such as self-stimulation, can distract the worker's attention and result in errors. Furthermore, a task may be too difficult given the worker's cognitive level. In addition, a possibility that cannot be overlooked is that the work supervisor or support personnel have placed such a heavy emphasis on productivity that quality suffers.

A determination must be made about the reason for the low quality work and a solution must then be prepared. If the worker is rushing through the task, or is being rushed, then the focus must shift from rewarding speed to rewarding accuracy. This shift can either be formal, through a behavior modification plan, or informal, through monitoring and feedback.

Sometimes it is necessary to insert self-checks into task performance. For example, Linda had a job in a tee-shirt factory. She often skipped necessary steps, resulting in defective merchandise. Finally, she was provided with a list of steps and was taught to refer to the list between steps. Once she reliably incorporated all of the steps, the checklist was faded from use.

If work quality is low because of interfering behaviors, such as self-stimulation, stimulation with work materials, wandering, or other off-task behaviors, then a behavior modification plan may be needed. The plan would most likely provide positive reinforcers based on accuracy.

Poor work quality may be due to the fact that the task is too difficult given the cognitive limitations of the worker. If the task is too difficult, it might be possible to restructure the task so that it can be done by an easier method. It might also be possible to create an arrangement in which the worker does part of the task. For example, Janice is a worker with autism and severe mental retardation. She was hired to price items in the stockroom of a retail store, but she was not able to learn how to set the price gun because of her cognitive deficits. She was able to keep the job because her job coach or a co-worker would set the price gun for her whenever necessary; she could then use it to price hundreds of items of merchandise.

Social Skills Problems

Social skills deficits, discussed in detail in Chapter 4, are common to individuals with autism. They can have an impact on a job in two ways. First, they can be job threatening if social skills are required to perform the job duties. For example, a hostess in a restaurant is required to interact with customers; if she does not have the skills to do so, she may lose her job. Second, social skills deficits can also interfere with interpersonal relationships among employees and between an employee and his or her supervisor. These problems can limit the employee's integration at work.

These difficulties can often be remedied by providing social skills training or additional support. Occasionally, adaptations to the task can also be made that eliminate the need for social interactions as part of the job duties. Jeffrey provides a good example of this solution. Jeffrey, a man with mild mental retardation and autism, works at a housewares store straightening and stocking shelves on the sales floor. He used to ignore customers who approached him with inquiries. One customer proceeded to follow him through the store, insisting that he answer her question. He remained unimpressed with her efforts and persisted in ignoring her. Because Jeffrey was working on the sales floor, it was expected that he would respond to customer inquiries. Jeffrey was taught that when a customer made an inquiry, he needed to either provide the information or direct the person to the service desk at the front of the store. Jeffrey was able to learn the correct response through social skills training that included instruction, demonstration, role-play, and feedback. Training was conducted at work 3 times per week for 3 weeks, then faded.

Sometimes it is not possible to teach the worker the social skill and an adaptation may be necessary. Albert is a worker with autism and profound mental retardation who has no verbal language skills. Albert works in a toy store straightening and stocking shelves. Because Albert is incapable of responding to customer inquiries, management agreed that Albert would not wear the store uniform. Without the uniform, he was less likely to be approached by customers.

Poor Appearance

Many workers with autism have fastidious personal hygiene; however, some are inattentive to their personal appearance and their hygiene. They either forget to attend to these issues, do so incompletely, or choose not to concern themselves with hygiene at all. Additionally, some people with autism have idiosyncratic clothing preferences—they may prefer to wear ill-fitting clothing, the same outfit for many days on end, clothes that are inappropriate for the weather, or clothes that are simply out of place at work. One man with autism was extremely fond of his tuxedo and often wore it to his factory job.

Hygiene and grooming issues can sometimes be resolved with instruction; for example, if the worker is not aware of the necessity of wearing clothes without rips, instruction and discrimination training can solve the problem. A worker with autism may be incapable of achieving acceptable hygiene and grooming without supervision and support. For example, a worker with severe mental retardation might need assistance with bathing and toothbrushing. For these workers, poor hygiene and grooming is most likely due to inattentive or insufficient support.

It may be that the person with autism is capable of performing the hygiene and grooming tasks, but inattentive or forgetful. Often, reminders in the forms of verbal prompts, written schedules, picture schedules, and checklists are effective in improving hygiene. Usually, reinforcers, other than praise, are not needed to achieve good hygiene and grooming.

Personal Items

Some workers with autism have favorite items that they enjoy carrying with them. These might be items such as pens, pencils, crayons, magazines, drawings, paper, or clothing. Although these items look acceptable in moderation, if the worker carries too much, it appears peculiar. One man with above average intelligence regularly went to work with three shopping bags of clothing and other irrelevant items. Another man would take dozens of pens with him and then lay them all out around his work area. Because these items were not needed to complete the task, they created a mess and a distraction that the employer considered unacceptable. Excess baggage can often be eliminated by setting limits on the amount of the item that the worker can carry. For example, the worker who carried the three shopping bags to work was told he could take one backpack to work and that any other belongings needed to remain at home. His residential counselor needed to provide periodic monitoring to ensure compliance. The man who carried an excess of pens and paper to work was told he could take three pens, three pencils, and one pad of paper.

Poor Attendance and Tardiness

Workers with autism usually do not have problems with poor attendance and tardiness. Autism is often associated with rigid adherence to routines, which means workers with autism often become upset if they cannot go to work when they expect to or if they arrive late. However, if the worker does have a problem with tardiness, it can often be solved by examining the morning routine and ensuring that enough time is allotted for the worker to leave for work on time. It might be necessary for the worker to adjust his or her sleeping and wake-up schedule. Occasionally, there are problems with the travel habits of the worker that cause him or her to be late on a regular basis. One man with autism often missed his bus because he loitered excessively in the convenience store near the bus stop. Another worker with autism would arrive at the bus stop and if the bus was not there he would walk to his job several miles away. That worker needed additional travel training, which included teaching him to wait at the bus stop until the bus arrived.

Rarely will workers with autism feign illness to avoid work. However, if this does happen, it is necessary to examine the reasons for avoiding work. It might be necessary to change motivational factors or, if possible, to change jobs. One woman complained excessively of somatic problems and would then stay home and watch television all day. She was informed that if she felt she was ill, she would need to go to the doctor and would need a doctor's excuse to miss work. This requirement eliminated the problem.

Aberrant Behavior

Aberrant behavior, sometimes seen in people with autism, can be job threatening or can inhibit social integration at work. Aberrant behaviors can be self-stimulatory behaviors such as finger flicking and rocking. They may also involve unusual interactions with objects, such as kissing trees, drinking from puddles, licking objects, or spitting on objects. Some workers with severe autism and mental retardation might use an employer's property in unusual ways, such as flipping objects or hoarding work materials.

Aberrant behavior can often be ameliorated with training, a behavior management program, or both. Individuals with autism often respond well to being taught to restrict certain behaviors to certain time periods or certain places. Or, a reinforcement plan may be used to encourage more acceptable work-related behaviors. Depending upon the frequency of the aberrant behavior, it also may be necessary to increase support until the individual learns more acceptable work habits.

Disruptive Behavior

Perhaps the most job-threatening behaviors that can occur at work are those that are disruptive to the workplace. Screaming, yelling, loud voice volume, running through the workplace, grabbing other's work materials, and making excessive demands on co-workers are examples of job-threatening behaviors that have been displayed by workers with severe autism. Other examples include lying on the floor and refusing to get up, disrobing, and public masturbation. Toileting problems can also be disruptive to the work environment, especially those that involve urinating or defecating in areas other than the toilet.

Disruptive behaviors can easily lead to job loss. In many cases, the job can be saved by quick action on the part of support personnel to stem the disruption caused by the behavior. If that behavior has been especially disruptive, it might be necessary for the employee to take several days off from work. During this period of time, the adequacy of the supports can be assessed. Support may need to be increased or the support personnel may need additional training. It is probably also necessary to do a functional assessment of the disruptive behavior and develop a behavior plan based on that functional assessment. Support personnel must then be trained to implement the plan so that the worker, with trained support, can return to his or her job. However, there may still need to be emergency measures in place to deal with the disruption, should it occur again, in a way that minimizes its effects on co-workers.

Melvin's case provides a good example of the management of disruptive behavior. Melvin is a man with limited verbal skills, severe autism, and profound mental retardation. He has a job unboxing merchandise in a stockroom. He would often lie on the floor, pull his pants down, and masturbate. He would also scream repetitive demands throughout the day (e.g., "Want Coke, want

Coke."). A functional assessment was done for Melvin and it appeared that the behaviors served the functions of obtaining attention, avoiding work, obtaining food or drink, and self-stimulation. A behavior plan was developed that provided frequent reinforcers of food, drinks, and attention for on-task behavior, remaining dressed, and working quietly. The plan also included a structured system of prompting should Melvin lie on the floor. The prompting involved physical intervention to prevent his disrobing and lying on the stockroom floor. Within several weeks, the disruptive behaviors were dramatically reduced and he began to display acceptable levels of productivity.

Destructive Behavior

Some individuals with severe autism may display destructive behavior at work, including aggression, self-injury, and property destruction. Related to destructive behavior are behaviors that result in loss or misuse of the employer's or co-worker's property, including pica, theft, throwing work materials, or damaging work materials.

The procedures for maintaining employment and managing these behaviors are similar to those for disruptive behavior. A functional assessment must be performed and a behavior plan implemented that decreases the frequency of misbehavior and encourages more cooperative behavior. Support staff must be sufficiently trained and measures must be put into place that prevent damage to persons and property. Individuals with outbursts of destructive behavior have enjoyed long-term employment with the support of well-trained personnel and the implementation of behavior plans based on functional assessments.

Refusal to Work

Occasionally, a worker with autism will refuse to work. Refusal may be based on any one of a variety of factors, such as inability to do the job, failure to understand the directions, disinterest in the job, or lack of motivation. An instructional assessment must first be conducted to ensure that the worker understands the job and is capable of performing the job duties. If he or she does not, then instructional procedures can be implemented. If the worker is disinterested or unmotivated, then a self-management plan or other behavior management plan is needed to encourage the person to work. If the worker is disinterested in the task and interest cannot be raised by providing motivation, then it may be necessary to seek employment that is more compatible with the worker's interests.

SWITCHING JOBS

Some workers with autism have good skills and are highly employable; however, some workers have difficulty finding steady work. If job loss occurs, months or even years of unemployment can ensue. Some of the characteristics associated with autism make job procurement and job success difficult. These difficulties make it advisable to try to keep a given job, even if the conditions are not ideal.

There are numerous reasons why workers may want to switch jobs: higher pay, more hours, more appealing job duties, and more stability. Although there might be compelling reasons to stay in a currently held job, often there are risks that outweigh the possible benefits of switching. It is not an unusual situation for a worker with autism and a history of self-injury to maintain a job for several years, then switch companies in search of more hours. However, the new company may not be as tolerant of self-injury or some other characteristic and, subsequently, the worker loses the job and months of unemployment follow.

If workers with severe autism and aberrant, disruptive, or destructive behavior have held a job under tolerant management, job switching should be avoided. There are often unrecognized supports that exist at jobs for workers with these difficulties. Tolerant managers, tolerant co-workers, informal systems of support, and positive reinforcement are often present and critically needed, even when a job coach is available. These supports can take months or even years to develop, and they are not easily duplicated. Temptations related to higher salaries, more interesting work, or more stable employment should typically be resisted in favor of keeping a job that has proven to be stable and tolerant.

LOSING A JOB

Occasionally workers with autism lose their jobs. Individuals with mental retardation, severe autism, and challenging behaviors may be fired many times, especially during the first few years in the job market. There are numerous reasons for firings, as well as productive responses to being fired to ensure future employment.

Reasons

Workers with autism can be fired for a variety of reasons already discussed in this chapter. Administrative difficulties, including lack of support, transportation problems, poor job match, or insufficient support can all lead to termination. Employer-initiated factors, including unsteady work, financial problems, layoffs, relocation, or bankruptcy can result in job loss. Co-worker problems can also occasionally lead to job separation. Worker-initiated problems, such as poor job performance, aberrant behavior, disruptive behavior, destructive behavior, social skills problems, or work refusal can all lead to job loss.

Responses to Job Loss

Agencies that support workers with autism must be prepared for job turnover. Workers with autism may go through several jobs during their first few years in the job market, but this period of instability is usually followed by long-term employment. The agency should respond to each occasion of job loss by asking the following questions:

1. Was support sufficient? If not, what else may be needed?
2. Were the job expectations clear? If not, how can they be clarified in the future?
3. Was the job developed properly? If not, what other procedures need to be in place?
4. Was this a poor job match? If so, what job match should be sought in the future?

Some workers with autism may have years of uneven job performance prior to finding a good match and a long-term employment situation. Even if one long-term employment situation is not found, a worker with autism can still spend the majority of his or her adult life employed. The supporting agency must always assume employability and continue to assist the individual with autism to seek and keep a job.

A worker with autism should be assisted to view job loss not as failure, but as part of the process of attaining long-term employment. Job separation should be handled in a matter-of-fact way so that the worker can be encouraged to concentrate on the task of obtaining and keeping the next job. See Table 5.1 for a summary of potential problems and solutions in the work environment.

SUMMARY

Most workers, with and without autism, encounter job problems during their careers. Workers with autism are especially prone to job problems because of the language and behavioral characteristics associated with autism. Additionally, workers with autism often have support needs, and the provision of those supports presents problems that can be beyond the worker's control. Vocational problems may be due to administrative causes, employer factors, and co-worker factors. Worker-initiated problems can also occur, including problems with performance; social skills; and aberrant, disruptive, or destructive behavior. Many problems can be solved through analysis of the cause and implementation of additional strategies, adaptations, or supports. Some cases of job problems lead to job loss. A proper analysis of job loss may lead to more successful employment in the future.

Table 5.1. Work problems and potential solutions

Category	Problem	Potential solutions

Administrative	Poor job match:
	  task too difficult
	  worker not interested
	  behavior and social difficulties made worse
		Carefully follow job matching procedures.
		Alter job tasks to make them simpler.
		Increase level of support through behavior program and social skills training.

	Unclear expectations at onset:
	  high productivity requirements
	  nature of job tasks
		Clarify expectations prior to employment.
		Try to observe tasks prior to employment.
		Increase level of supervision.
		Increase instructional support.
		Implement behavior program to increase productivity.
		Renegotiate pay based on productivity.
		Limit number of job tasks.

	Lack of agency support:
	  not enough support planned to meet job requirements
	  problems with staff expertise
		Increase level of support as necessary.
		Improve expertise of support personnel with training.
		Improve program implementation by frequent observation and feedback.
		Do not go to work unless adequate support personnel are available.

	Transportation problems: tardiness	Arrange for later starting time that coincides with transportation services.

	Parent or guardian difficulties:
	  disapprove of job
	  poor interactions with employer
		Discuss job position at team meeting with parents.
		Define roles for parents, support personnel, and employer.

		Establish procedure for handling parental concerns through the supported employment agency.
Employer-initiated	Bankruptcy or company dissolution	Begin looking for new job immediately.
		Get recommendation from employer.
	Seasonal slowdown	Assess possibility of slowdowns during initial job interview.
		Find alternative temporary employment.
		Provide sufficient support to make worker valuable to employer.
	Financial problems	Find alternative temporary employment.
		Find part-time employment to fill in work schedule gaps.
		Provide sufficient support to make worker valuable to employer.
	Relocation	Move with company if possible.
		Seek new job position.
	Changes in management personnel who supported employees with autism	Arrange similar supports from other sources.
		Meet with new management personnel to build rapport and provide education on workers with autism and supported employment.
Co-worker–initiated	Teasing co-worker with autism	Teach worker with autism acceptable responses to teasing.
		Have support personnel intervene for worker with autism.
		Teach more acceptable social skills and behaviors to worker with autism to avoid teasing.

(continued)

Table 5.1. (continued)

Category	Problem	Potential solutions
Co-worker–initiated (continued)		
		Contact management staff to intervene if necessary.
	Bossing and harassment	Teach worker with autism how to respond to co-worker.
		Support personnel can provide instructions prior to a co-worker giving directions.
		Support personnel can intervene on behalf of the worker with autism.
		Contact management staff if necessary.
	Resentment	Provide co-worker training on autism.
		Maintain pleasant, helpful demeanor.
		Assist co-worker to view worker with autism more positively.
	Uneasiness	Educate co-worker on nature of autism.
		Encourage social interaction if co-worker is willing.
		Remove worker with autism from work area when disruptive.
Worker-initiated	Low productivity:	Provide training to learn new task.
	difficulty learning new tasks	Job coach assists in task completion initially to keep productivity high.
	short attention span	
	distractibility	Consider short unpaid teaching period.
	low cognitive levels	Behavioral intervention to encourage on-task behaviors and decrease interfering behavior.
	interfering behavior	
	lack of motivation	Differential reinforcement of high rates of productivity.
	motivated to work slowly	

Problem	Strategies

Low quality work:
  careless errors due to hurrying
  interfering behaviors
  task too difficult
  high productivity rate resulting in errors
	Frequent reinforcement for working.
	Avoid reinforcing low rates of productivity.
	Reward accuracy, not speed.
	Provide task analysis for self-checking.
	Behavior management to reduce interfering behaviors and increase on-task behaviors.
	Restructure job tasks to make them simpler.

Social skills problems:
  lack of social skills
  inappropriate social behaviors
  withdrawal
	Social skills training.
	Adaptation to environment to eliminate need for social skills.
	Behavior management to encourage and reinforce appropriate social skills.
	Full-time support of job coach to bridge social skills gap.

Poor hygiene and appearance	Teach hygiene and dressing skills. Provide assistance at home as necessary.
Personal items taken to work	Provide briefcase or backpack to limit what can be taken to work. Set limits on amount of items that can be taken to work.
Poor attendance and tardiness	Allow enough time for morning routine. Provide travel training. Provide motivation to go to work. Eliminate motivation to stay at home.
Aberrant behaviors	Behavior management plan based on functions. Restructure the time and place for these behaviors.

(continued)

Table 5.1. (continued)

Category	Problem	Potential solutions
Worker-initiated (continued)		
	Disruptive behaviors	Behavior management plan based on functions. Quick response is needed from support personnel to remove the person from the situation. Increase support at work. Provide additional training to support personnel. Re-evaluate functions of behaviors.
	Destructive behaviors	Behavior management plan based on functions. Teach support personnel in nonaversive, physical interventions to prevent damage or injury. Back-up system to ensure extra help to manage problems.
	Refusal to work: inability to do job failure to understand instructions lack of motivation	Assess ability to do job and understand instructions. Provide additional instruction. Create a behavior management plan to increase motivation.

CHAPTER **6**

Jobs in Manufacturing

Workers with autism successfully work at a variety of jobs in the manufacturing field, including jobs at companies that produce computer cables, air conditioning parts, electronic parts, laminated products, venetian blinds, fuses, posters, and silk-screened clothing. These jobs consist of assembly tasks in which the worker assembles either pieces that will eventually fit together or entire objects. Workers may also have other duties, such as lamination, rolling and labeling posters, and enlarging and copying microfiche. Some individuals with autism are able to perform these jobs without assistance. Other workers need their work to be adapted so that they are able to complete their tasks.

ADVANTAGES OF MANUFACTURING JOBS

Work Environment

Manufacturing jobs often are done in relatively large rooms in which a number of workers are given enough work space to perform their tasks. Workers are well spaced out (i.e., at least 5 feet from each other). Typically, manufacturing jobs do not take place in small rooms or under crowded conditions. Workers with autism do well in large spaces, with co-workers at a comfortable distance from them. Because of the comfortable spacing, there are few encounters with co-workers, such as one worker jostling another, a worker accidentally picking up another person's tools or work materials, or one worker making undue demands on another because of space limitations. Therefore, the social skills of workers with autism are not strained in these environments. Additionally, because of the wide spacing, if a co-worker has a difficulty or does something unusual, this break from routine does not disrupt the routine or work rhythm of the worker with autism, and vice versa.

The work environment in manufacturing firms is often very task-oriented. Usually, there are high production quotas and close supervision by management. A visit to a manufacturing site reveals workers sitting or standing quietly at their work stations, working steadily. Although there might be occasional banter between employees, this is not common because most workers are intent on achieving their productivity and accuracy requirements. This type of environment has instructional and social advantages for the worker with autism. All the visual and auditory cues are task related, and as such can serve as powerful prompts that on-task behavior is expected.

Nature of the Tasks

Individuals with autism often have strengths in the areas of visual-motor coordination and fine and gross motor control. It is not unusual for a person with autism whose overall cognitive functioning is considered to be in the mild range of mental retardation to have fine motor skills that are above average. Manufacturing jobs usually require manipulation of objects, and good visual-motor control and fine or gross motor control are imperative.

Manufacturing tasks tend to require good visual discrimination, not only in the performance of the tasks, but also in quality control. Workers with autism are often adept at the visual requirements of assembly tasks and are frequently better than their co-workers without disabilities at discerning errors in production.

Furthermore, workers with autism can be adept at memorizing sequences, and, therefore, can quickly learn the steps involved in complex, multistep manufacturing tasks. Their good visual-motor skills allow for rapid execution of those steps, which means their productivity levels can very well exceed those of co-workers.

Cognitive Demands

Many manufacturing jobs require a certain level of cognitive functioning. Some of the more skilled jobs may not be suitable for individuals with severe or profound mental retardation. Some jobs require that the worker have near-average intelligence. There are many workers with autism who have these cognitive levels. However, if they do not, these jobs might prove too difficult.

Manufacturing tasks also offer a comforting degree of sameness and routine, which workers with autism tend to appreciate. Once a task is mastered by a worker with autism, the steps of the task typically remain the same, with no unexpected surprises or changes. This reliance on sameness does not imply, however, that the worker must do the same task all day long. A worker with autism is capable of learning numerous tasks and performing them well in the manufacturing environment. What does stay the same is how each individual task is executed.

Related to the degree of sameness is the repetitive nature of the tasks. Workers with autism who are dependent on routine often do better in jobs in which the tasks are repetitive. Because they are not only tolerant of repetitive tasks, but are appreciative of them, they are valuable workers to employers in manufacturing who often experience high turnover rates due to employee boredom.

Work Materials Manufacturing jobs provide workers with the opportunity to use a variety of tools and materials. These jobs might involve using materials at different temperatures, and using materials that have a variety of consistencies, including metals, chemicals, and other solutions. Workers with autism often enjoy this variety.

Volume of Work Manufacturing jobs provide a steady work flow, which can be an advantage to the worker with autism. Keeping busy is an antidote to behavior problems, such as self-stimulation, wandering, and even self-injury. A worker with autism who has nothing to do might stand and rock, pace, or even engage in mild self-injury such as self-scratching. However, if the worker is steadily engaged in a task, these behaviors are less likely to occur.

Social Requirements

Workers in manufacturing jobs are usually insulated from unusual or unpredictable social events involving unfamiliar people. Some individuals with autism become either overly curious, distracted, or possibly upset when approached by strangers or when strangers enter their work environment. Typically, the only individuals who frequent the manufacturing environment are workers or supervisors. These environments lack the constant flow of people that occurs in other jobs in which customers come and go. However, if unfamiliar people do enter the workplace, the area is typically large enough that the visit does not intrude on anyone's work area.

In addition, manufacturing jobs do not involve a great deal of social interaction as part of the job requirements. Because workers with autism may have difficulty with language as well as social skills, jobs that do not make social demands on them are desirable. The task itself, assembling products, does not involve social interactions or verbal interactions other than interactions that are instructional or supervisory in nature.

Social interactions that do occur in manufacturing environments—greeting co-workers upon arrival, short conversations at break or at lunch, and saying good-bye—are predictable, routine, and consistent with the social skills level of workers with autism.

DISADVANTAGES OF MANUFACTURING JOBS

Nature of the Tasks

Accuracy Manufacturing tasks must be completed with a high level of accuracy. Sloppy work is usually not tolerated and can lead to dismissal if it persists. Although some workers with autism work with a high degree of precision, others are prone to being quick and sloppy. If workers with the latter tendency have a manufacturing job, it might be necessary to implement instructional or motivational strategies to ensure and reinforce accuracy.

Production Requirements Some manufacturing environments have high production requirements. If the required rate is too fast for the worker with autism, termination may result. One way of lessening this possibility is to come to an agreement about production requirements prior to accepting the job. If the production rate is unrealistic for the worker, then serious thought should be given to accepting the job. If the worker is capable of learning to do the task at a sufficiently high rate of speed, then instructional and motivational strategies can be used to teach and strengthen a fast work rate.

Need for Flexibility Workers with autism tend to be resistant to change or to learning a new way to do a task. In manufacturing, a worker may be taught a certain way to do a task and then carry out the task that way for weeks, months, or even years. Yet, sometimes a change is required in the way the task is performed. This change puts the worker with autism in the position of having to accept a change in a very established routine. This type of change can be met with resistance, which may lead to termination; however, it is unusual for a worker with autism to absolutely refuse to change the manner in which the task is performed. If necessary, specialized instructional and motivational procedures can be implemented to encourage the flexibility necessary to maintain employment.

The manufacturing task itself may require a certain amount of flexibility. For example, some manufacturing firms make complex products, which require many parts and components. The worker might spend the morning working on one component, then be directed to work on another component in the afternoon. Some workers have difficulty changing from one task to another, especially if it is an abrupt change; however, many workers with autism, with training, have acquired the flexibility required to adapt to the changes that may occur in a manufacturing job.

Social Requirements

Although the social climate of a manufacturing job is generally favorable for workers with autism, there can be challenges. One challenge involves visitors to the workplace. From time to time, customers or the company's owner or president may visit the site. Some workers with autism may have difficulty dealing with visitors as they are not a part of the typical routine. These social problems can be anticipated and prevented by social skills instruction or by close supervision during the visit.

Occasionally, co-workers may present problems for a worker with autism. Because manufacturing jobs involve at least several people working in one room, some co-workers may resent having to work with individuals with disabilities. This resentment can be revealed through negative comments, teasing, or subtle, rude treatment. These co-workers may also attempt to interfere with the individual's work by making frequent critical remarks or by complaining to management. These cases are not frequent and they are not limited to manufacturing jobs. Usually, once the co-workers become more familiar with the worker with autism, they become more accepting. If the situation does not improve, a support person or manager may need to intervene. In rare cases, the worker with autism must continue to work with the harassment.

Other Disadvantages

Manufacturing firms often depend on contracts from outside sources for their work flow. For example, a firm that makes computer cables is dependent on contracts from computer firms that need those cables. Occasionally, the availability of work is disrupted because of a lull in the need for the product. This may result in days in which the workers are sent home early or told not to come in at all. In extreme cases, the lack of work can result in layoffs or even terminations. An uncertain work schedule can be stressful for a worker with autism; however, most workers, if sufficiently supported, can adapt to these situations.

A final disadvantage is that manufacturing jobs often hold little or no opportunity for advancement. The next step up in manufacturing jobs is often a supervisory or managerial position, which typically requires social and communication skills that many workers with autism do not have.

JOBS IN MANUFACTURING

Individuals with autism fill a variety of manufacturing jobs and do well economically, socially, and vocationally in such jobs. These jobs can be especially rewarding because the workers produce an object or part of an object; that is, they have something to show for their efforts. Descriptions of manufacturing jobs that are held by workers with autism are provided on the following pages. Workers with a range of skills and deficits fill these jobs.

Computer Cable Assembler

Job Description: A computer cable assembler works in assembly line production of computer cables designed to customer specifications.

Worksite Description: This is a medium-size company that manufactures and installs computer cables and connections. The company employs about 15 workers who work in the same area assembling cables.

Employees with Autism

Worker 1: Speaks in full sentences, average intelligence, poor social skills (including perseveration of bizarre speech topics, talking loudly to self, and not asking for assistance), pacing

Worker 2: Speaks clearly in sentences, average to low-average intelligence, pacing, talking loudly to self, severe problems with social and language skills, poor personal grooming

Job Tasks

- Measure and cut cable according to specifications
- Strip the ends of each cable with a razor blade
- Operate a crimping machine
- Place pins in the connection by matching a numbered slot to a colored wire
- Assemble hood over connection
- Label cable for length and add assembler's initials
- Test cable using a volt meter

Equipment, Machinery, and Hand Tools Needed to Complete Job Tasks

- Hand-operated cable measurement device
- Hydraulic crimping machine
- Volt meter
- Razor blade
- Wire cutters

Potential Problems in Job Completion

- Some problems with attending to task
- Erratic social behavior

Modifications and Accommodations to Site or Task

- Initial support from a job coach
- Task analysis done by job coach
- Written schedules
- Self-management plans
- Social skills training and training to ask for assistance

MANUFACTURING

Laminator

Job Description: A laminator feeds materials into a laminating machine at a consistent rate.

Worksite Description: This job is in a small private company with a small office and sales area adjoining the relatively large laminating area. There are approximately eight employees, one with autism.

Employee with Autism

Worker 1: Speaks in full sentences, average intelligence, problems with social and language skills

Job Tasks

- Feed materials into a laminating machine
- Cut laminated materials
- Round corners on laminated materials
- Attach stands to the back of laminated materials
- Maintain a clean work area

Equipment, Machinery, and Hand Tools Needed to Complete Job Tasks

- Laminating machine
- Hand-held cornering machine

Potential Problems in Job Completion

- Inconsistent work load
- Social skills problems

Modifications and Accommodations to Site or Task

- Initial supervision from a job coach
- Use of natural supports in the form of extra co-worker assistance
- Written schedule
- Social skills training

Venetian Blind Assembler

Job Description: A venetian blind assembler works in a warehouse assembling venetian blinds.

Worksite Description: This job is with a small, family-owned business that manufactures venetian blinds, curtains, and curtain rods. There are approximately 10 workers, 1 with autism.

Employee with Autism

Worker 1: Speaks in complete sentences, borderline intellectual functioning, yelling, and cursing

Job Tasks

- Cut vertical blind bars
- Assemble vertical blinds
- Assemble curtain rods

Equipment, Machinery, and Hand Tools Needed to Complete Job Tasks

- Sturbridge machine

Potential Problems in Job Completion

- Social skills problems

Modifications and Accommodations to Site or Task

- Drop-in supervision from job coach
- Social skills training

Bulk Mailing Clerk

Job Description: A bulk mailing clerk assembles laboratory supplies for educational and vocational use and mails them.

Worksite Description: The company is located in a three-story townhouse where there is a reception area and bulk mailing table on the first floor and a laboratory for assembling kits in the basement. The company employs approximately 15 workers; 6 people work in the same area with the 2 workers with autism.

Employees with Autism

Worker 1: Speaks clearly in sentences, average intellectual functioning, problems with social and language skills, aggression upon provocation

Worker 2: Speaks clearly in sentences, mild mental retardation, self-injury, property destruction, aggression, and difficulties with social use of language, including perseveration

Job Tasks

- Count, sort, and label test tubes, DNA markers, and dyes
- Assemble and label kits
- Box kits for mailing
- Make boxes
- Collate pamphlets or catalogs
- Stuff envelopes
- Adhere adhesive mailing labels

Equipment, Machinery, and Hand Tools Needed to Complete Job Tasks

- Test tubes
- Dye kits
- DNA marker kits
- Boxes
- Envelopes
- Labels

Potential Problems in Job Completion

- Difficulty getting to work on time
- Aggression
- Remaining in assigned location
- Talking loudly

Modifications and Accommodations to Site or Task

- Hours are flexible if employees arrive late
- Full-time supervision by a job coach
- Self-management (Worker 1)
- Behavior management plans, including positive reinforcement, written schedules, social skills training, alternate sensory stimuli, extinction procedures

Electronic Component Assembler

Job Description: An electronic component assembler works on assembly line manufacturing fuses for the marine industry.

Worksite Description: This is a small, family-owned business that occupies 15 rooms, 9 of which are used by the electronic component assemblers. There are approximately 25–30 workers in the company. There are 15 workers on the assembly line, including 2 with autism.

Employees with Autism

Worker 1: Speaks in complete sentences but speech is unclear, low-average cognitive functioning, problems with social and language skills, off-task behaviors, noncompliance

Worker 2: Speaks clearly in sentences, mild mental retardation, throws objects, aggression, self-injury, inappropriate sexual comments, clothes tearing, and yelling

Job Tasks

- Wrap wires on small lamp around fuse
- Dip lamps and fuse in solder
- Clean threads on electrical bodies
- Assemble electrical bodies by putting clips, screws, and nuts into place

Equipment, Machinery, and
Hand Tools Needed to Complete Job Tasks

- Tweezers
- Phillip's screwdriver
- Flathead screwdriver
- Wire cutter
- Soldering pot

Potential Problems in Job Completion

- Some materials are caustic or hot and require careful handling.
- Some co-workers make fun of speech and behavior of workers with autism.
- Work is sporadic and layoffs are frequent.
- Salary is too low, considering length of employment.
- Supervisor shows favoritism toward workers without disabilities.

Modifications and Accommodations to Site or Task

- The job coach, for safety reasons, cleans materials and tools for wrapping and dips lamps in a cleaning machine with a solvent.

- Behavior management plans, including positive reinforcement, social skills training, self-management, and guidelines for managing aggression (Worker 1)
- Social skills instruction and self-management plan (Worker 2)

Mailing Clerk

Job Description: A mailing clerk packages microfilm in envelopes for distribution.

Worksite Description: This job is with a medium-size company that reproduces microfilm, printed material, and blueprints. The company employs approximately 40 workers. There are 10 employees in one room packaging microfilm, including 2 workers with autism.

Employees with Autism

Worker 1: Speaks clearly in sentences, moderate mental retardation, noncompliance, self-injury, self-stimulation, aggression

Worker 2: Speaks clearly in sentences, moderate mental retardation, aggression (including hair pulling, lunging, hitting, kicking, scratching, banging other people's heads against walls, property destruction, self-injury, cursing, and name calling)

Job Tasks

- Stuffs envelopes with microfilm

Equipment, Machinery, and Hand Tools Needed to Complete Job Tasks

- Envelopes
- Microfilm

Potential Problems in Job Completion

- Behavior problems interfering with productivity

Modifications and Accommodations to Site or Task

- Job coach to supervise productivity and for behavior management
- Behavior management plans, including positive reinforcement, social skills training, graduated prompt system, alternate sensory stimuli, and extinction procedures

Microfilm Reproducer

Job Description: A microfilm reproducer enlarges and copies microfiche and films new microfiche from original material in an office environment.

Worksite Description: This job is with a medium-size company that reproduces microfilm, printed material, and blueprints. The company employs approximately 40 workers, with 10 in a room packaging microfilm, including 2 workers with autism.

Employees with Autism

Worker 1: Speaks clearly in sentences, high-average cognitive functioning, extremely uncooperative—frequent task refusal and program participation refusal, difficulty relating to employers and co-workers, late for work, uses phone inappropriately during work hours

Worker 2: Speaks in complete sentences, limited intellectual functioning, yelling and cursing, talks loudly to self

Job Tasks

- Enlarge microfiche
- Copy microfiche
- Film new microfiche
- Photocopy

Equipment, Machinery, and Hand Tools Needed to Complete Job Tasks

- Micrographic machine
- Static camera
- Microfiche
- Photocopy machine

Potential Problems in Job Completion

- Work refusal, low productivity (Worker 1)

Modifications and Accommodations to Site or Task

- Job coach to supervise productivity and for behavior management
- Behavior management plans, including positive reinforcement, social skills training, and guidelines for redirection to task

Furniture Finisher

Job Description: A furniture finisher finishes furniture to fill customer orders or for placement on the sales floor.

Worksite Description: This is a small, family-owned business that produces furniture. The store employs approximately 15 workers, including 2 with autism.

Employees with Autism

Worker 1: Speaks clearly in sentences, low-average cognitive functioning, limited communication and social skills, tantrums

Worker 2: Speaks clearly in sentences, low-average intelligence, pacing, talks loudly to self, limited social and language skills

Job Tasks

- Create flat surface with filling paste
- Sand unfinished furniture
- Select finish to be used by using a number code system
- Apply stains and polishes to wooden headboards
- Apply polish and buff

Equipment, Machinery, and Hand Tools Needed to Complete Job Tasks

- Stains and polishes
- Filler paste
- Rags
- Sandpaper

Potential Problems in Job Completion

- Matching codes for finishes
- Maintaining attention to quality
- Slow productivity due to meticulous attention to detail
- Using sandpaper after the grit is worn off

Modifications and Accommodations to Site or Task

- Assistance of job coach

Poster Roller

Job Description: A poster roller rolls, packages, and labels posters and assembles novelty pins.

Worksite Description: This is a large warehouse that manufactures and distributes posters and pins of rock music stars and other personalities. It has approximately 10 employees, 2 with autism.

Employees with Autism

Worker 1: Speaks in full sentences, severe mental retardation, stealing, darting from work, property destruction, aggression

Worker 2: Speaks clearly in sentences, borderline intellectual functioning, limited social and language skills, difficulty following instructions, distracted by visitors

Job Tasks

- Roll posters
- Label posters by stock number and title
- Package posters in shipping boxes (100 posters to a box)
- Insert wire pin backs into metal pins
- Pack pins in shipping boxes

Equipment, Machinery, and Hand Tools Needed to Complete Job Tasks

- Plastic bags
- Foot- or hand-operated electric rolling machine
- Wire and metal pin backs
- Boxes

Potential Problems in Job Completion

- Worksite not heated during cold weather
- Behavior problems interfering with productivity

Modifications and Accommodations to Site or Task

- Dress warmly
- Supervision by job coach for productivity and behavior management
- Behavior management plans, including positive reinforcement, instructional guidelines, guidelines for redirection, and extinction procedures

Electronic Component Assembler

Job Description: An electronic component assembler works in a stockroom counting electronic components into sets of 50 or 100, and pulls listed items from stock.

Worksite Description: This job is with a manufacturer of electronic components for the railway industry. There are approximately 30 workers, including 3 employees with autism.

Employees with Autism

Worker 1: Speaks in complete sentences, borderline intellectual functioning, limited social and language skills, difficulty asking for assistance

Worker 2: Speaks clearly in sentences, average intellectual functioning, problems with social and language skills, aggression upon provocation, yells at others, interrupts, tells others what to do, often makes vulgar gestures

Worker 3: Speaks clearly in complete sentences, mild mental retardation, inappropriate social conversations, speaks too loudly, talks to self, self-injury, aggression, property destruction

Job Tasks

- Count electronic components into sets of 50 or 100
- Pull listed items from shelves

Equipment, Machinery, and Hand Tools Needed to Complete Job Tasks

- Electronic components
- Bags
- Calibration scale
- Tape

Potential Problems in Job Completion

- Difficulty with accuracy
- Difficulty leaving the bathroom in a timely manner following breaks

Modifications and Accommodations to Site or Task

- Supervision by job coach for productivity and behavior management
- Accuracy improves with instruction to work slowly and deliberately
- Behavior management plans, including self-rating, positive reinforcement, and social skills training

Screen Printing Worker

Job Description: A screen printing employee works in the print shop, checking tee-shirts for errors, and folding, stacking, counting, and boxing tee-shirts.

Worksite Description: This job is with a small, family-owned business. There is a small sales area, an office downstairs, an office upstairs, a print shop area, a loading dock, and silk screen and storage areas. There are approximately 13 workers, including 3 with autism.

Employees with Autism

Worker 1: Speaks in full sentences, severe mental retardation, stealing, darting from work

Worker 2: Speaks in complete sentences but speech is unclear, low-average cognitive functioning, screaming, jumping, hand flapping, spinning, rapid verbalizations, motor rituals (especially spinning while walking)

Worker 3: Speaks clearly in sentences, low-average cognitive functioning, limited social and language skills, perseveration on inappropriate topics

Job Tasks

- Inspect tee-shirts for errors
- Count tee-shirts
- Fold and box tee-shirts
- Take trash out
- Sweep the work area
- Open boxes with razor blade
- Dust off machines
- Take masking tape off silk screens

Equipment, Machinery, and Hand Tools Needed to Complete Job Tasks

- Hot-air dryer
- Razor
- Scissors
- Silk screens
- Broom

Potential Problems in Job Completion

- Finding errors
- Counting
- Sexual comments directed toward co-workers
- Agitated by co-workers teasing and arguing with each other
- Company moved

Modifications and Accommodations to Site or Task

- Supervision by job coach
- Tables, machinery, and the job coach were positioned to prevent bolting.
- The job coach completes steps that cannot be completed by the worker, such as counting and looking for errors.
- Behavior management plans, including hourly ratings, positive reinforcement, redirection guidelines, social skills training, extinction procedures, and guidelines for managing dangerous behavior

Assistant Subassembly Worker

Job Description: An assistant subassembly worker assembles heating and air conditioning units.

Worksite Description: This is a medium-size company that manufactures heating and air conditioning units. There are approximately 30–40 workers, including 3 with autism.

Employees with Autism

Worker 1: Speaks clearly in sentences, low-average cognitive functioning, limited communication and social skills (including difficulty greeting people, sharing work space, and asking for assistance), tantrums

Worker 2: Speaks in full sentences, borderline cognitive functioning, poor personal grooming, limited social and language skills (including difficulty asking for help or more work), poor motor coordination

Worker 3: Speaks clearly in sentences, low-average intelligence, pacing, talks loudly to self, limited social and language skills, low production rate due to being distracted, gazing into space, wandering away from work area

Job Tasks

- Flare pipe
- Cut pipe or wire
- Ream pipe
- Sand pipe
- Polish pipe joints
- Bend pipe
- Mark parts
- Rivet
- Drain line assembly
- Fold, collate, and shrink wrap
- Swedge pipe
- Sweep parking lot
- Paint cabinet
- Assemble refrigeration units
- Tape metal coils
- Fold cardboard strips to make corners
- Clean floors and bathrooms
- Inventory—count pieces produced and put them in boxes
- Seal refrigerator basepans
- Clean paint off incorrectly painted metal
- Dispose of nonreusable crates and parts
- Stack materials for the stock area
- Move stock to specified areas

- Assemble CBR covers
- Glue insulation over vent covers
- Measure and cut rubber gaskets
- Measure and cut insulator strips
- Place tape over gaskets to protect the paint
- Clean and color air conditioning units
- Drill
- Shear
- Tap bolts
- Assemble cable
- Sort hardware

Equipment, Machinery, and Hand Tools Needed to Complete Job Tasks

- Tape measure
- Ink stamper
- Pipe cutter
- Reaming instrument
- Sandpaper
- Grinding machine
- Sharp object (knife, pen)
- Pipe bending tool
- Model parts
- Tweezers
- Canned ink and ink roller brush
- Auger
- Flaring tool
- Swedging tool
- Needle nose pliers
- Slip joint
- Side cutter
- Scissors
- Vise grips
- Rubber mallet
- File
- Screwdriver
- Hammer
- Adjustable and open wrench
- Ruler
- Earplugs
- Toolbox
- Sealant, contact glue, solvent

- Stand-up or hand riveter
- Drill
- Shearing machine
- Chemicals to clean and color
- Tap and dye tools
- Counter sink
- Blueprints
- Enamel spray

Potential Problems in Job Completion

- Failing to ask for assistance when needed
- Each step must be carried out to exact specifications.
- Errors must be found and corrected.
- Airborne particles cause frequent nosebleeds.
- Units dipped in tanks for specified amount of time
- Rude to co-workers

Modifications and Accommodations to Site or Task

- Wearing a face mask to prevent nosebleeds
- Social skills training
- Self-management

CASE STUDY—BEVERLY

• • • • • • •

Employee Description

Beverly is 36 years old and her intelligence level as measured by a standard intelligence test indicates that she has mild mental retardation, and she also has severe autism. She can speak in complete sentences, although her speech has a flat inflection and no affect. She can talk on a few topics and uses functional language with difficulty to get what she wants or to communicate her concerns. Beverly is also socially withdrawn in that she rarely initiates social interactions and prefers to be alone.

Beverly has a history of severe behavior problems. She hits and kicks other people, rips her clothing, scratches her hands and face, and throws objects at others. Her aggression can be severe and poses a serious danger to other people. In addition, she sometimes leaves her work area, yells at others, and refuses to follow directions.

Employee History

As an infant, Beverly spent 2 years in a foster home before being placed in a residential school for people with mental retardation. Because of her behavior problems, she was transferred to a state institution for people with mental retardation and after several years was transferred to an out-of-state residential school. Beverly returned to her home state at the age of 18 years and was committed to a state mental hospital. She remained there until the age of 21 when she entered a residential and supported employment program for people with autism. At the time Beverly entered the program, she had never lived or been educated in an integrated environment and had received no vocational training.

Description of Company and Job

Beverly obtained employment at a small manufacturing firm that produces electronic parts for the defense industry. The firm relies heavily on government defense contracts and employs about 25 people in either the manufacturing or sales division. The manufacturing tasks take place in one large room with several workers at large tables. Although there is no assembly line, much of the work is done in an assembly line manner.

Beverly was hired by this firm as a component assembler. She has good visual-perceptual skills and attention to detail, and her job capitalized on her strengths. Her lack of social skills and her language deficits were not an obstacle for employment as she was hired to assemble various electronic fuses for use in military and commercial vehicles. One job task involved carefully wrapping the wires on a tiny lamp around wires on a fuse and then cutting the wires and soldering the end. She also has to use hand-held tools, such as tweezers and screwdrivers, and small components, such as washers, screws, and springs, to assemble fuse bodies.

Setting Up the Job

Once the job was secured, the job coach and agency supervisors spent about 1 week learning to do the jobs and writing task analyses. The tasks required exacting precision, so it was important that correct task analyses be written. In addition, once Beverly learns to perform a task a certain way, it is difficult to teach her a new way; therefore, it was important that it be taught correctly from the start. Because Beverly has trouble handling changes, the job coach also paid attention to learning the work schedule so that Beverly could be informed of the times of certain activities. The social demands of the job and the work environment were also assessed.

Establishing Employment Supports

Upon entering the supported employment program, Beverly had an interdisciplinary team meeting to establish vocational goals and determine her need for supports.

Determination of Supports   It was determined that although Beverly has strengths, including relatively good use of language, because of her cognitive deficits and her behavior problems, she would not be able to learn her job duties in the same manner as her co-workers without disabilities at the firm. In addition, her team determined that because of her outbursts of intense aggression and property destruction, she needed specialized supervision and monitoring to prevent injury to herself and others and to ensure that property was not damaged. Therefore, the team agreed that Beverly required full-time supervision by a job coach because of her severe behavior problems and her cognitive and language deficits.

Description of Job Coach Duties   The job coach supervised her and one other adult with autism on a full-time basis during their workday. The job coach taught Beverly to take the bus to work, instructed her on the job tasks, supervised her work performance, assisted her in remaining on task and in her work area, and helped her manage her behavior problems.

Description of Behavior Management Plan   A psychologist consulted with Beverly's supported employment supervisor and job coach to develop a behavior management plan. The purpose of the plan was to assist Beverly in exhibiting acceptable behavior at work, with a decrease in self-injury, aggression, and property destruction and an increase in more acceptable social and work behaviors.

A functional assessment was done that identified several possible functions of Beverly's aggression, self-injury, and property destruction. These functions included escaping from task, avoiding change, and obtaining assistance. It was also apparent that Beverly lacked the social skills to more appropriately handle stresses in her environment.

Beverly's behavior management plan included strategies for assisting her to handle changes and difficulties. It also had preventive components, such as the job coach being aware of when Beverly was having difficulty or becoming upset and assisting her to deal with the problem without an outburst. To encourage more acceptable behavior, her plan included hourly ratings on the following targeted behaviors: respecting herself (i.e., no self-injury), respecting others (i.e., no aggression), respecting property (i.e., no property destruction), keeping her voice at an appropriate volume (i.e., no yelling), holding interesting conversations (i.e., no conversation on inappropriate topics), following directions related to work tasks, and working steadily. Because Beverly seemed unaware of what types of conversations were acceptable at work, discrimination training was initiated to teach her to discriminate interesting conversations from uninteresting conversations. (Uninteresting conversations were defined as talk about aggression, sexual activity, and self-injury.)

Because Beverly has good reading skills, these rules were written out for her and periodically she and her job coach rated her performance on each behavior. She was praised for earning positive ratings. Over time, Beverly was taught to rate herself independently, and a new item, "Rates Self Accurately," was added to the report card.

This program was effective in reducing Beverly's behavior problems, but she continued to have sporadic problems, such as self-injury and clothes tearing, when she was alone. Procedures were developed to assist Beverly to stop from scratching herself or tearing her clothes should she have the urge to do so. Twice per day Beverly and her job coach practiced how she should control herself if she became upset. Additionally, because Beverly's aggression and property destruction could be severe, the job coach was trained in nonaversive management of aggressive behavior so that she could prevent injury to Beverly or others should an outburst occur.

During her employment, Beverly displayed some behavior problems that had specific antecedents. When something went wrong, she would become upset and act out rather than communicate what was bothering her so that assistance could be provided. For instance, if a tool broke at work, she would yell and scratch herself instead of asking for help to get a new tool. Social skills instruction was implemented to help Beverly disclose when she was having a problem. The job coach used modeling, role-play, practice, and feedback to help her practice disclosing problems. The job coach also closely monitored Beverly to see if something upsetting had occurred in order to prompt her to reveal what was bothering her. Gradually, Beverly began to tell the job coach what was bothering her rather than acting out.

Several other problems came up during the length of her employment. For example, Beverly had difficulty accepting suggestions from others and switching tasks at work, so social skills training was provided to assist her in both of these skills. Sometimes Beverly would arrive at work poorly groomed or not bring important items such as her purse with her keys and money to work. To address these problems, Beverly was given two checklists—one for grooming and one for what to bring to work. She reviewed these prior to leaving home for work. Finally, when traveling to work Beverly became the victim of unwanted advances from a male stranger who would touch her and follow her home. Assertive social skills training was implemented to teach her to tell him to leave her alone. These skills effectively discouraged his advances.

Because of low productivity rates, Beverly began her job earning a percentage of minimum wage based on her productivity. Therefore, one of her goals was to increase her productivity rate while maintaining good work quality. Beverly was placed on a productivity program that called for reinforcing high rates of productivity. In addition, one of her rated items was to work steadily. As a result of these strategies, Beverly's productivity improved and she was given a raise to minimum wage.

Outcomes

Although there were sporadic layoffs over the years, Beverly was employed at the electronics company for a total of 9 years during a 10-year period. Beverly was laid off only after several workers without disabilities also had been laid off. During periods of layoff, Beverly was employed as a food service worker and as an assembler of conference materials, but she always expressed a preference for her job as an electronic component assembler. It was gratifying that she was often one of the first employees rehired by the manufacturing firm when they were awarded a new contract. Beverly's salary increased from $1.75 per hour to $3.62 per hour during her employment.

Beverly's ability to perform her job without supervision gradually improved and she became able to do job tasks without job coach assistance. She gradually became more independent and proficient in her work. Although she still had sporadic behavior problems throughout that time with incidents of aggression, property destruction, and self-injury at work, these incidents were managed effectively by her job coach and were not job threatening. On a few occasions, Beverly left work early or did not go to work for a day because of behavior difficulties.

Beverly's employment at the manufacturing firm was terminated when the company went out of business due to economic conditions. She has since found another job that she performs well and seems to enjoy. She has continued to need a full-time job coach because of the intensity of her behavior problems when they occur. When Beverly is supervised by a job coach who is structured, gentle but firm, and who runs her behavior management plan consistently, she is able to maintain employment with a minimum of problem behaviors.

Her current employer is pleased with her performance, and the outlook for continued employment at her present job is high. In addition, her ability to handle changes and difficult interpersonal situations has improved and she has continued to also improve her social as well as her vocational functioning.

CHAPTER 7

Jobs in Retail

Workers with autism are employed in various retail environments including clothing outlets, hardware stores, housewares stores, department stores, and drug stores. Typically, their jobs involve unpacking merchandise; hanging merchandise; pricing merchandise; packing merchandise; sorting merchandise by size or color; inserting security sensors; or preparing merchandise for shipping, display, or sale. They are also involved in stocking shelves, restocking shelves, straightening displays, tagging merchandise, filling orders, retrieving merchandise from the stockroom, sorting merchandise, collecting damaged items, peeling stickers from incorrectly priced items, and organizing merchandise. Workers with autism typically do not directly serve customers as salespeople, sales managers, or cashiers. Some workers with autism move merchandise from the stockroom to the sales floor. Occasionally, they stock and shelve on the sales floor and provide directions to inquiring customers.

ADVANTAGES OF RETAIL JOBS

Some jobs in retail are ideally suited to workers with autism. These are primarily jobs that involve working with merchandise rather than working directly with customers or buyers. Such jobs do not require skilled labor and can be performed by people with autism and profound mental retardation. In addition, these jobs often do not require verbal skills.

Work Environment

People with autism who work in retail often have jobs in the stockroom of stores. The stockroom provides a good environment for many (not all) workers with autism who have idiosyncratic behaviors or vocalizations. Stockrooms are typically large and partitioned by shelves of stock. In this environment, problem behaviors are not directly observed by other workers or by customers. In addition, because of the size of stockrooms and the relative seclusion of each employee's work station, verbal self-stimulation may not be heard by co-workers. Similarly, workers with autism are not as likely to be bothered by the behavior or conversations of their co-workers in this environment.

The work environment of retail stockrooms is often casual. Dress is casual and comfortable and typically there are no rigid standards of behavior. The work environment is conducive to moving around—the spaces are large and the job often involves moving merchandise from one area to another. This can be especially appealing because many workers with autism prefer to move about; they find it difficult to remain seated at a table or in one place for long periods of time.

Most retail jobs give the employee some opportunity to go out on the sales floor. In these instances, workers with autism often enjoy seeing and manipulating the merchandise on display.

Furthermore, retail jobs often have built-in sources of reinforcement for workers with autism who need motivation, such as vending machines, break rooms, cafeterias, and snack bars. There might even be popcorn stands, candy counters, and other areas that sell special treats that can be used as reinforcers.

Nature of the Tasks

Some retail jobs involve simple, one- or two-step tasks that can be performed by individuals with severe or profound mental retardation and autism. Jobs that involve preparing merchandise for sale, stocking shelves, and similar tasks can be done by workers with these severe disabilities. Among these jobs are tasks such as unpacking boxes, sorting clothing by color, putting items into boxes, removing the plastic from articles of clothing, breaking down boxes, moving boxes, placing items on shelves, and hanging articles of clothing.

There are also more difficult tasks involved in retail jobs that individuals with better cognitive functioning can perform, such as pricing merchandise and shelving items according to written descriptions or numerical or alphabetic codes. There are also jobs filling orders in which the worker must be able to read the order, obtain the correct merchandise, and place the merchandise in a shipping box. These latter tasks can be performed independently by workers with better cognitive skills or they can be done with the assistance of a job coach by workers with autism who have more severe problems. For example, a job coach might set the price on the pricing gun, then the worker with autism can use the gun to put price labels on merchandise. Or, a job coach can obtain the necessary items and the worker can box them.

Retail tasks often do not require a high degree of precision and, therefore, are well suited to workers with autism who do not have meticulous work habits. For example, placing items in a box does not require the same degree of precision that is involved in making computer cables or electronic parts in a manufacturing job. Removing plastic from clothing can be done in one grand gesture; it does not require precise movements or a high degree of accuracy.

Retail tasks often involve gross motor skills, but do not necessarily require good fine motor skills. Many individuals with autism do well with gross motor tasks, such as carrying, lifting, boxing, and unpacking boxes.

An important advantage of some retail tasks is that they typically do not require verbal skills. Individuals with autism who are nonverbal are able to perform a variety of tasks related to merchandise preparation without having to speak. Instructions can be provided through demonstration and graduated guidance; therefore, good language comprehension is not necessary.

Type of Merchandise A unique advantage of retail jobs is that in some cases the merchandise being sold is of interest to the worker with autism. For example, one individual with autism who enjoyed books and merchandise about Batman obtained a job in a toy store. On his breaks he would spend time with the Batman merchandise, and on payday he would use part of his earnings and his employee discount to purchase such merchandise. Another young man with autism was particularly fond of candy and obtained a job keeping the candy shelves in a drug store stocked and straightened. One young woman with autism who liked soap and cleaning products worked in a drug store where she was able to purchase such items with her employee discount.

Volume of Work Work in a stockroom is generally steady. This is an advantage for workers with autism who do best socially and behaviorally when they are busy. Work in a retail store is varied, and if there are no new shipments of merchandise to handle, the worker can perform other tasks such as stocking shelves, restocking, straightening shelves, and cleaning the stockroom.

Social Requirements

Socially, retail stocking jobs are very casual. Workers have ample opportunity to move about and perhaps, greet co-workers as they do so. There are usually break rooms and cafeterias in which opportunities for social interaction during breaks or lunch exist.

The casual social atmosphere of these jobs is often appealing to workers with autism who have difficulty meeting rigid social norms, but who enjoy social interaction. However, if a worker tends to be more socially withdrawn, greeting co-workers throughout the day is not necessary.

DISADVANTAGES OF RETAIL JOBS

Work Environment

The retail work environment can be problematic if the employee with autism must work on a busy sales floor. Unsettling events are likely to occur, such as an occasional rush of customers through the store, unruly children, and loudspeaker announcements. Some workers with autism are sensitive to these occurrences and may react with inappropriate comments, shouting, or even self-injury. The effects of these events can be mitigated by training the worker how to deal with them; gradually desensitizing the worker to the events; or providing gentle instruction and, if necessary, positive reinforcement for responding appropriately.

Nature of the Tasks

Customer Relations   Workers with autism may have difficulties in retail jobs that require providing a direct service to the public. Although some individuals with mild autism might be able to handle such a requirement, many workers, especially those with limited verbal skills, would not be able to function in such a capacity. Therefore, retail jobs that require a great deal of interaction with customers are not suitable for workers with autism. Even jobs that require a small amount of customer interaction can be problematic for some workers with autism.

Althouth some jobs are primarily stocking jobs, there may be times when the worker is required to go out onto the sales floor. This can be problematic and there have been cases in which workers with autism refused to answer customer questions, walked away while customers were talking, and, in an extreme case, a normally mild mannered man with autism became so upset at a customer's insistent questioning that he pushed her. If workers with autism are nonverbal, they will clearly not be able to respond to customers' questions and they will need to be situated away from customers. If they must work near customers, they will need the support of a job coach or a co-worker who can intervene and assist the customer. If workers with autism are verbal, they can be taught how to respond to customers' questions. Some workers may be able to direct them to the merchandise they are asking about. Other workers with autism may need to be taught to simply direct the customer to the information desk.

Workers with severe behavior problems can have difficulty at work if they display these behaviors in view of customers. Occasional episodes of aggression, self-injury, or screaming can be job threatening if done in view of customers.

Seasonal Nature of the Work   Some retail work is seasonal. There are retail stores that are very busy between Thanksgiving and Christmas, and then have a major slowdown in January and February. Other stores, such as home improvement supply stores, are slow in the winter and busy in the spring. Slowdowns can affect workers by providing inconsistent work schedules. For example, workers might report to work and be told that there is not enough work that day. Or, their full-time jobs might be reduced to part-time during slowdowns. Occasionally, a worker is laid off for months at a time. Although the seasonal nature of the work is not necessarily a reason to turn down the job, it is a factor that needs to be considered in vocational planning. Sometimes workers can take a temporary job during their layoff, then resume the retail job when sales pick up.

Retail work can also involve periods of time within the day, week, or month when there is no work to be done. For example, there may be a slow period between shipments that leaves the employee without work for several hours or even several days. Furthermore, stores occasionally take several days to do inventory, during which time the employees not involved with the inventory do not work.

Merchandise-Related Issues   There are several problematic issues related to the merchandise at retail jobs. These issues relate primarily to workers with severe disabilities who also have difficulty handling property. The first issue is that some individuals with autism destroy property. Property destruction can include deliberately breaking glass and other breakable items, throwing objects, kicking boxes and other objects, and tearing clothing. If an individual has a history of severe property destruction, a retail job may not be appropriate. However, if the behavior is well managed and if adequate support and supervision are provided, it is possible that an individual with a history of property destruction can succeed in a retail environment.

The second issue is that merchandise usually requires special care on the part of the retail worker. So, even if the worker does not exhibit property destruction, he or she must take care not to damage the merchandise inadvertently. Workers with hygiene problems or workers who have self-stimulation behavior, such as smearing saliva, might soil or damage merchandise. Additionally, some workers with autism who have severe behavior problems are on schedules of positive reinforcement, with food serving as a potent reinforcer. Edible reinforcers can cause smudges or stains on merchandise. These issues are not necessarily job-threatening, but they need to be considered during the selection of a retail job, and as a support issue if the job is accepted.

Third, some individuals with autism display pica (i.e., eating inedible objects). This behavior, if uncontrolled, can cause problems in retail environments. One worker with autism who had problems with pica was fired from his job because he began eating the buttons off the clothes that he was preparing for display. This same individual would attempt to eat pins, clips, and other small metal objects that were found in his workplace. Yet, if the individual is well supported and an effective behavior plan is consistently run, pica can be controlled in retail environments.

A final merchandise-related problem that can occur is stealing merchandise or unauthorized use of merchandise. In businesses that sell food, this may be seen when workers with autism who are nonverbal and have more severe levels of mental retardation eat the merchandise. Food-related problems have been solved in several cases by using that same type of food that is sold as a frequent reinforcer for on-task behavior, or by providing that food at work breaks or at lunch. For example, one man who had a problem with taking crackers from his employer was provided with several packages of crackers at the beginning of the workday. He kept these crackers in his pocket and helped himself throughout the day. In other cases, higher functioning individuals who have difficulty with stealing might deliberately take desired items and hide them in their purse or briefcase. One young woman who had problems with hoarding shampoo stole shampoo from the drug store in which she worked. A behavior plan was put into place and the behavior was controlled.

JOBS IN RETAIL

Individuals with autism work in numerous retail environments. Individuals who were once considered unemployable because of severe autism, profound mental retardation, and serious behavior problems have succeeded in retail jobs, as well as persons with less severe disabilities. Descriptions of retail jobs that are filled by workers with autism are provided on the following pages.

Inventory Clerk

Job Description: An inventory clerk works in a warehouse filling catalog orders for customers.

Worksite Description: This job is in the warehouse of a small discount outlet that sells children's clothing through catalog sales. There are approximately 10 employees in the warehouse, 2 with autism.

Employees with Autism

Worker 1: Speaks in complete sentences but speech is unclear, low-average cognitive functioning, screaming, jumping, hand flapping, spinning, rapid verbalizations, motor rituals (especially spinning while walking)

Worker 2: Speaks in complete sentences, mild mental retardation, ritualistic behaviors, stealing, eavesdropping, poor money management skills

Job Tasks

- Locate items in stockroom from a list to fill customer orders

Equipment, Machinery, and Hand Tools Needed to Complete Job Tasks

- Inventory list for customer orders
- Cart with bins
- Clipboard

Potential Problems in Job Completion

- Employee does not ask for help
- Low productivity

Modifications and Accommodations to Site or Task

- Job coach to assist with productivity and behavior management
- Social skills training on asking for assistance
- Instruction on money management (Worker 2)
- Monitoring by job coach to prevent stealing

Receiving/Stock Clerk

Job Description: A receiving/stock clerk works in the stockroom preparing price tags and pricing merchandise

Worksite Description: This job is with a large catalog discount store, which is part of a chain. The store employs approximately 30 workers, including 2 employees with autism.

Employees with Autism

Worker 1:   Speaks clearly in sentences, average intellectual functioning, problems in social and language skills, aggression upon provocation

Worker 2:   Speaks clearly in full sentences, mild mental retardation, self-injury, property destruction, aggression, jumping from moving vehicles, yelling, throwing things

Job Tasks

- Make price tags
- Open boxes of merchandise
- Apply price tags to merchandise and repack boxes
- Price merchandise using a pricing gun
- Pull up computer printouts of orders
- Fill orders by locating merchandise in stockroom
- Stock shelves with merchandise

Equipment, Machinery, and
Hand Tools Needed to Complete Job Tasks

- Order forms
- Map used to locate items in the warehouse
- Pricing gun

Potential Problems in Job Completion

- Task is complicated.

Modifications and Accommodations to Site or Task

- Job coach to assist with training, productivity, and behavior management
- Task analysis to break task into steps
- Self-management plan, including self-rating and written schedule (Worker 1)
- Behavior plans, including periodic ratings and positive reinforcement

RETAIL

Receiving/Stock Clerk

Job Description: A receiving/stock clerk works in the stockroom pulling plastic off clothing and hanging it up for placement on the sales floor.

Worksite Description: This job is with a large retail department store that is part of a chain. The store employs approximately 50 workers. Twenty employees work in the stockroom, including two with autism.

Employees with Autism

Worker 1:   Communicates using sounds and gestures, profound mental retardation, screaming, yelling, throwing work on the floor, self-injury, hyperactivity, self-stimulation, task refusal, noncompliance, prompt dependence

Worker 2:   Speaks clearly in sentences, moderate mental retardation, property destruction, self-injury, aggression (including hair pulling, lunging, hitting, kicking, scratching, and banging other people's heads against walls)

Job Tasks

- Pull plastic covering off clothing
- Choose the appropriate hanger and pad it if necessary
- Hang clothing on the appropriate hanger, then on racks

Equipment, Machinery, and Hand Tools Needed to Complete Job Tasks

- Clothing hangers
- Clothing racks

Potential Problems in Job Completion

- Long hours
- Choosing the correct hanger for the clothing
- Asking for assistance

Modifications and Accommodations to Site or Task

- Job coach to assist with training, productivity, and behavior management
- Adjusted hours
- Instruction on asking for assistance
- Behavior plans, including positive reinforcement, social skills training, extinction procedures, and guidelines for managing dangerous behavior

Receiving Clerk

Job Description: A receiving clerk works in the stockroom sorting, hanging, and ticketing clothing for placement on the sales floor.

Worksite Description: This job is with a large discount clothing outlet that is part of a chain. The store employs approximately 50 workers. Ten employees work in the stockroom, including three with autism.

Employees with Autism

Worker 1:   Speaks clearly in sentences, moderate mental retardation, non-compliance, self-injury, self-stimulation, aggression

Worker 2:   Speaks clearly in sentences, low-average cognitive functioning, limited social and language skills, perseveration on inappropriate topics

Worker 3:   Communicates using limited manual signs and pictures, severe mental retardation, self-injury, aggression (including grabbing, biting, and pinching), property destruction, refusal to comply with directions, pica, public masturbation, feces smearing, spitting, food stealing, licking glass surfaces

Job Tasks

- Check in deliveries of merchandise
- Open boxes of merchandise
- Sort deliveries to correct department
- Ticket merchandise
- Hang merchandise
- Sort hangers

Equipment, Machinery, and Hand Tools Needed to Complete Job Tasks

- Pricing gun
- Clothing hangers
- Clothing racks

Potential Problems in Job Completion

- Worksite littered with small nonedibles

Modifications and Accommodations to Site or Task

- Job coach to assist with training, productivity, and behavior management
- Keep work area as clean as possible and provide close supervision to prevent eating of inedibles.
- Behavior management plans, including positive reinforcement, self-management procedures, periodic ratings, prompt hierarchy, noncontingent reinforcers, alternate sensory stimuli, extinction, and guidelines for managing dangerous behavior

Stock Clerk

Job Description: A stock clerk prices and reprices items in the stockroom for placement on the sales floor.

Worksite Description: This job is with a large retail store that is part of a local chain. The store employs approximately 30 workers, including 3 employees with autism.

Employees with Autism

Worker 1: Speaks in sentences but speech is unclear, profound mental retardation, prompt dependency, self-injury, tantrums, deficits in communication skills (including loud echolalia and perseverative verbalizations)

Worker 2: Speaks in full sentences, moderate mental retardation, aggression, property destruction, difficulties in social communication (including repetitive questions and standing too close while speaking)

Worker 3: Speaks clearly in full sentences, mild mental retardation, swearing, aggression, stealing, urinating in inappropriate places, undressing in public, inappropriate sexual behaviors

Job Tasks

- Price merchandise
- Change prices on merchandise as necessary
- Break down boxes
- Compact trash

Equipment, Machinery, and Hand Tools Needed to Complete Job Tasks

- Pricing gun
- Boxes
- Trash compactor

Potential Problems in Job Completion

- Noisy worksite can be distracting.
- No chairs are available, which makes the task more difficult.
- Behavior problems can be disturbing to the public and other employees.
- Work area is near the loading dock, which is exposed to the weather.

Modifications and Accommodations to Site or Task

- Job coach to assist with training, productivity, and behavior management
- Bring in chairs
- Limit contact with the public
- Behavior management plans, including positive reinforcement, periodic ratings, social skills training, communication guidelines, extinction, and guidelines for managing dangerous behavior

Stock Clerk

Job Description: A stock clerk prepares and organizes merchandise for display and sales.

Worksite Description: This job is with a medium-size discount drug store that is part of a local chain. There are approximately 20 employees, including 2 with autism.

Employees with Autism

Worker 1: Speaks in sentences but speech is unclear, profound mental retardation, prompt dependency, self-injury, tantrums, problems with communication skills (including loud echolalia and perseverative verbalizations)

Worker 2: Speaks clearly in full sentences, mild mental retardation, swearing, aggression, stealing, urinating in inappropriate places, undressing in public, inappropriate sexual behaviors

Job Tasks

- Straighten shelves so merchandise faces forward and is flush with the shelf
- Collect damaged items and empty boxes
- Price merchandise with a pricing gun
- Break down empty boxes and take them to the trash compactor
- Peel stickers from incorrectly priced items

Equipment, Machinery, and
Hand Tools Needed to Complete Job Tasks

- Pricing gun
- Trash compactor
- Shopping cart

Potential Problems in Job Completion

- Employee makes loud noises
- Employee unable to load stickers into pricing gun or set prices on gun
- Customers ask for directions

Modifications and Accommodations to Site or Task

- Job coach to assist with training, productivity, and behavior management
- Employee is removed from the sales floor when loud.
- The job coach sets the pricing gun and puts on the stickers.
- Worker taught to tell customers to ask up front or have the job coach provide assistance
- Behavior management plans, including positive reinforcement, self-management, social skills training, and voice volume training (Worker 1)

RETAIL

Stock Clerk

Job Description: A stock clerk prepares merchandise for placement on the sales floor of a large home and garden store.

Worksite Description: This job is with a large retail home and garden store that is part of a local chain. The store employs approximately 50 employees. Fifteen employees work in the stockroom, including 3 with autism. Occasionally, the employees with autism work on the sales floor.

Employees with Autism

Worker 1:   Speaks clearly in sentences, moderate mental retardation, aggression (including hitting, kicking, hair pulling, scratching, clothes tearing, and biting)

Worker 2:   Speaks clearly in sentences, average intellectual functioning, poor social skills and language problems, aggression upon provocation

Worker 3:   Speaks clearly in full sentences, low-average cognitive functioning, resistance to doing scheduled tasks, threats of self-punishment and self-injury (including hitting self, grabbing self by neck, and head banging)

Job Tasks

- Check off merchandise as it arrives
- Price items
- Attach security tags
- Open boxes and repack items after pricing
- Organize merchandise according to category
- Restock items on the sales floor
- Consolidate merchandise by placing older items on the top of the pallet and newer items on the bottom
- Remove damaged items from shelves
- Rebag broken bags of merchandise
- Load customers' cars
- Break down boxes for trash compacting
- Sweep
- Water plants

Equipment, Machinery, and Hand Tools Needed to Complete Job Tasks

- Pricing gun
- Security tags
- X-ACTO knife
- Ladder
- Shopping carts and flatbeds

- Trash compactor
- Rolling trash cans and dumpster
- Brooms, shovels
- Garden hose
- Dollies
- Rolling carts

Potential Problems in Job Completion

- Work area is near the loading dock, which is exposed to the weather.
- Lifting heavy merchandise
- Answering customers' questions
- Ritualistic behavior and need to sit in a particular seat at lunch
- Rocking back and forth on ladder

Modifications and Accommodations to Site or Task

- Employee is directed to tell customers to ask at the front desk or the job coach answers questions.
- Job coach lifts heavy items.
- Dress appropriately for the weather

Stock Clerk

Job Description: A stock clerk works in the stockroom hanging clothes and attaching sensors to merchandise for placement on the sales floor.

Worksite Description: This job is with a large chain department store. The store employs approximately 40 workers, 10 of whom are stock clerks, including 3 employees with autism.

Employees with Autism

Worker 1:   Speaks clearly in sentences, moderate mental retardation, aggression (including hair pulling, lunging, hitting, kicking, scratching, banging other people's heads against walls, property destruction, and self-injury)

Worker 2:   Speaks clearly in full sentences, mild mental retardation, crying, yelling, squealing, task refusal

Worker 3:   Communicates using limited manual signs and pictures; severe mental retardation; significant difficulties in social, language, and toileting skills

Job Tasks

- Unpack clothing
- Remove plastic and tissue paper from clothing
- Hang clothing on hangers, then on racks
- Place electronic security sensors on clothing
- Keep work area clean and discard trash

Equipment, Machinery, and Hand Tools Needed to Complete Job Tasks

- Security sensor tags
- Security sensor gun
- Racks
- Various types of hangers

Potential Problems in Job Completion

- Difficulty choosing the correct hanger for clothing
- Works slowly and produces low quality work

Modifications and Accommodations to Site or Task

- Job coach to assist with training, toileting (Worker 3), productivity, and behavior management
- Ribbons on hangers provide visual cues for choosing the correct hanger
- Behavior management plans, including positive reinforcement, social skills training, prompt hierarchy, extinction, and procedures for managing dangerous behavior

Inventory Clerk

Job Description: An inventory clerk prepares merchandise for placement on the sales floor and stocks merchandise on the sales floor.

Worksite Description: This job is with a medium-size retail store. The store employs approximately 12 workers, including 1 with autism.

Employee with Autism

Worker 1:   Speaks in full sentences, mild mental retardation, task refusal, property destruction, sulking, aggression (including kicking co-workers and spitting)

Job Tasks

- Price merchandise with a pricing gun
- Stock shelves on sales floor
- Return merchandise to the shelves
- Sweep floor
- Dispose of trash

Equipment, Machinery, and Hand Tools Needed to Complete Job Tasks

- Pricing gun
- Broom
- Garbage cans

Potential Problems in Job Completion

- Behavior problems, including refusal to work and aggression

Modifications and Accommodations to Site or Task

- Job coach to assist with training, productivity, and behavior management
- Behavior management plans, including positive reinforcement, social skills training, prompt hierarchy, extinction, and procedures for managing dangerous behavior

Assistant Subassembly Worker

Job Description: An assistant subassembly worker assembles merchandise to fill customer orders and for display in the store.

Worksite Description: This job is with a large retail toy store that is part of a local chain. The store has a large sales floor and a stockroom in the back. There are approximately 30 employees, including 1 with autism.

Employee with Autism

Worker 1:   Speaks in full sentences, severe mental retardation, delayed echolalia, difficulty remaining on location during tasks, yelling, stealing, urinating and defecating in clothing

Job Tasks

- Assemble bicycles
- Assemble merchandise for display
- Price merchandise using a pricing gun
- Locate merchandise to be stocked on store shelves
- Sweep floors

Equipment, Machinery, and Hand Tools Needed to Complete Job Tasks

- Wrench
- Screwdriver
- Hammer
- Ratchet
- Pliers
- Broom

Potential Problems in Job Completion

- Refusal to do certain tasks, such as sweeping floors

Modifications and Accommodations to Site or Task

- Job coach to assist with training, productivity, and behavior management
- Behavior management plans, including positive reinforcement, social skills training, prompt hierarchy, and toileting procedures
- Rarely asked to sweep floors

Stock Clerk

Job Description: A stock clerk works in the stockroom preparing merchandise for placement on the sales floor and cleaning up the stockroom.

Worksite Description: This job is with a large retail company that is part of a national chain. The store employs approximately 40 workers, 6 as stock clerks, including 3 with autism.

Employees with Autism

Worker 1: Speaks clearly in sentences, moderate mental retardation, noncompliance, self-injury, self-stimulation, aggression, poor hygiene and grooming, low productivity, difficulty squeezing pricing gun handle

Worker 2: Speaks clearly in full sentences, mild mental retardation, crying, yelling, squealing, task refusal, inappropriate language, prompt dependence

Worker 3: Communicates using key words, severe mental retardation, spitting, lying on the floor, noncompliance, disrobing in public, throwing objects

Job Tasks

- Unload deliveries from truck to a conveyor belt
- Restack boxes of merchandise
- Price merchandise using a pricing gun
- Remove price tags from merchandise
- Hang clothing on hangers, then on racks
- Collect shopping carts from the store aisles and parking lot
- Load merchandise into customers' cars
- Sweep the warehouse floor
- Break down boxes and carry them to the trash compactor
- Dispose of debris in the trash compactor

Equipment, Machinery, and Hand Tools Needed to Complete Job Tasks

- Pricing gun
- Hangers
- Clothing racks
- Trash compactor
- Conveyor belt
- Broom

Potential Problems in Job Completion

- Stockroom is often crowded and passage through is difficult.
- Pricing became computerized.

Modifications and Accommodations to Site or Task

- Job coach to assist with training, productivity, and behavior management
- Keep work area as uncluttered as possible
- Behavior management plans, including positive reinforcement, prompt hierarchy, alternate sensory stimuli, extinction, and procedures for managing dangerous behavior

Stock Clerk

Job Description: A stock clerk works in the stockroom sorting, hanging, and attaching sensors to clothing for placement on the sales floor.

Worksite Description: This job is with a small retail company that is part of a national chain. The store employs approximately 20 workers, 3 with autism.

Employees with Autism

Worker 1:   Speaks in complete sentences but speech is unclear, low-average cognitive functioning, difficulties with social and language skills, off-task behaviors

Worker 2:   Communicates using sounds and gestures, profound mental retardation, screaming, yelling, throwing work on the floor, self-injury, hyperactivity, self-stimulation, task refusal, noncompliance, prompt dependency

Worker 3:   Speaks clearly in sentences, mild mental retardation, throwing objects, aggression, self-injury, inappropriate sexual comments, tearing clothes, yelling

Job Tasks

- Sort mixed racks of clothing
- Replace shipping hangers with display hangers
- Attach electronic security sensors to clothing
- Break down boxes for disposal in dumpster

Equipment, Machinery, and Hand Tools Needed to Complete Job Tasks

- Pricing gun
- Hangers
- Clothing racks

Potential Problems in Job Completion

- Management turnover very high

Modifications and Accommodations to Site or Task

- Job coach to assist with training, productivity, and behavior management
- Behavior management plans, including positive reinforcement, periodic ratings, social discrimination instruction, social skills training, prompt hierarchy, extinction, and procedures for managing dangerous behavior

Stock Clerk

Job Description: A stock clerk works on the sales floor sorting, folding, and stacking linens for display.

Worksite Description: This job is with a mid-size retail company that is part of a national chain. The store employs approximately 20 workers, including 2 workers with autism.

Employees with Autism

Worker 1:   Speaks in full sentences, mild mental retardation, task refusal, property destruction, sulking, aggression, works slowly

Worker 2:   Communicates using limited sign language, severe mental retardation, self-injury, aggression, self-stimulation, noncompliance, prompt dependence

Job Tasks

- Sort linen by style, size, color, and manufacturer
- Fold linens, then place them on shelves or hang them on hooks
- Price linens
- Stock shelves with linens as necessary

Equipment, Machinery, and Hand Tools Needed to Complete Job Tasks

- Linens
- Pricing gun

Potential Problems in Job Completion

- Contact with public
- Necessary to sit on the floor, which blocks the aisles

Modifications and Accommodations to Site or Task

- Job coach to assist with training, productivity, and behavior management
- Position workers to block as little space as possible
- Behavior management plans, including positive reinforcement, periodic ratings, prompt hierarchy, extinction, and procedures for managing dangerous behavior

Stock/Receiving Clerk

Job Description: A stock/receiving clerk prepares merchandise in the stockroom for placement on the sales floor of a drug store.

Worksite Description: This job is with a medium-size retail store that is part of a chain. There are approximately 20 employees, 2 with autism.

Employees with Autism

Worker 1:   Speaks clearly in complete sentences, low-average intelligence, aggression, limited social and language skills, property destruction, screaming, infrequent physical aggression

Worker 2:   Speaks in complete sentences, mild mental retardation, displays ritualistic behaviors, shoplifting, eavesdropping, poor money management skills, sometimes works slowly, task refusal

Job Tasks

- Match items according to color and size
- Locate price, price item, and mark shelf with price
- Stock shelves in the warehouse
- Move merchandise as directed
- Discard empty boxes
- Sweep

Equipment, Machinery, and Hand Tools Needed to Complete Job Tasks

- Conveyor belt
- Broom
- Price book
- Price gun

Potential Problems in Job Completion

- Answer customer requests
- Difficulty asking for instructions after task completion

Modifications and Accommodations to Site or Task

- Job coach to assist with training, productivity, and behavior management
- Teach employee to direct customer to the front desk
- Behavior management plans, including self-management, self-rating, social skills training, and positive reinforcement

RETAIL

Stock Clerk

Job Description: A stock clerk prices and stocks merchandise on the sales floor of a drug and variety store.

Worksite Description: This job is with a large retail store that is part of a local chain. There are approximately 35 employees, 2 with autism.

Employees with Autism

Worker 1: Speaks clearly in complete sentences, low-average intelligence, aggression, limited social and language skills

Worker 2: Speaks in complete sentences, mild mental retardation, ritualistic behaviors, stealing, eavesdropping, poor money management skills

Job Tasks

- Price items with pricing gun
- Straighten merchandise on store shelves
- Re-stock merchandise on store shelves
- Set aside damaged items
- Return misplaced merchandise to the correct locations

Equipment, Machinery, and Hand Tools Needed to Complete Job Tasks

- Pricing gun

Potential Problems in Job Completion

- Customers ask questions.
- Store aisles are narrow and working in the aisles blocks them.
- Employees need to carry out all tasks in the store.

Modifications and Accommodations to Site or Task

- Social skills training to direct customers to front, or the job coach directs customers
- Job coach to assist with training, productivity, and behavior management
- Behavior management plans, including self-management, self-rating, social skills training, and positive reinforcement

Car Washer

Job Description: A car washer washes customers' cars at the dealership as a service offered to the car owners.

Worksite Description: The job is with a medium-size car dealership. The dealership has a large lot, show room, parts department, repair shop, and detail shop. The dealership employs approximately 50 workers, 20 in the service area, including 3 workers with autism.

Employees with Autism

Worker 1:   Speaks in sentences but speech is unclear, profound mental retardation, prompt dependence, self-injury, tantrums, problems with communication (including loud echolalia and perseverative verbalizations)

Worker 2:   Speaks in sentences but speech is unclear, moderate mental retardation, crying, self-induced vomiting, toilet stuffing, urinating and defecating in clothing

Worker 3:   Speaks in complete sentences but speech is unclear, moderate mental retardation, noncompliance, wandering away from tasks, screaming, loud perseverative echolalia

Job Tasks

- Rinse car with hose
- Wash car with soap using a mitt
- Dry exterior of car with a chamois cloth
- Wash the windows
- Remove floor mats from the car and shake them to remove dirt
- Vacuum rugs and upholstery

Equipment, Machinery, and Hand Tools Needed to Complete Job Tasks

- Hose
- Soap
- Bucket
- Rags
- Chamois cloth
- Paper towels
- Window cleaner
- Vinyl cleaner
- Vacuum

Potential Problems in Job Completion

- Weather (rain or heat) interferes with work.
- Cars must be driven to washing area.
- Work is seasonal.
- Hose is shared with service department and it is necessary to wait sometimes.

Modifications and Accommodations to Site or Task

- Job coach to assist with training, productivity, and behavior management
- Job coach drives cars to washing area.
- Behavior management plans, including positive reinforcement, voice volume training, prompt hierarchy, and extinction

Stock Clerk

Job Description: A stock clerk works in the stockroom preparing clothing for display on the sales floor of a department store.

Worksite Description: This job is with a large, multilevel department store that is part of a national chain. The store employs approximately 100 workers, 10 in the stockroom, including 3 workers with autism.

Employees with Autism

Worker 1: Communicates using limited manual signs and pictures, severe mental retardation, self-injury, aggression (including grabbing, biting, and pinching), property destruction, pica, refusal to comply with directions, public masturbation, feces smearing, spitting, food stealing, licking glass surfaces

Worker 2: Speaks clearly in full sentences, mild mental retardation, self-injury, property destruction, aggression, bolting from moving vehicles, yelling

Worker 3: Communicates using key words, profound mental retardation, noncompliance, refusal to move, severe self-injury (including head banging)

Job Tasks

- Remove plastic from clothing
- Attach electronic security sensors to clothing
- Hang clothing on hangers, then on racks
- Break down boxes and carry them to the trash compactor
- Count items to check inventory

Equipment, Machinery, and Hand Tools Needed to Complete Job Tasks

- Hangers
- Clothing racks
- Trash compactor
- Security sensors

Potential Problems in Job Completion

- Disturbing customers with behavior problems
- Part of task requires counting

Modifications and Accommodations to Site or Task

- Job coach to assist with training, productivity, and behavior management
- Task was modified so all work took place in the stockroom.

- For employees who cannot count, the job coach must carry out that part of the task.
- Behavior management plans, including positive reinforcement, alternate sensory stimuli, liberal snacking program, prompt hierarchy, and extinction procedures for managing dangerous behavior

Stock Clerk

Job Description: A stock clerk prices and stocks merchandise on the sales floor of a toy store.

Worksite Description: This job is with a large retail store that is part of a local chain. There are approximately 35 employees. There are eight stock clerks, including four workers with autism, at each store.

Employees with Autism

Worker 1: Speaks clearly in complete sentences, borderline range of intellectual functioning, sporadic self-injury, aggression

Worker 2: Speaks in sentences but speech is unclear, mild mental retardation, task refusal, does not initiate tasks

Worker 3: Communicates using limited manual signs and pictures, profound mental retardation, self-injury, feces smearing

Worker 4: Speaks clearly in sentences, borderline mental retardation, limited social and language skills, difficulty following instructions, distracted by visitors

Job Tasks

- Unload delivery trucks
- Price items with pricing gun
- Stock merchandise on store shelves
- Straighten merchandise on store shelves
- Return misplaced merchandise to the correct location
- Collect damaged merchandise

Equipment, Machinery, and Hand Tools Needed to Complete Job Tasks

- Shopping carts and flat carts
- Trash compactor
- Pallets

Potential Problems in Job Completion

- Customers ask questions.
- Store aisles are narrow and working in the aisles blocks them.
- Employees need to carry out all tasks in the store.
- Crying children
- Finding items in the storage room and using a ladder

Modifications and Accommodations to Site or Task

- Job coach to assist with training, productivity, and behavior management
- Social skills training to direct customers to the front, or the job coach directs customers
- Directed to another aisle if crying child approaches
- Job coach provides assistance for finding items in storage and using a ladder
- Position merchandise and self to block the aisle as little as possible
- Behavior management plans, including positive reinforcement, self-management, social skills training, prompt hierarchy, extinction, and procedures for managing dangerous behavior and preventing bolting

Stock Clerk

Job Description: A stock clerk works in the stockroom preparing merchandise for placement on the sales floor.

Worksite Description: This job is with a large discount retail company that is part of a national chain. The store employs approximately 20 workers per shift, 5 of whom are stock clerks, including 3 with autism.

Employees with Autism

Worker 1: Communicates using limited manual signs and pictures, severe mental retardation, self-injury, aggression (including grabbing, biting, and pinching), property destruction, pica, refusal to comply with directions, public masturbation, feces smearing, spitting, food stealing, licking glass surfaces, trying to lie down and sleep on the job during work hours

Worker 2: Speaks in complete sentences, mild mental retardation, ritualistic behaviors, shoplifting, eavesdropping, poor money management skills, shopping during work hours when on sales floor

Worker 3: Speaks in full sentences, severe mental retardation, stealing, darting from work area

Job Tasks

- Unload deliveries onto a conveyor belt
- Open boxes
- Price merchandise using a pricing gun
- Remove plastic from clothing
- Hang clothing on hangers, then on racks
- Sort hangers by type and size
- Break down boxes

Equipment, Machinery, and Hand Tools Needed to Complete Job Tasks

- Pricing gun
- Clothing hangers
- Clothing racks
- Trash compactor
- Conveyor belt

Potential Problems in Job Completion

- Stockroom is often crowded and passage through is difficult, which inhibits the use of nonaversive physical management.
- Many small nonedibles on site
- Long hours

Modifications and Accommodations to Site or Task

- Shorten hours
- Keep area clean of nonedibles
- Behavior management plans, including positive reinforcement, social skills training, alternate sensory stimuli, prompt hierarchy, extinction, and procedures for managing dangerous behavior

CASE STUDY #1—JERRY
• • • • • • • • •

Employee Description

Jerry is a 30-year-old man with autism and severe mental retardation. He has good visual motor skills, good visual discrimination, and excellent fine motor control although he exhibits significant social withdrawal and cannot communicate verbally. Jerry also displays several behaviors that provide him with sensory feedback. These include spitting on his hands and on objects such as work materials, kissing and licking smooth cool surfaces such as glass or tiles, and playing in toilet water or his own urine. His most dangerous behavior is pica; he tends to eat objects such as paper clips, pieces of plastic or glass, paper, bits of twigs, and bottle caps. Jerry sees an object on the floor and quickly grabs it and puts it in his mouth before he can be prevented from doing it. An x-ray several years ago revealed various foreign objects in his stomach. Jerry also had surgery on one occasion to remove embedded objects from his intestine.

In addition, Jerry sometimes ruminates his food, masturbates in public, and smears his feces in the bathroom. Occasionally, Jerry is aggressive toward others; he hits, bites, pushes and grabs others, and in some cases has caused injury to other people.

Employee History

Jerry lived at home and attended segregated special education schools in the local public school system until the age of 21 years. He then entered a supported employment program for people with autism and moved into a group home for people with mental retardation and other developmental disabilities. The supported employment program was the first integrated experience of his life.

Description of Company and Job

Jerry has held several jobs as a receiving and stock clerk in retail stores. Most of these jobs have been with large, national department store chains. His current job, which he has held for 5 years, is in a retail store that sells clothing.

Jerry works in the stockroom and receiving area of the store. His job duties are opening boxes of clothes, removing the plastic coverings, hanging the clothes on hangers for display on the sales floor, and applying price and security tags. Jerry also sorts the hangers according to size and takes out the trash. Previously, Jerry unloaded delivery trucks and organized boxes of merchandise in the stockroom.

Setting Up the Job

An initial vocational assessment of Jerry revealed obvious problems with language and socialization and strengths in visual-motor skills. It was also noted that he was very strong and not averse to hard physical labor such as moving boxes. Because of this pattern of strengths and weaknesses, the employment specialist sought a job position that required visual-motor skills with minimal language requirements.

In setting up the work environment, special attention was given to safety considerations. Because Jerry would dart away from staff and grab inedible objects to eat, the work environment was arranged to limit the areas to which he had access. Because of the nature of the work environment, it was possible to rearrange boxes of merchandise so that Jerry could not easily leave his work area to find inedibles. This was done with the permission of the stockroom supervisor. The job coach and Jerry then worked to keep this smaller area free of inedibles. This was done by frequently vacuuming or sweeping the work area.

Establishing Employment Supports

Before admitting Jerry into the supported employment program, staff interviewed his parents and school personnel and read his records to determine the level of support needed.

Determination of Supports   Because of the severity of Jerry's pica behavior and aggression, it was clear that he would require continual supervision and monitoring to ensure his safety and the safety of others. In addition, the absence of language and social skills meant that high levels of assistance would be necessary for him to negotiate the demands of an integrated work environment. It was agreed that he could share a job coach with another worker with autism who needed less supervision.

Description of Job Coach Duties   The job coach's primary responsibility with Jerry was to teach him his job duties and assist him in performing those duties while preventing him from harming himself. The job coach was required to implement a behavior plan at work to help eliminate pica and he was responsible for keeping the work environment clear of potentially dangerous objects.

Description of Behavior Plan   Jerry required intensive behavioral interventions to retain employment. A functional assessment revealed that he engaged in pica primarily for self-stimulation. Antecedents to aggression included being abruptly or repeatedly told to do something or having his schedule disrupted by visitors. Jerry was also likely to bite others if they tried to prevent him from eating inedibles. Finally, he was sensitive to negative feedback and often became aggressive when criticized. It was thought that aggression served the purpose of escaping from undesirable situations such as demands and criticisms, and that the function of his pica was self-stimulation.

A psychologist consulted with supported employment staff and developed a behavior program based on the above functions. The program called for reinforcers approximately every 15 minutes for specific target behaviors that emphasized appropriate use of his hands (e.g., hands on work, hands at side), staying in his work area, having his mouth clear of inedibles, and responding to verbal instructions. Reinforcers were chosen that provided Jerry with desired sensory feedback. Food reinforcers that are crunchy, such as carrots, pretzels, and granola, and sensory reinforcers that provide tactile or olfactory stimulation, such as lotions, massage oils, and colognes, were used. Because Jerry's pica was so dangerous, he was given free access to snacks as alternate sensory stimuli. This was done by attaching a snack pouch to his belt and filling it with crunchy foods. If Jerry wanted a snack, he simply opened the pouch and ate one. Jerry had almost continual access to snacks in the pouch because they were replenished once an hour. Data were taken separately on the number of incidents of pica, aggression, and leaving his work area. With the reinforcement procedures and access to snacks, Jerry quickly learned that he no longer had to eat inedibles to obtain oral stimulation.

A key component to Jerry's behavior program was a set of very specific guidelines on how staff were to manage his pica. Preventive procedures included keeping his work area clean and maintaining a constant awareness of hazards in the environment. It was helpful that Jerry was a neat worker. In addition, staff were instructed to keep an eye on the position of Jerry's hands and to quickly redirect him should he attempt to eat an inedible item. Regular observations by behavioral staff instructors ensured that job coaches received specific ongoing feedback about their adherence to the guidelines. Staff were also instructed to supervise Jerry's use of the bathroom to ensure that it was kept neat and clean.

Description of Instructional Procedures Although Jerry was a hard worker, he had some difficulty meeting acceptable employer's standard productivity rates and performing tasks accurately. For instance, he had difficulty putting the price tag through the seams of the clothing. A productivity program that called for reinforcing high rates of work was implemented. Accuracy was addressed by using structured task analyses as well as a prompt hierarchy to teach correct placement of price tags. With these procedures, Jerry's productivity rate and work quality improved.

Outcomes

During the past 9 years, Jerry has held jobs as a receiving and stock clerk at five different retail stores. He was laid off from three of these jobs because of a lack of work and terminated at one because of his behavior problems. Since Jerry started working in retail, he has worked for a total of 6 years and 9 months, and he has been unemployed for a total of 15 months. He currently works 25 hours per week for $4.90 per hour. Because of sporadic dangerous behaviors, his lack of verbal language, and his profound mental retardation, Jerry continues to need the assistance of a full-time job coach. He is still on a behavior management plan, but the frequency of reinforcers has been reduced.

CASE STUDY #2—HOWARD
• • • • • • • • • •

Employee Description

Howard is a 36-year-old man who scores within the normal range of intelligence on a standard intelligence test, even though he has severe autism. Howard speaks in complete sentences and often initiates conversation; however, he only speaks on a few topics, namely baseball and hit songs. He displays difficulty understanding the nuances of language and communication. For example, he sometimes asks personal questions of others and interrupts others while they are talking. Howard also has some maladaptive social skills, including clinging to others, inappropriately touching others, and invading personal space such as private offices without permission.

Howard has a history of severe behavior problems. He has hit and grabbed people, threatened others, destroyed property, and yelled and cursed at others. Howard is also hyperactive and easily distracted. Although these behaviors have improved, he has difficulty sitting still for brief periods of time and attending to his work tasks.

Employee History

Howard lived with his parents and attended segregated schools for children with developmental disabilities. He remained in such schools until age 21 when he was placed in a supported employment program designed for individuals with autism. At the same time, he moved into a group home for adults with autism.

Howard held several job positions briefly before settling into one job as a warehouse stock clerk in a retail store. He worked for less than 6 months each as a bulk mailing clerk, newspaper recycling worker, book sorter, air conditioning assembler, and tee-shirt manufacturer. Howard also worked for more than a year each as a bindery worker in a printing company, as a beverage warehouse worker, and as an electronic component assembler. Although he lost these jobs for a variety of reasons, his behavior, slow work speed, and poor work quality certainly had an impact on the decision to let him go. It was clear that Howard had not found a job position and employment environment that suited him.

Description of Company and Job

Howard eventually was placed in a job in a retail store warehouse. The store sold lighting fixtures and other electrical supplies that were stored in the warehouse. The warehouse also supplied lights and electrical components to different stores in the same chain. Howard's job was to price merchandise for display, re-stock shelves in the store and the warehouse, sweep and clean the warehouse, and fill supply orders from the other stores. To do this last job, Howard had to read stock numbers on a computer printout, find requested items on the warehouse shelves, and count out the correct number of items. He then placed the requested items in a bin and labeled the bin with the store's location.

Setting Up the Job

Howard's employment specialist thought that this new retail job was a good match for him for several reasons. Howard had excellent reading skills and this job required that he read computer printouts to select items by stock numbers. In previous jobs, Howard had displayed difficulty sitting still, but this position allowed him to move around the warehouse collecting electrical supplies. Finally, most of the work for this job took place in the warehouse rather than on the retail sales floor. This meant that should he have behavior problems, they were less likely to be job threatening than if they occurred in front of customers.

After securing the job, the job coach spent several days on the job learning the job tasks without Howard. The job coach became familiar with how to fill orders from the computer printouts and with what to do if requested supplies were not available. The job coach also assessed the social demands of the work environment.

Establishing Supports

When he entered the supported employment program, Howard's interdisciplinary team met and reviewed his behaviors and skills to determine necessary levels of support.

Determination of Supports The team agreed that Howard needed the full-time supervision of a job coach because of his severe behavior problems and his inappropriate social behaviors. It was clear from previous jobs that Howard required a high level of structure and constant supervision to ensure the safety of others and to retain employment. Therefore, Howard had a job coach who supervised him and one other adult with autism on a full-time basis. Because Howard's problems were sporadic, he was paired with another worker with autism who also had sporadic behavior problems. It was unlikely that both workers would act out at the same time and emergency back-up was always available should this occur.

Description of Job Coach Duties The job coach's duties were to teach Howard his work tasks, to supervise his work, and to assist him in remaining on task. The job coach was also responsible for teaching appropriate social skills, implementing Howard's behavior management plan, and intervening when inappropriate social behaviors occurred. Howard also needed instruction on how to use the bus to travel to and from work.

Description of Behavior Plan A psychologist consulted with Howard's supported employment staff and developed a behavior change plan for Howard that was based on the functions of his behavior. Concerning antecedent events, Howard had trouble handling changes in the environment, including changes in staff, normal routine, and the weather. In contrast, he did well in structured environments with clear expectations and consequences. In the absence of structure, Howard was likely to get into trouble by entering people's offices, cursing, yelling, and not working. Howard was also sensitive to corrections or criticism from his job coach and would become aggressive if the job coach told him to stop doing something that he wanted to do. Concerning consequences, Howard sometimes received extra attention in the form of conversation and counseling in an effort to calm him down.

Howard was placed on a behavior plan to increase acceptable work and social behaviors and to decrease his aggression, yelling, cursing, and property destruction. The plan included a self-management component that involved a system of self-monitoring and self-rating. Howard was taught to rate himself hourly on the following targeted behaviors: keeping hands and feet to self (i.e., no aggression), speaking softly (i.e., no yelling), correct use of property (i.e., no property destruction), having interesting conversation (i.e., no cursing or threats), and working steadily to complete his assigned tasks. Targeted behaviors were written out for him, and each hour he rated his performance on each behavior. Initially, the job coach monitored his ratings and provided corrective feedback; however, over time, Howard learned to do the ratings himself. Currently, the job coach continues to provide occasional praise for the targeted behaviors.

Howard also chooses his own weekly reinforcer for good performance on his ratings. At the beginning of each week, Howard lists three activities that he would like to do at the end of the week. If he earns 90% of his points and has no dangerous behavior problems, he can choose an activity he would like to do with his job coach. Because Howard's aggressive behavior can be severe, the job coach was trained in nonaversive management of aggressive behavior so that he could prevent injury to Howard or others should an incident occur.

Description of Instructional Procedures Although Howard had the skills necessary to do his job, he frequently wandered off task and paced aimlessly around the warehouse. To encourage on-task behaviors, an item for working steadily was included on his hourly ratings. Howard was given credit for that item if he worked diligently on his job tasks. He was also praised for attending to his work and for working quickly.

Howard usually walked through the warehouse with his head down looking at the floor rather than at where he was going. To help in his social adjustment to work, it was important that he walk with his head held up. Howard was given social skills instruction to practice walking with his head up. The counselor explained why it was important to walk with his head up and demonstrated the skill to Howard who then practiced it himself. Throughout the day, Howard was reminded to walk with his head up and was praised if he did so independently. This program succeeded in teaching him to walk with his head up, which meant that he could look at his work and greet co-workers.

Howard quickly learned what bus to take to and from work; however, he displayed many problem behaviors that made independent travel difficult. These included rushing to get a seat, bumping into and pushing other passengers, and yelling to the driver to let him off. A self-rating system for use only on the bus was developed for Howard. He was taught to rate himself on the following behaviors: taking a transfer, walking slowly to his seat, keeping his limbs and backpack to himself (i.e., not pushing or bumping into other passengers), sitting quietly in his seat or standing quietly, and ringing the bell to get off or walking quietly to the front of the bus if the bell was broken. Howard's job coach reviewed these behaviors with him prior to getting on the bus and then taught Howard to rate himself at the end of the bus ride. After Howard was earning all his points regularly, the job coach faded out supervision on the bus and did occasional covert checks of Howard's behavior on the bus. Covert checks revealed that Howard independently displayed appropriate behaviors on the bus.

Outcomes

Howard earned $5.00 per hour at this retail job and worked about 25 hours per week. Aggression became rare, and Howard was employed at the job for almost 5 years, until the company moved and downsized the number of employees. Due to the effective management of Howard's difficulties by his job coach, behavioral incidents did not prove job threatening. Since leaving this job, Howard had seasonal work as a retail stock clerk in a home and garden store and now works as a bulk mailing clerk. He continues to run his own behavior plan but still needs a full-time job coach because of the danger posed by his now infrequent behavior problems. His current employer is pleased with his job performance and the outlook for continued employment at his present job is high.

CHAPTER 8

Jobs in Printing and Bulk Mailing

The fields of printing and bulk mailing provide good employment opportunities for workers with autism. These workers are hired by printing companies to do a range of tasks involved in the manufacturing of books and other printed materials. Job duties include collating, separating books into stacks, binding books, wrapping books, and punching holes into books. People with autism may work at specialty printing companies, such as those that specialize in name labels, greeting cards, and business cards. At these jobs, workers have been involved in tasks that are specific to the production of the specialty item, for example, cutting sheets of mailing labels and making name badges. Workers with autism are also hired by bulk mailing firms to do jobs such as applying mailing labels to envelopes, collating materials, collecting and sorting inserts, wrapping packages, and stuffing envelopes. Some workers hold these jobs independent of support, whereas others need full-time assistance from a job coach to perform the tasks satisfactorily.

ADVANTAGES OF PRINTING AND BULK MAILING JOBS

Printing and bulk mailing jobs have proven to be ideal for some workers with autism. The nature of the tasks and work materials are often of interest to people with autism, and the nature and sequences of the tasks are often compatible with the worker's need for consistency and routine.

Work Environment

Printing companies often provide spacious work areas where an employee normally works at a large table that is situated at a comfortable distance from co-workers. Similarly, bulk mailing companies often provide ample space for the employee to work. In both settings, the employee is often working with large stacks of paper products that demand a large work area. Having a spacious work area is advantageous for a worker with autism because it reduces the social demands that would occur if the employees worked close together.

Employees in printing and bulk mailing firms often need to operate machinery, such as binding machines, hole punching machines, and shrink wrap machines. These machines are typically operated by one person at a time, which is an advantage for workers with autism who generally work best when their actual task performance is not too heavily intertwined with that of co-workers.

The work environment in printing and bulk mailing companies, similar to manufacturing, is often highly task-oriented. Production requirements can be high, which provides the worker with a steady stream of work. Because the work is primarily with paper products and these are plentiful throughout the workplace, there are strong visual cues that remind the worker with autism to attend to task. Piles of paper, stacks of cards, and the sight of other workers binding, sorting, collating, or wrapping these materials all provide strong stimulus control for task completion.

In addition, the large machines in printing companies that operate on a regular basis tend to produce a high background noise level. This high noise level masks or obscures potential loud talking, shouting, or unconventional vocalizations of workers with autism. Because co-workers often find loud verbalizations more disruptive than self-injury or aggression, the natural noise level of a print shop or bulk mailing firm can be an advantage.

Nature of the Tasks

Printing and bulk mailing tasks are favorable for workers with autism who have sufficient visual-motor coordination and fine and gross motor control. Workers with autism and mental retardation often have splinter skills in fine motor control and visual-motor coordination and are well suited for work in these environments.

The tasks involved in printing and bulk mailing work require very precise stacking or boxing skills. Books are often separated into stacks and pages must be lined up exactly. Greeting cards might need to be stacked, boxed, then wrapped. Greeting cards also must be lined up exactly for the finished product to be acceptable. Many workers with autism enjoy this process, stopping to straighten a stack of papers or other material that appears disorderly. Workers with autism appreciate order, and in printing and bulk mailing firms they are being paid, in part, to keep order among stacks, piles, and boxes of papers.

Printing and bulk mailing settings also have the advantage of providing a great deal of sameness, which can be comfortable for workers with autism. For example, Martha works in a printing company binding books. Each day, she works with the same book-making materials: covers, interior pages, bindings, and machinery. She does not have to make daily adjustments in terms of the kinds of materials she works with or the kinds of tasks she does. Evan, a man with severe autism, has an even higher degree of uniformity in his work environment where he produces business cards. Whereas Martha might be working with books of different sizes, shapes, and colors, Evan works exclusively with business cards.

Another advantage of printing and bulk mailing jobs is that the sequence of tasks is often the same, with little or no need for flexibility. If a worker is performing the sequencing for covering a book, the steps will not vary from job to job. This sameness in the order and sequence of tasks is an advantage for the worker with autism who might have difficulty with flexibility.

Printing and bulk mailing tasks often have a well-defined beginning and end, and a well-defined completed product. Workers with autism appear to enjoy work with concrete outcomes.

Volume of Work   Printing and bulk mailing jobs typically have a steady supply of work. Unless the employer is experiencing financial problems, the work flow is steady throughout the day and the worker is not usually subjected to down time.

Long-Term Stability   Printing companies have been outstanding in offering long-term employment stability to workers with autism. If the worker is proficient at the task, there is a great likelihood of long-term employment. One man with autism and moderate mental retardation has been employed at a printing company for 13 years to date. Another man with autism who had a history of bolting from his job in a stockroom to run through the sales floor, for which he was fired, obtained a job in a printing company that specializes in making labels. This environment, which has few intrusions and distractions and has highly routine work, has provided this man with long-term, stable employment. Printing companies are often moderate- or small-size family businesses with owners who are devoted to their employees, including those with autism.

Social Requirements

Printing and bulk mailing environments have the advantage of stimulating cooperation between the worker with autism and other company employees. Often, the work is done in a modified assembly line fashion. For example, when producing business cards, one worker cuts them and then hands them to another worker who boxes them. A third worker prepares them for mailing. This arrangement gives a worker with autism the opportunity to depend on and be depended on by other workers.

Although these environments stimulate dependence and cooperation, they do not require a great deal of social interaction. Many workers with autism can perform the task extremely well and prove themselves to be reliant co-workers without much or any social interaction. These environments have the advantage of not requiring social interaction for cooperation to take place. Peter is a man with severe autism who is nonverbal. He wraps and boxes cards in a greeting card company where other workers must depend on his work in order to do their own. Peter can do the job well and in a manner that his co-workers can rely on.

Printing and bulk mailing firms have the advantage of allowing the worker with autism to work with the same co-workers each day, without the intrusion of unfamiliar people, customers, or other outsiders. Although there may occasionally be visitors or customers coming through the work area, these visits are not frequent and it is not an integral part of the employee's job to greet them, provide them with assistance, or engage in other discourse with them.

Furthermore, printing companies do not have the same high turnover rate that retail and warehouse businesses often experience. This stability provides workers with autism the time to develop a rapport with their co-workers. Likewise, other print shop employees have the opportunity to develop a relationship with the workers with autism over a long period of time. This relationship allows co-workers to better understand the disability and to develop a high tolerance for disruptive behaviors when they occur.

DISADVANTAGES OF PRINTING AND BULK MAILING JOBS

Many workers with autism have enjoyed long-term stability in printing and bulk mailing jobs; however, there are some requirements and features of these jobs that can function as disadvantages for some workers with autism.

Nature of the Tasks

Although for some workers with autism the high degree of precision required in printing jobs is an advantage (e.g., precise stacking, cutting, and positioning), for others it is a disadvantage. It might be possible to improve precision with instructional or motivational techniques; however, if the worker has difficulty meeting high demands for accuracy and precision and lacks interest in doing so, printing work may not be appropriate.

Work Materials Printing and bulk mailing jobs require that particular care be taken to preserve the quality of the printed material. Folded, bent, soiled, or torn products are unacceptable. Some workers with autism have behavioral habits that are damaging to these products. For example, individuals who have pica may enjoy eating paper. Others may engage in paper tearing, ripping the corners from paper, or stuffing paper in their pockets. These behaviors may be for self-stimulation or as part of long-standing rituals.

Production Requirements Printing and bulk mailing jobs often have high production requirements. If the work of the employees is interdependent, then it is especially critical that production requirements be met because if one worker falls behind in production, it could hamper the output of the shop. Prior to accepting printing and bulk mailing jobs, it is necessary to make a careful assessment of what the production requirements are and to match those requirements with the capabilities of the worker.

Social Requirements

Although printing company workers are fairly well insulated from outsiders, occasionally customers or important visitors may walk through the work area. Disruptive social behaviors on the part of the worker with autism can threaten the well-being of the company. Ernest, for example, is a man with autism and low-average intelligence. He was a good worker, except when female visitors entered his work area. When this occurred, Ernest would put down his work, dash over to the female visitor, and attempt to hug her. Often, these women were important customers. If Ernest's job coach attempted to intervene, Ernest would scream and become violent. Fortunately, a social skills program that taught Ernest to remain in his work area when female visitors came through and a reinforcement plan to reward such behavior were successful in teaching him a more acceptable response to female visitors.

Cognitive Requirements

Individuals with autism and profound or severe mental retardation might have difficulty meeting the cognitive demands of printing company tasks. Some jobs require that the individual have near-average intelligence, although there are workers with autism and mental retardation who have succeeded in printing companies. Bulk mailing jobs typically do not have the same cognitive requirements as printing jobs, especially if the worker has strengths in fine motor skills or visual-motor coordination. Workers with mental retardation and autism who are sufficiently supported can often succeed in bulk mailing jobs. Printing company jobs may require higher cognitive skills, even if the worker is being supported.

PRINTING AND BULK MAILING JOBS

Descriptions of both printing jobs and bulk mailing jobs that are held by workers with autism are provided on the following pages.

Assembly Assistant

Job Description: An assembly assistant assembles and distributes products for conventions and conferences.

Worksite Description: This job is with a small, family-owned business that manufactures products for conventions and conferences. The work takes place in a small warehouse with approximately 10 employees, 3 of whom have autism.

Employees with Autism

Worker 1:   Speaks in full sentences, moderate mental retardation, aggression, property destruction, problems with social communication (including repetitive questions and standing too close while speaking)

Worker 2:   Communicates using key words, moderate mental retardation, aggression, darts from staff, takes others' work and belongings

Worker 3:   Speaks clearly in sentences, moderate mental retardation, self-injury, yelling, echolalia, perseverative speech

Job Tasks

- Cut sheets of mailing labels
- Apply address stickers to envelopes
- Pull pins from defective plastic badges
- Stack and count perforated pages
- Count clips, chains, and prize ribbons
- Heat-seal perforated pages in plastic
- Assemble cardboard boxes
- File edges of plexiglass name plates
- Empty trash cans
- Sweep work area
- Vacuum work area

Equipment, Machinery, and Hand Tools Needed to Complete Job Tasks

- Paper cutter
- Heat-sealing machine
- Plastic wrap
- Dull-edged scraping instrument for filing plexiglass
- Plastic badges and pins
- Boxes
- Mailing labels
- Envelopes
- Double-sided tape

- Perforated pages
- Vacuum
- Broom

Potential Problems in Job Completion

- Employer stops workers mid-task to perform other jobs, causing disruption and lowered productivity.
- Dangerous equipment is a safety hazard to workers.
- Workers are expected to become proficient at performing a large number of tasks.
- Counting tasks are difficult for one worker.

Modifications and Accommodations to Site or Task

- Job coach present to assist with production and behavior management
- To avoid injury, the job coach performs tasks requiring dangerous equipment. Sharp objects are replaced with blunt objects when possible.
- A counting system was developed to help workers with counting tasks.
- Behavior management plans, including positive reinforcement, hourly ratings, social skills training, extinction procedures, and written schedules

Bindery Worker

Job Description: A bindery worker prepares business cards for distribution.

Worksite Description: This job is with a small, family-owned business that manufactures business cards. There are 10 employees in the company and 5 in the immediate work area, including 2 workers with autism.

Employees with Autism

Worker 1: Speaks clearly in complete sentences, mild mental retardation, inappropriate social conversations, speaks too loudly, talks to self, self-injury, aggression, property destruction

Worker 2: Communicates with limited sign language, profound mental retardation, jumping up and down, hand flapping, aggression, screaming, whining

Job Tasks

- Check business cards for defects
- Box business cards
- Empty the garbage
- Vacuum and clean work area

Equipment, Machinery, and
Hand Tools Needed to Complete Job Tasks

- Boxes for business cards
- Vacuum cleaner

Potential Problems in Job Completion

- Self-stimulation interfering with productivity

Modifications and Accommodations to Site or Task

- Job coach to assist with productivity and behavior management
- Behavior management plans, including positive reinforcement, self-rating, written schedule, social skills training, and extinction procedures

Bindery Worker

Job Description: A bindery worker completes various steps in the assembly of books, booklets, pamphlets, and other printed matter.

Worksite Description: The job is with a medium-size, family-owned printing company. There are 16 rooms in the company, 4 of which are used by the employees. There are approximately 40 workers in the company, including 3 with autism. Four to eight other employees work in the bindery and perform similar jobs.

Employees with Autism

Worker 1: Speaks in sentences but speech is unclear, mild mental retardation, problems with social skills, outbursts, clothes tearing, toileting problems, self-induced vomiting, rumination

Worker 2: Speaks in complete sentences, borderline cognitive functioning, limited social and language skills, provides unwanted instruction to coworkers

Worker 3: Speaks clearly in sentences, mild mental retardation, limited social and language skills, leaves work area to accost visitors, temper tantrums, takes items from others

Job Tasks

- Separate and stack books from the printer
- Collate inserts into brochures
- Punch holes in book covers
- Bind booklets
- Wrap books in plastic using a shrink-wrap machine
- Keep inventory of completed work
- Retrieve materials from storage
- Assemble cardboard boxes
- Sweep work area

Equipment, Machinery, and Hand Tools Needed to Complete Job Tasks

- Binding punch
- Tape gun
- Tape dispenser
- Jacks
- Binding machine
- Carts and skids for moving materials
- Razor blades and scissors
- Shrink-wrap machine
- Broom

Potential Problems in Job Completion

- Conversation among co-workers in the immediate vicinity sometimes distracts the workers from their tasks.
- Female visitors cause a problem for a worker who has a history of grabbing females.
- Co-workers criticize and make fun of workers with autism.

Modifications and Accommodations to Site or Task

- Job coach to assist with productivity and behavior management
- Job coach positioning and behavior program to prevent grabbing females (Worker 3)
- Behavior management plans, including training on asking for assistance, social skills training, and positive reinforcement (Worker 3)

Office Clerk

Job Description: An office clerk prepares reports for mailing.

Worksite Description: This job is with a medium-size company that provides clerical and bulk mailing services. There are approximately 200 workers in the company, approximately 30 employees work in the immediate vicinity, and the company employs 3 workers with autism.

Employees with Autism

Worker 1:   Speaks in complete sentences but speech is unclear, low-average cognitive functioning, problems with social and language skills, off-task behaviors

Worker 2:   Speaks clearly in sentences, mild mental retardation, throws objects, aggression, self-injury, inappropriate sexual comments, clothes tearing, yelling

Worker 3:   Speaks clearly in sentences, average intellectual functioning, problems with social and language skills, and aggression upon provocation

Job Tasks

- Collate reports
- Label envelopes
- Sort mail
- Stuff envelopes

Equipment, Machinery, and Hand Tools Needed to Complete Job Tasks

- Stapler
- Labels
- Envelopes

Potential Problems in Job Completion

- Work involves standing for long periods of time.
- Sufficient training is not provided by supervisors.

Modifications and Accommodations to Site or Task

- The job coach helps with tasks to increase production rate.
- Behavior management plans, including self-rating, social skills training, and guidelines for management of dangerous behavior

Bulk Mailing Clerk

Job Description: A bulk mailing clerk completes bulk mailing tasks.

Worksite Description: The work takes place at a small company that handles bulk mailing contracts. The company employs three other workers who perform the same jobs as the three workers with autism.

Employees with Autism

Worker 1:   Speaks in sentences but speech is unclear, profound mental retardation, prompt dependency, self-injury, tantrums, problems with communication (including loud echolalia and perseverative verbalizations)

Worker 2:   Speaks in full sentences, borderline cognitive functioning, poor personal grooming, limited social and language skills

Worker 3:   Speaks clearly in full sentences, mild mental retardation, swearing, aggression, stealing, urinating in inappropriate places, undressing in public, inappropriate sexual behaviors

Job Tasks

- Sort envelopes by zip code
- Collate mailing materials
- Stuff envelopes
- Stamp envelopes using a stamping machine

Equipment, Machinery, and Hand Tools Needed to Complete Job Tasks

- Stamping machine
- Envelopes

Potential Problems in Job Completion

- Employer arrives late to work or does not show up at all.
- Lack of supervision and organization at worksite causes confusion.
- Job requires standing for long periods of time.

Modifications and Accommodations to Site or Task

- Workers were given chairs.

Bulk Mailing Clerk

Job Description: A bulk mailing clerk assembles printed materials and prepares them for mailing.

Worksite Description: The job is with a medium-size company that handles government contract work. The work takes place in an office environment. There are approximately 20–25 workers in the company; 5 or more employees work in the immediate area and perform the same tasks, and there are 3 workers with autism on a regular basis and 5 others who are called in when extra employees are needed.

Employees with Autism

Worker 1: Speaks clearly in sentences, mild mental retardation, self-injury, property destruction, aggression, problems with social use of language (including perseveration)

Worker 2: Speaks in complete sentences but speech is unclear, low-average cognitive functioning, problems with social and language skills, off-task behaviors

Worker 3: Speaks clearly in complete sentences, borderline range of intellectual functioning, presents sporadic self-injury and aggression

Job Tasks

- Collate booklets and pamphlets
- Place booklets in three-ring binders
- Place inserts in folder flaps
- Refold incorrectly folded items
- Label flyers
- Assemble boxes
- Seal envelopes
- Sort mail according to destination

Equipment, Machinery, and Hand Tools Needed to Complete Job Tasks

- Tape gun
- Mailing bins
- Envelope moistener
- Knife for opening boxes
- Three-ring binders
- Labels
- Boxes
- Envelopes
- Flyers

- Inserts
- Booklets and pamphlets

Potential Problems in Job Completion

- Work is sporadic as it is on a contract basis.
- Sharp objects used for opening boxes are a safety hazard to workers.

Modifications and Accommodations to Site or Task

- The job coach assists with productivity and behavior management.
- The job coach opens boxes to prevent injury.
- The job coach receives task instructions from the manager and passes them on to workers to avoid confusion.
- The job coach helps the employees to set up work materials and organize the work area.
- Social skills training
- Behavior management plans, including positive reinforcement, written schedules, redirection guidelines, and extinction procedures

Bindery Worker

Job Description: A bindery worker completes various steps in the process of manufacturing books and other printed material.

Worksite Description: This job is with a printing company that has several locations. The work takes place in a factory where employees are seated at a large table. There are about 20 employees in the work area and the company employs 3 workers with autism.

Employees with Autism

Worker 1:   Speaks clearly in complete sentences, mild mental retardation, inappropriate social conversations, speaks too loudly, talks to self, self-injury, aggression, property destruction

Worker 2:   Speaks in complete sentences, borderline cognitive functioning, limited social and language skills, no significant behavior problems

Worker 3:   Speaks in complete sentences, mild mental retardation, ritualistic behaviors, stealing, eavesdropping, poor money management skills

Job Tasks

- Collate
- Separate booklets
- Fold papers
- Stack papers
- Label book spines
- Band books
- Package materials for shipping
- Strip print negatives from paper backing
- Clean printer and printing area

Equipment, Machinery, and Hand Tools Needed to Complete Job Tasks

- Printer
- Boxes for packing
- Tags
- String
- Labels
- Rubber bands

Potential Problems in Job Completion

- Some tasks require organizing similar looking materials into different categories. These tasks are difficult for Worker 2.
- Work at the company is sporadic—there is not always work for the employees.

Modifications and Accommodations to Site or Task

- Job coach to assist with productivity and behavior management
- Behavior management plans, including self-rating, positive reinforcement, social skills training, written schedules, and extinction procedures

Bulk Mailing Clerk

Job Description: A bulk mailing clerk completes bulk mailing tasks.

Worksite Description: This job is for a small bulk mailing company. The work takes place on long tables in a small room. The company has a total of 18 workers; 10 employees perform the same tasks as the workers with autism. The company employs 2–4 workers with autism at any one time

Employees with Autism

Worker 1: Communicates using sounds and gestures, profound mental retardation, darts from work area, jumps up and down (sometimes on furniture), grabs food from others, pica, noncompliance, self-stimulation

Worker 2: Speaks in complete sentences but speech is unclear, moderate mental retardation, property destruction, aggression, severe self-injury (including hitting self, head banging, ear banging, arm banging, kicking self, and finger picking)

Worker 3: Speaks in sentences but speech is unclear, profound mental retardation, prompt dependency, self-injury, tantrums, unconventional verbalization (including loud echolalia and perseverative verbalizations)

Job Tasks

- Stuff envelopes
- Label envelopes
- Fill boxes with envelopes
- Heat-seal plastic envelopes

Equipment, Machinery, and Hand Tools Needed to Complete Job Tasks

- Envelopes
- Labels
- Boxes
- Heat-sealer

Potential Problems in Job Completion

- Behavior problems interfere with productivity.

Modifications and Accommodations to Site or Task

- Job coach to assist with productivity and behavior management
- Behavior management plans, including positive reinforcement, prompt hierarchy, and extinction procedures

Greeting Card Processor

Job Description: A greeting card processor assembles greeting cards and promotional displays for greeting cards.

Worksite Description: This job is with a company that manufactures and sells greeting cards. The work takes place in a small warehouse. There are five employees, including three with autism, who work in the immediate vicinity of one another.

Employees with Autism

Worker 1: Speaks clearly in complete sentences, low-average intelligence, aggression, limited social and language skills

Worker 2: Speaks in complete sentences but speech is unclear, low-average cognitive functioning, screaming, jumping, hand flapping, spinning, rapid verbalizations, motor rituals (most notably spinning while walking)

Worker 3: Speaks clearly in complete sentences, mild mental retardation, inappropriate social conversations, speaks too loudly, talks to self, self-injury, aggression, property destruction

Job Tasks

- Glue plastic crystals onto greeting cards
- Collate cards, envelopes, and inserts
- Heat-wrap greeting cards
- Box heat-wrapped greeting cards
- Assemble cardboard promotional displays

Equipment, Machinery, and Hand Tools Needed to Complete Job Tasks

- Heat-wrapping machine
- Cards, envelopes, and inserts
- Glue
- Display box

Potential Problems in Job Completion

- Low productivity

Modifications and Accommodations to Site or Task

- Job coach to assist with productivity and behavior management
- Behavior management plans, including positive reinforcement, self-management, social skills training

Bulk Mailing Clerk

Job Description: A bulk mailing clerk completes bulk mailing tasks.

Worksite Description: This job is with a medium-size bulk mailing company. The work takes place in a large mailing room. There are about 40 employees in the company; 20–30 employees work in the immediate area, and there are 2 workers with autism.

Employees with Autism

Worker 1:   Speaks in full sentences, borderline cognitive functioning, poor personal grooming, limited social and language skills

Worker 2:   Speaks clearly in full sentences, average intelligence, self-injury, limited social and language skills, repetitive inappropriate conversations, invades other people's personal space and privacy (including reading personal written material)

Job Tasks

- Fold letters
- Tear perforated edges from items to be mailed
- Staple
- Stuff envelopes
- Address envelopes
- Seal envelopes
- Sort mail
- Shingle envelopes

Equipment, Machinery, and Hand Tools Needed to Complete Job Tasks

- Rubber stamps
- Stapler
- Envelopes
- Labels

Potential Problems in Job Completion

- Workers are periodically laid off due to economic downturns.

Modifications and Accommodations to Site or Task

- Periodic assistance from a job coach
- Social skills training
- Behavior management plan, including self-rating

Bindery Worker

Job Description: A bindery worker has a variety of tasks related to the manufacturing of books and other printed material.

Worksite Description: This job takes place at a large printing company that handles government contracts. The company has 10 rooms and the majority of work takes place in a large printing room. The company has approximately 75 employees, including 3 workers with autism.

Employees with Autism

Worker 1:   Speaks clearly in full sentences, average intelligence, self-injury, limited social and language skills, repetitive inappropriate conversations, invades other people's personal space and privacy (including reading personal written material)

Worker 2:   Speaks clearly in sentences, low-average intelligence, pacing, talks loudly to self, limited social and language skills

Worker 3:   Speaks clearly in sentences, moderate mental retardation, self-injury, yelling, echolalia, perseverative speech

Job Tasks

- Catch books as they come off the drill press and binder
- Collate
- Separate books
- Feed book covers into the binder
- Make booklets on the saddle machine
- Stitch books on the foot stitcher
- Load pockets on the Macey machine
- Feed shrink-wrap machine
- Assemble cardboard boxes
- Apply stickers to boxes
- Separate printing negatives from paper backing

Equipment, Machinery, and Hand Tools Needed to Complete Job Tasks

- Saddle machine
- Binder
- Shrink-wrap machine
- Dollies
- Racks
- Skids
- Tape machine
- Drill press
- Collator

- Hand stapler
- Foot stitcher
- Macey machine

Potential Problems in Job Completion

- Dangerous equipment poses a hazard to workers.

Modifications and Accommodations to Site or Task

- Temporary increase in job coach supervision to avoid injury from dangerous equipment
- Behavior management plans, including social skills training and self-management
- Procedures to increase independence and fade out job coach

CASE STUDY—RANDY

Employee Description

Randy is a 37-year-old man with autism and mild mental retardation as measured by a standard intelligence test. Randy speaks in complete sentences but converses on only a few perseverative topics and has great difficulty using language to communicate functionally. His speech also has a monotone, robot-like quality often seen in people with autism. He has difficulty engaging in a social interaction for more than several minutes. Prior to intervention, he would frequently walk off in the middle of a conversation while the other person was still speaking. However, Randy has excellent visual-motor skills, including good visual-motor coordination and good fine motor coordination.

Employee History

Compared to many people with autism, Randy's history of education and habilitation was relatively stable. From the ages of 6 to 14 years, he attended a segregated residential school designed specifically for children with autism. He then transferred to a local public school that provided special education services in a segregated environment. At the age of 21, Randy began attending a vocational center for people with mental retardation that provided training in adaptive skills and prevocational and vocational activities. After 4 years in this program, Randy was still unemployed. Because of the lack of progress, Randy was transferred to a supported employment program.

Description of Company and Job

Randy began working at a printing company as a bindery worker soon after he was transferred to the supported employment program. The printing company is a medium-size, family-owned business. Initially, the company employed about 20 workers; it has since expanded to a staff of approximately 40 workers. The work area consists of a large warehouse that is divided into several smaller areas according to the type of job and the equipment being used. Randy performs a variety of jobs that are related to binding books. These include separating books to prepare them for binding, collating books and covers, binding the books, shrink-wrapping groups of books, and boxing books. In addition, Randy sometimes puts inserts into brochures, makes cardboard boxes, breaks down cardboard boxes, takes out the trash, and sweeps the work area. These jobs all require visual-motor skills, but they require little reliance on social or language skills.

Setting Up the Job

Because of the variety and the complexity of tasks involved in the job, a priority in setting it up was to perform task analyses. This was done by job coaches and agency supervisors prior to Randy starting work. In addition, employee standard productivity rates were measured by having agency staff perform the various job tasks while recording their productivity.

Establishing Employment Supports

Randy's interdisciplinary team met to determine the kinds of supports that he would need to succeed at work.

Determination of Supports   The nature of support needed was determined by examining several different factors. Although Randy was generally calm and cooperative, he did have occasional outbursts that were characterized by extreme agitation, yelling, clothes tearing, and occasionally slapping his face. In addition, Randy had periods of time during which he was anxious and distractable. During these times, he would frequently wander away from what he was doing or ask repetitive questions about what was bothering him rather than do his work. Randy was sometimes sexually inappropriate in public and would soil or urinate in his clothes or on the floor.

Randy also had serious language and social difficulties, and was clearly unable to handle the language and socialization demands of the printing company. He had a long history of education and vocational training in segregated environments where he did not learn functional language or socialization skills. At the age of 25 years, his job at the printing company was his first integrated experience.

Finally, Randy had never traveled independently in the community and needed extensive travel training. For all of these reasons, Randy's interdisciplinary team decided that he needed the full-time supervision of a job coach.

Description of Job Coach Duties   Initially, the job coach was responsible for supervising all aspects of Randy's vocational life. Job coach duties included transporting him to work, teaching him how to do binding and other work tasks, assisting him in remaining on task to meet productivity goals, supporting and assisting him in communicating with co-workers and supervisors, and helping him to manage his behavior problems. As time passed and Randy became proficient at his work, job coach duties evolved into assisting him in negotiating the language and social demands of the environment and assisting him in controlling his behaviors.

Description of Behavior Plan   Randy's behavior management plan was developed to address his various behavior problems and the functions of these behaviors. Because Randy's behavior changed over time, procedural components of his program were added and deleted as necessary. Initial behaviors of concern were his difficulty remaining on task and his tendency to become agitated. He also had incidents of urinating on the floor at work and exposing himself in public.

Randy was placed on a behavior management plan that emphasized instruction regarding appropriate places to urinate and appropriate places to expose his genitals. He was given daily discrimination training during which his job coach presented different locations and Randy and he would discuss which locations were acceptable for these activities and which were not.

Randy's productivity was low during his first 18 months on the job, and he attained productivity rates of only 60% of that of his co-workers without disabilities. He was placed on a differential reinforcement for high rates of behavior (DRH) schedule of positive reinforcement. He and his job coach measured his production rate several times daily and graphed the rate. He was praised for increases in productivity in his five main job tasks: separating books, binding books, covering books, wrapping books, and punching covers. Additionally, his job coach praised him when he worked quickly. His productivity gradually increased to acceptable rates.

Despite Randy's increase in production, he continued to have episodes of ceasing his work and wandering away from his work area or simply gazing into space for extended periods of time. To remedy this problem, the job coach began posting cards in his view that said "Work" or "Break." He was taught that when the "Work" card was posted, he was to work on his tasks, but when the "Break" card was posted, he could stop his work and leave his work area.

Because of his pervasive problems with social skills and language, Randy has received extensive social skills training for many years. Initially, he rarely said anything to anyone. Social skills were practiced in role play with his job coach and then with his co-workers and supervisors. Specific social skills include greeting others in the morning, engaging others in conversation, asking questions of others, waiting for answers to his questions, terminating conversations, and saying "Good-bye" to others in the evening. He has made significant gains in communication and social skills and recently his supervisor commented on how much more he speaks to others.

Travel Training   One of Randy's goals was to travel to and from work independently. This was accomplished by accompanying him on the bus many times to assist him in mastering all the steps of a bus ride. It was especially difficult to motivate him to look out the window to see when it was time to transfer to a different bus, but gradually he learned how to do it. For many weeks, the job coach followed the bus in her car. Randy then began to take the bus independently and did well for several months. Gradually, he began to come to work late and retraining was started. Randy's job coach followed him in the morning and discovered that if he arrived at the bus stop and the bus did not immediately come, Randy would walk to work. If the regular bus driver was on the route, he would see Randy several blocks away and would stop and pick him up. However, if there was a substitute bus driver, he would not know to pick Randy up. On those mornings, he arrived to work up to an hour late. After retraining, Randy was able to stand at the bus stop and wait until the bus arrived.

Outcomes

Randy made substantial gains in his work productivity and behavior at work. He has now been employed by the same company for 13 years and receives an hourly wage of $11.00 per hour. He works a minimum of 33 hour per week. In addition, he has met acceptable rates of productivity. Although he does not receive health insurance, he does receive other benefits such as vacation and sick leave. His social skills have improved so that now he greets co-workers and supervisors, and converses with them about work and nonwork topics. Because of sporadic behavior problems and concerns of his employer, Randy continues to have a full-time job coach at the company who also supports one other employee with autism.

Jobs in Food Service

ood service is a traditional area of employment for people with mental
retardation. Interestingly, most workers with autism have not been employed in food service establishments. Many of the skills needed for traditional food service jobs are not usually strengths for workers with autism.
However, they have had some success in this field by preparing food, cleaning
restaurants, doing kitchen clean-up tasks, setting tables, preparing silverware
and napkins for placement on tables, washing dishes, and distributing advertisement flyers for pizza delivery services.

ADVANTAGES OF FOOD SERVICE JOBS

There have been workers with autism who have done well in food service jobs
following years of troublesome employment histories. Food service is a field
that offers a wide variety of job duties, and good matches can be found for
workers with autism. Food service jobs offer several advantages for people with
autism.

Work Environment

People with autism typically do well when working in environments that allow
for solitary job performance, and there are food service jobs that provide this
kind of environment for the worker. Peter and Mark, two workers with autism,
were hired by a busy restaurant to wash dishes and roll silverware. Both workers had occasional problems with self-injury and screaming, so they required a
work area that provided some privacy. Their work area in the busy restaurant is
a relatively private section of the kitchen where there is a sink and a table for
rolling silverware. Linda, a middle-age woman with autism who occasionally
had episodes of pouting and work refusal, also did best when working in a more
secluded area. Her job rolling baking potatoes in aluminum foil allowed her to
work at her own table in the kitchen.

Some jobs in food service are done prior to the restaurant opening or prior
to the customer lunch rush. In those jobs, the worker may have the empty restaurant as a workplace. Such an environment has the advantage of being large,

quiet, and lacking in distractions or disruptions. For example, one man with autism and severe mental retardation had a history of high frequency head banging. He was also very sensitive to disruptions in his environment. He held a job doing cleaning tasks at a restaurant specializing in children's birthday parties. He worked part time—he finished work every day by 11:00 A.M., prior to the restaurant opening. A job in a restaurant filled with children would have been impossible for him, but a large, quiet restaurant was ideal. If he did have occasional bouts of self-injury, there were no customers to witness the incidents.

Some food service jobs involve distribution of advertisement flyers to residences in the community. Because the work is done outdoors, it is an ideal job for workers with autism who prefer being outside. In addition, for workers who have difficulty remaining in one location, the job is ideal because it involves constant movement from one location to the next. Furthermore, if behavior problems do occur, or if productivity slows for some reason, there is no disruption to co-workers as these are relatively solitary jobs.

Nature of the Tasks

Many food service jobs involve tasks that are repetitive and fairly simple to accomplish. Workers with autism who are resistant to change appreciate such jobs. Sorting silverware; folding napkins; wrapping silverware in napkins; refilling salt and pepper shakers, condiment containers, sugar containers, and napkin holders; cleaning menus; and delivering flyers are all examples. Workers with autism have also been hired for food preparation tasks that follow set routines, such as rolling baking potatoes or cutting vegetables. Some of these jobs may involve relatively complex preparation tasks, such as making pizzas. These jobs do not require social expertise or creativity, only the ability to follow a set sequence of tasks. Often, written cues are provided and the worker only needs to read and follow the instructions.

In addition, jobs in food service are often attractive to workers with autism because they enjoy the food products that are sold by their employers. For example, the man who worked in the children's party restaurant described earlier was often allowed to eat birthday cake or was given brownies or coke by the store manager to snack on while working. Workers who deliver flyers for pizza delivery services are given free pizza from time to time. Two workers with autism who work part time in the kitchen of a seafood restaurant are often allowed snacks such as shrimp or baked potatoes. These snacks and meals can be more reinforcing than paychecks for many workers with autism.

Social Requirements

Many workers with autism have difficulty in jobs that involve social interaction or verbal communication. They also have difficulty in jobs that require interaction with unfamiliar people, such as customers, or jobs that must be done in pairs or groups. There are food service jobs that do not involve these sorts of interactions. For example, flyer distribution, cleaning tasks, dish washing, food preparation, container refilling, or table setting can all be done without a great deal of interaction with co-workers and without customer interaction.

Cognitive Requirements

Some individuals with autism and profound mental retardation have difficulty learning and performing any but the most simple of tasks. There are jobs in food service that these workers can perform, such as flyer distribution. This task can be accomplished by workers with severe autism, profound mental retardation, and no verbal skills. Job coaches are primarily needed to serve as a guide on the worker's route and to ensure the safety of the worker.

There are other simple jobs in food service, such as making boxes for pizzas, rolling silverware, sorting silverware, and filling salt and pepper shakers that can be accomplished by workers with severe mental retardation. Many of these tasks require only one, two, or three steps, and can be done independently or with minimal assistance.

Many workers with autism may have average or above-average intelligence. For these workers, there are food service jobs that can be challenging but realistic. These include jobs with multistep tasks, such as pizza preparation. Jobs such as these enable workers to use a variety of skills, such as reading and measuring, as well as to perform a range of cooking tasks, such as stirring, kneading, chopping, and baking. Food service jobs also can provide variety for workers, even though they involve set, routine ways of performing individual tasks. These jobs are suitable for workers with autism who enjoy variety, but depend on the repetitiveness of individual tasks.

DISADVANTAGES OF FOOD SERVICE JOBS

Although there are some food service jobs that provide good matches for workers with autism, most jobs in food service have insurmountable disadvantages for most workers with autism. These disadvantages include aspects of the job environment, hygiene issues, social requirements, production requirements, deadlines, flexibility, and hours.

Work Environment

Although there are some food service jobs that can be performed in an isolated area, many must be performed in small work areas, such as crowded kitchens and between the aisles of busy restaurants. Many workers with autism prefer to work in larger work areas and do not like being confined to small work spaces or crowded areas. If the worker enjoys pacing and does not like being confined to a small space, many food service jobs would be unsuitable.

Food service jobs often require the worker to work within close proximity to co-workers. Some jobs require the workers to work elbow-to-elbow. Many individuals with autism prefer not to work in close quarters with others and would find this work environment aversive. Bumping into co-workers or grazing co-workers or customers can be upsetting and may even serve as an antecedent to a behavioral outburst. Furthermore, some workers with autism have problem behaviors, such as self-injury. These behaviors can cause a major disruption to the work environment if they occur in close proximity to co-workers or customers. For example, a worker with autism who throws an object in a warehouse is not likely to hit another worker; however, a kitchen worker who hurls a pot across the kitchen places co-workers at risk. Given the small and close quarters of many food service jobs, behavioral outbursts that are tolerated in other environments are job threatening in food service environments.

Food service jobs also may require the worker to work among customers. Even if the worker is simply busing or setting tables, or replacing condiment containers, these tasks might be done in the dining room of a busy restaurant frequented by customers of all ages and using varying levels of voice volume. Many workers with autism become upset by a large number of people, especially when they are talking, laughing, or crying (e.g., small children). Additionally, behavior problems, such as self-injury, aggression, shouting, or other unusual behaviors, are not tolerated in the dining room of a restaurant.

Food service environments also have the disadvantage of having dangerous, sharp, or hot equipment in close proximity to workers. For workers with autism who do not follow directions well, or who have occasional behavioral outbursts, these hot or sharp items can be problematic. If a behavioral outburst occurs, the worker, co-workers, equipment, and possibly customers are all at risk.

Nature of the Tasks

Although some food service tasks are ideal for workers with autism, many tasks in food service are difficult for them to perform. Taking orders, explaining the menu, operating a cash register, and food preparation may be difficult for workers with cognitive or communication limitations that are associated with autism. Behavior problems that can be associated with autism, such as self-stimulation, stereotypy, or verbal or motor rituals, make it difficult to complete many food service tasks satisfactorily. A worker who interrupts his sorting task in a stockroom to finger flick can still perform the sorting task acceptably and be considered a good worker. Yet, a worker who interrupts his delivery of food to a customer's table or the busing of that table with finger flicking would be considered an unsuitable employee.

Many food service jobs such as planning menus, preparing meals, and meeting customer requests require good judgment and creativity. Although workers with autism may have average or above-average intelligence and perform certain rote motor tasks at speeds greater than the acceptable employer's standard productivity rate, they may have great difficulty solving new problems or performing tasks that require creativity and judgment.

Production Requirements   Food service jobs can have high production requirements that are beyond the capacity of many workers with autism. Even if an employee works fairly quickly, the exacting nature of the restaurant schedule can be problematic. Production requirements in food preparation jobs are important in at least two aspects of the work. First, when the customer orders a meal, there is some expectation of timely service of that meal. Yet, a worker with autism may have problems meeting the time requirements and be too slow in preparing the food. Second, productivity also depends on attention to the task. If food is left cooking too long or if a worker is too slow to perform the next step in the cooking process, the food can be ruined.

Some food service jobs take place prior to the restaurant opening or between meals when the restaurant is closed. Even jobs during these times have production requirements because the tasks must be done prior to the restaurant opening again. For example, a worker who performs janitorial tasks in a restaurant must complete his or her routine by the time the restaurant opens. If there are productivity or behavior problems, the restaurant may not be in order when customers arrive. In another example, two workers with autism were employed by a restaurant to prepare silverware and to peel vegetables and shrimp prior to opening for lunch. These tasks need to be completed by a certain time or the management is not prepared to serve its lunch customers.

Flexibility   Many food service jobs require flexibility on the part of the worker. A food service worker may be told to peel potatoes and then be told to switch to cleaning shrimp, depending on the customers' orders. Or, a food service worker may routinely prepare pizza in one way, then abruptly be told to change the manner of preparation to suit a particular customer. Because autism is often characterized by resistance to change, abrupt changes in routine can be difficult for these workers. In the kitchen of a restaurant, changes need to be made quickly, which creates a significant challenge for individuals who lack flexibility.

Direct customer service jobs, such as a waiter or waitress, demand a degree of flexibility that is beyond the capacity of many workers with autism. Direct service workers need to be accommodating to many different personality types and be able to deal with many different kinds of changes, shifts, and transitions, such as a constant turnover in customers, customers who change their orders, or customers who have a complaint about some aspect of the meal.

Hygiene Issues   Many workers with autism have excellent hygiene and grooming habits. However, for workers who have problems in these areas, food service jobs are unsuitable. For example, rectal digging is a problem that occasionally occurs among individuals with autism, as are masturbation, spitting, and smearing saliva. Although these behavior problems can be well controlled through behavior management, if there is any risk that they may occur, employment in food service cannot be considered.

Conditions of Employment   Food service jobs often have conditions of employment that are not advantageous to workers with autism. They often require very early morning hours, late afternoon or evening hours, and weekend hours. These hours can be problematic if they do not coincide with those of the supported employment program. In addition, many food service jobs that have proven to be suitable for workers with autism are only part time because they are performed prior to the restaurant opening or between meals.

Furthermore, food service jobs are often low paying, have no benefits, and provide little opportunity for advancement. If workers have communication or cognitive limitations, it is unlikely they could perform the tasks of higher level positions, such as manager, host or hostess, chief cook, or kitchen supervisor.

Social Requirements

Many food service jobs have social requirements that are beyond the ability of some workers with autism. Jobs such as waiters, waitresses, or dining room hosts or hostesses require social and communication skills that many workers with autism do not have. Even jobs such as busing tables can entail interactions with customers that would be difficult for a worker with autism.

Although most kitchen jobs do not require interactions with customers, there are social demands in terms of relationships with co-workers that can be difficult for many workers with autism. Because employees in the kitchen often work in close proximity to each other, and because their jobs can be interdependent, there are often social or communication requirements that are difficult for a worker with autism to meet.

JOBS IN FOOD SERVICE

The food service field offers a variety of jobs, some of which are well suited to workers with autism. Some workers with autism with previously sporadic employment histories have had stable employment in the food service field. Descriptions of jobs that are held by food service workers are provided on the following pages.

Janitorial Worker

Job Description: A janitorial worker does janitorial work in a restaurant.

Worksite Description: This job is with a medium-size restaurant that is part of a national chain. There are approximately 30 employees at each restaurant. The company employs three workers with autism. Nine employees work on the same shift.

Employees with Autism

Worker 1:   Communicates with sounds and gestures, profound mental retardation, self-injury, aggression, property destruction

Worker 2:   Communicates using sounds and gestures, profound mental retardation, screaming, self-stimulation, aggression, property destruction, noncompliance, lack of independence performing tasks

Worker 3:   Communicates using key words, profound mental retardation, noncompliance, refusal to move, severe self-injury (including head banging)

Job Tasks

- Retrieve materials for cleaning bathroom from storage closet
- Wipe down bathroom mirror, sink, and toilet surfaces
- Clean toilet with toilet brush
- Mop bathroom floor
- Dispose of soiled water and return cleaning supplies to closet
- Clean windows
- Polish brass
- Take chairs down from tables

Equipment, Machinery, and Hand Tools Needed to Complete Job Tasks

- Cleansers
- Cleaning rags
- Mops
- Bucket
- Brush

Potential Problems in Job Completion

- Some tasks require multiple steps and judgment about when the task has been completed correctly.

Modifications and Accommodations to Site or Task

- Job coach to assist with training, productivity, and behavior management
- Job coach provides additional instruction and monitoring for difficult tasks.
- Behavior management plans, including positive reinforcement, alternate sensory stimuli, noncontingent reinforcers, graduated guidance, prompt hierarchy, extinction, and procedures for managing dangerous behavior

Food Service Worker

Job Description: A food service worker prepares food and assists in cleaning the restaurant.

Worksite Description: This job is with a medium-size seafood restaurant that is part of a chain. There are 22 employees. The company employs two workers with autism. Five employees work on the same shift as the workers with autism.

Employees with Autism

Worker 1: Speaks in full sentences, mild mental retardation, task refusal, property destruction, sulking, aggression

Worker 2: Speaks clearly in sentences, moderate mental retardation, noncompliance, self-injury, self-stimulation, aggression

Job Tasks

- Roll silverware in napkins
- Shell shrimp
- Roll potatoes in foil
- Polish brass rails
- Clean laminated menus
- Wash dishes

Equipment, Machinery, and Hand Tools Needed to Complete Job Tasks

- Trays
- Stacking carts
- Sink
- Sponges
- Cleansers
- Polishing agents and cloths
- Napkins
- Silverware
- Aluminum foil

Potential Problems in Job Completion

- Low productivity

Modifications and Accommodations to Site or Task

- Job coach to assist with training, productivity, and behavior management
- Job coach works beside employees to increase productivity.
- Behavior management plans, including periodic rating, positive reinforcement, prompt hierarchy, written schedule, extinction, and procedures for managing dangerous behavior

Flyer Distributor

Job Description: A flyer distributor delivers coupon flyers door to door in residential neighborhoods.

Worksite Description: This job is with a national pizza delivery chain. Employees with autism work alone in the community with their job coaches; there are one to three employees with autism for every job coach.

Employees with Autism

Worker 1: Speaks in sentences but speech is unclear, moderate mental retardation, crying, self-induced vomiting, toilet stuffing, urinating and defecating in clothing

Worker 2: Communicates using sounds and gestures, profound mental retardation, darting, jumping up and down (sometimes on furniture), grabbing food from others, pica, noncompliance, self-stimulation

Worker 3: Communicates using sounds and gestures, profound mental retardation, screaming, self-stimulation, aggression, property destruction, noncompliance, lack of independence performing tasks

Worker 4: Communicates with sounds and gestures, profound mental retardation, self-injury, aggression, property destruction

Job Tasks

* Hang advertisement flyers on doorknobs

Equipment, Machinery, and Hand Tools Needed to Complete Job Tasks

* Advertisement flyers

Potential Problems in Job Completion

* Marketing budget varies from month to month; at times there are no flyers to be delivered.
* Low productivity
* Traffic creates a danger to workers.
* The job requires fine motor control.
* Some workers walk slowly.

Modifications and Accommodations to Site or Task

* Job coach to assist with training, productivity, and behavior management
* Workers wear backpacks that the job coach can hold onto to prevent darting into traffic.
* Hand-over-hand assistance is given to workers who lack fine motor skills.
* Behavior management plans, including positive reinforcement, alternate sensory stimuli, prompt hierarchy, extinction, and procedures for managing dangerous behavior

Food Service Worker

Job Description: A food service worker is involved in various food preparation and kitchen clean-up tasks in a restaurant.

Worksite Description: This job takes place in a large seafood restaurant with a sit-down dining area and a bar. There are 40 employees. The company employs two workers with autism who work in the kitchen with about five other employees.

Employees with Autism

Worker 1:   Speaks in full sentences, severe mental retardation, delayed echolalia, difficulty remaining on location during tasks, yelling, stealing, urinating and defecating in clothing

Worker 2:   Speaks in complete sentences but speech is unclear, severe mental retardation, darting from location, grabbing people, loud and perseverative yelling, difficulty following directions, tearing clothing, property destruction, self-injury, aggression (including hitting, kicking, and biting)

Job Tasks

- Chop onions
- Shred onions
- Peel carrots
- Weigh pasta
- Chop celery
- Load dishwasher
- Sweep

Equipment, Machinery, and Hand Tools Needed to Complete Job Tasks

- Chopper
- Scales
- Vegetable peeler
- Broom
- Dishwasher

Potential Problems in Job Completion

- High level of activity in kitchen is distracting.
- Workers must stand for long periods of time.
- Manager assistance is needed to get started; at times, the manager is unavailable.
- Tasks require use of judgment and understanding concepts such as more and less.

Modifications and Accommodations to Site or Task

- Job coach to assist with training, productivity, and behavior management
- Stools were provided to workers.
- Job coach found containers that hold various weights of pasta so that weighing is not necessary.
- Behavior management plans, including periodic ratings, positive reinforcement, prompt hierarchy, extinction, and procedures for managing dangerous behavior

Food Service Worker

Job Description: A food service worker fills salt and pepper shakers to be used on airline food trays.

Worksite Description: This job is with a large food service company that contracts with several airlines. There are more than 100 employees who work in the same area, including one with autism.

Employee with Autism

Worker 1: Speaks in complete sentences but speech is unclear, moderate mental retardation, property destruction, aggression, severe self-injury (including hitting self, head banging, ear banging, arm banging, kicking self, and finger picking)

Job Tasks

- Clean salt and pepper shakers
- Refill salt and pepper shakers

Equipment, Machinery, and Hand Tools Needed to Complete Job Tasks

- Filling tool
- Wiping rags

Potential Problems in Job Completion

- Salt burns sores that worker has on his hands as a result of self-injurious behavior.
- Low productivity

Modifications and Accommodations to Site or Task

- Job coach to assist with training, productivity, and behavior management
- Job coach helps with task to increase productivity.
- Behavior management plans, including positive reinforcement, alternate sensory stimuli, close monitoring to prevent self-injury, picture schedule, and procedures for managing dangerous behavior

Food Service Worker

Job Description: A food service worker prepares food for a restaurant that specializes in pizza.

Worksite Description: This job is with a national pizza restaurant chain with a kitchen and a sit-down dining room. There are about 30 employees at each restaurant; five work the same shift as the four workers with autism.

Employees with Autism

Worker 1: Speaks in full sentences, borderline cognitive functioning, poor personal grooming, limited social and language skills

Worker 2: Speaks clearly in sentences, mild mental retardation, object throwing, aggression, self-injury, inappropriate sexual comments, clothes tearing, yelling

Worker 3: Speaks in complete sentences but speech is unclear, low-average cognitive functioning, problems with language and social skills, off-task behaviors

Worker 4: Speaks clearly in complete sentences, borderline range of intellectual functioning, sporadic self-injury, and aggression

Job Tasks

- Mix pizza dough
- Pull pizza dough with pulling machine
- Weigh and cut pizza dough
- Oil pizza pans
- Roll dough
- Press dough into pizza pans
- Put pizza pans away

Equipment, Machinery, and Hand Tools Needed to Complete Job Tasks

- Dough mixer
- Dough pulling machine
- Dough cutter
- Mixing bowls
- Pizza pans
- Rolling pin
- Scale
- Oil

Potential Problems in Job Completion

- Work takes place in a confined area, which makes it difficult to keep work area organized.

FOOD SERVICE

- Determining correct pan sizes and dough weights is difficult.
- One worker was upset by a mess created by flour.

Modifications and Accommodations to Site or Task

- Job coach to assist with training, productivity, and behavior management
- Behavior management plans, including positive reinforcement, written schedule, self-management, social skills training, and procedures for managing dangerous behavior

Flyer Distributor

Job Description: A flyer distributor goes door to door delivering advertisement flyers for a pizza restaurant and delivery service.

Worksite Description: This job is with a medium-size sit-down pizza restaurant chain. There are approximately 30 employees. Employees with autism work in the community in pairs.

Employees with Autism

Worker 1:   No meaningful communication, profound mental retardation, exhibits extreme prompt dependence in task initiation and completion, grabs others

Worker 2:   Communicates using limited manual signs and pictures, profound mental retardation, shrieking, running away, noncompliance, property destruction, grabbing at others, feces smearing, darting into traffic

Worker 3:   Communicates using key words with a vocabulary under 10 words, profound mental retardation, self-injury, aggression, refusal to comply with directions

Worker 4:   Communicates with sounds and gestures, profound mental retardation, self-injury, aggression, property destruction

Job Tasks

- Hanging flyers on doorknobs

**Equipment, Machinery, and
Hand Tools Needed to Complete Job Tasks**

- Advertisement flyers

Potential Problems in Job Completion

- Barking dogs on flyer route cause one worker to engage in self-injurious behavior.
- Hanging flyers requires fine motor control.
- There are no bathrooms available.
- Traffic causes a potential hazard.
- Some workers walk slowly, resulting in low productivity.

Modifications and Accommodations to Site or Task

- Job coach to assist with training, productivity, and behavior management
- Behavior program was developed to deal appropriately with barking dogs.
- Hand-over-hand assistance is given to workers who lack fine motor control.
- Workers wear backpacks that job coach can hold onto to prevent darting into traffic.
- Behavior management plans, including positive reinforcement, voice volume procedures, prompt hierarchy, extinction, and procedures for managing dangerous behavior

Food Service Worker

Job Description: A food service worker does various food service and janitorial tasks in a restaurant.

Worksite Description: This job is in a medium-size restaurant that is part of a national chain. There are about 25 employees. No co-workers work in the immediate area. The company employs three workers with autism.

Employees with Autism

Worker 1: Speaks in complete sentences but speech is unclear, moderate mental retardation, noncompliance, wandering away from tasks, screaming, loud perseverative echolalia

Worker 2: Communicates using limited sign language, severe mental retardation, self-injury, aggression, self-stimulation, noncompliance, playing in dish water

Worker 3: Communicates with limited sign language, profound mental retardation, jumping up and down, hand flapping, aggression, screaming, whining

Job Tasks

- Buff silverware
- Roll silverware in napkins
- Clean plastic menus
- Polish brass
- Stuff envelopes with letters
- Blow up balloons
- Fill salt and pepper shakers
- Wash pots, pans, and utensils
- Put clean dishes away

Equipment, Machinery, and Hand Tools Needed to Complete Job Tasks

- Cleaners and cloths
- Sink
- Dish soap
- Sterilization fluid
- Scrub brush
- Napkins
- Silverware
- Salt and pepper shakers

Potential Problems in Job Completion

- Washing dishes requires judgment about whether or not the item is clean.

Modifications and Accommodations to Site or Task

- Job coach to assist with training, productivity, and behavior management
- Behavior management plans, including positive reinforcement, alternate sensory stimuli, prompt hierarchy, extinction, and procedures for managing dangerous behavior

CASE STUDY #1—MICHAEL

Employee Description

Michael is a handsome 36-year-old man with autism and moderate mental retardation as measured by a standard intelligence test. Michael speaks in complete sentences, but his range of conversation is limited to a few topics. He frequently uses language to communicate his basic needs and wants, but rarely initiates conversation for social purposes. Although Michael is socially withdrawn and displays poorly developed social skills, at times he is personable and friendly to people he knows well.

Michael has a history of severe behavior problems. He is sometimes aggressive toward other people and has hit, kicked, pushed, and spit at others. His aggression can be severe and pose a serious danger to other people. Michael also scratches his own skin and has caused open sores. When agitated, he will yell loudly. Although usually cooperative, he sometimes refuses to do his assigned job tasks and can become aggressive if repeatedly prompted to do so. He frequently engages in self-stimulatory finger flicking and can become aggressive if this behavior is interrupted.

Employee History

Michael attended a series of public and private schools for people with developmental disabilities until he was 21 years old. He was then placed in a vocational training center that provided instruction in adaptive living skills and prevocational and vocational activities. Michael was expelled from this program because of his aggressive behaviors and transferred to another vocational training center. His behavior problems continued at this center and resulted in frequent suspensions. Although competitive employment was a goal in his individual program plan, he never attained employment. After 5 years in this program, Michael was transferred to a supported employment program for people with autism.

In the supported employment program, Michael has held several different job positions, primarily as a retail stock clerk in various stores. Unfortunately, he lost these jobs due to either economic layoffs or behavior problems. Between these jobs, he worked briefly as a newspaper deliverer and greeting card manufacturer, but left them to assume retail stock clerk positions that offered more hours and better wages. Therefore, although Michael was able to get jobs and keep them for a period of time, his employment history suggests that he has not found a suitable area of employment.

Description of Company and Job

Michael's employment specialist was aware of his employment history and decided to seek a job position in another type of business. Michael has good visual-motor skills and the ability to pay attention to a task for a brief period of time. With this in mind, the employment specialist found Michael a job in food service where he performs a limited number of tasks that require visual-motor skills. The company he works for is a local restaurant chain that employs approximately 25 workers per restaurant. Michael is responsible for wrapping silverware in napkins, wrapping potatoes in aluminum foil, cleaning laminated menus, shelling shrimp, and polishing brass fixtures. These jobs all rely on visual-motor skills and require little in the way of social or language skills.

Setting Up the Job

Setting up Michael's job in food service required that the employer actually develop a job position for Michael. The employment specialist's initial contact with the employer uncovered no job positions that seemed suitable for Michael; however, there were a number of job tasks that seemed suitable that were done by several different workers. The waiters and waitresses rolled napkins, the table busing staff cleaned menus, the kitchen staff rolled potatoes in aluminum foil, and the janitorial staff polished the brass. The employment specialist targeted these job tasks that Michael would be able to do, negotiated with the employer, and created a job position that matched Michael's abilities. Because these jobs could be done in about 10–12 hours a week at one restaurant, the employment specialist developed the same job position in another restaurant of the same chain.

Because of the variety of tasks that were to be done, the job coach started work before Michael and determined his daily and weekly schedule. Michael had some tasks such as potato rolling that needed to be done daily and other tasks such as brass polishing that needed to be done weekly.

Establishing Employment Supports

Supported employment staff assessed Michael prior to his entry into the program and determined that he would need ongoing support to succeed in competitive employment.

Determination of Supports The level of support needed was determined by examining several different factors. To begin with, although Michael is often calm and cooperative, he does have dangerous behavioral outbursts that are characterized by yelling and aggression. At his vocational training center, he sometimes chased staff around the parking lot while trying to hit them. In addition, Michael often engages in self-stimulation that severely interferes with his work productivity. Finally, Michael has language and social skill limitations that make it difficult for him to handle the language and socialization demands of integrated employment. His entire educational and vocational history took place in segregated environments where he did not learn functional language or socialization skills. For all of these reasons, Michael's interdisciplinary team decided that while he needs the full-time supervision of a job coach, the job coach can also supervise one other worker with autism.

Description of Job Coach Duties The job coach was responsible for teaching Michael how to do his work tasks, assisting him in remaining on task to meet productivity goals, supporting and assisting him in communicating with co-workers and supervisors, and helping him to manage his behavior problems. Because Michael disliked taking buses and his behaviors posed a danger to other passengers, the job coach also transported him to and from work.

Description of Behavior Plan Michael's behavioral program was developed to address his behavior problems and the functions of these behaviors. His main job-threatening behaviors included aggression, yelling, and task refusal. Antecedents to these behaviors included being abruptly told to do something, receiving critical feedback, and changes in the environment. Self-stimulation behaviors were frequent and interfered with his attention to job tasks. The consequences of these behaviors were that Michael no longer had to do his tasks and was able to avoid future requests to do tasks.

A psychologist consulted with Michael's supported employment staff to develop a behavior change plan. The purpose of the plan was to encourage more cooperative behavior at work by decreasing the frequency of aggression, yelling, and noncompliance, and by increasing work-oriented behaviors. The behavior plan included hourly ratings on the following targeted behaviors: keeps hands and feet to himself, respects his body (defined as no self-injury), speaks at a normal voice volume, and follows directions. Because Michael is able to read, these rules were written out for him, and he and his job coach rated his performance on each behavior hourly. If Michael displayed all targeted behaviors in 1 hour, he was given a small edible reinforcer.

Michael's behavior plan also included several other features to address the functions of his behaviors. Because criticism was often an antecedent to aggression, his job coach received instruction on how to noncritically redirect Michael should he misbehave. The job coach was also instructed on how to respond when inappropriate behaviors occurred to minimize attention to them. Finally, because Michael was sometimes aggressive during car rides, specific behavioral procedures were developed just for the car. These included specifying where he should keep his hands at the beginning of the trip and frequent praise for keeping his hands to himself and sitting in his seat.

Description of Instructional Procedures Michael has relatively good visual-motor skills, and, therefore, is capable of performing his job duties. However, his finger flicking interfered with his productivity. Because of this, instructional procedures were developed to encourage Michael to use his hands to do his work tasks. Basically, Michael was praised frequently for keeping his hands on his work and no comments were made about the finger flicking. If he did finger flick, a prompt hierarchy was used to redirect him back to the task at hand. The job coach would wait about 10 seconds to see if he would independently stop finger flicking and go back to work. If he did not, the job coach gave a general prompt of "What's next?". If he did not return to working, the job coach systematically progressed to gestural and physical prompts to encourage on-task behavior; however, only gentle physical assistance was provided. Michael was never forced to do his task. If he resisted, job coach staff would simply wait and try to redirect him in a few minutes. With these procedures his productivity increased while his self-stimulation decreased.

Because of his lack of basic social and language skills, Michael received specific social skills instruction on greeting his co-workers. This social skill was practiced in role play with his job coach and then with his co-workers and supervisors. Michael learned to greet his co-workers independently, which has helped to enhance his acceptance and integration on the job.

Outcomes

Michael has been employed as a food service worker for 2 years. He works approximately 10 hours a week at two separate restaurants for a total of 20 hours per week. He receives an hourly wage of $4.50. He has learned to do his job tasks but needs the supervision of a job coach to encourage on-task behaviors. Because of sporadic behavior problems, he continues to have a full-time job coach who also supervises one other employee with autism. Michael seems to have attained a job position that, with continued support, may suit him for many years.

CASE STUDY #2—DARREN
• • • • • • • • • •

Employee Description

Darren is a 27-year-old man with autism and profound mental retardation. He is nonverbal and although he rarely initiates social interactions unless he wants something, he likes social contact initiated by others. At times Darren is playful with others and will take someone's hand as a sign of affection. Darren is also hyperactive and has difficulty sitting still for even brief periods of time. He will run from staff, jump up and down, pace the floor, and sometimes flap his arms. In the community, this behavior is dangerous because he sporadically darts in front of cars. On one occasion, he was struck by a car. Even when he is seated, Darren fidgets constantly. He also has pica and tends to eat or drink anything that comes in a bottle, including cleaning fluids, correction fluid, hand lotions, and make-up. He also eats solid objects such as paper, push pins, and paper clips. Darren is very quick and will grab an inedible and put it in his mouth before staff have an opportunity to prevent him. Other behaviors of concern include grabbing food from others and urinating on the floor. Finally, Darren has very poor attention skills and will only pay attention to a task for brief periods of time, often less than several seconds.

Employee History

Darren spent the majority of his education in institutional schools for people with developmental disabilities. Most of these were out-of-state placements that provided year-round, 24-hour supervision. Following these placements, Darren spent 3½ years in a community-based residential school for adolescents with autism. This was Darren's first integrated, educational experience. At age 21, he was transferred from this program to a supported employment program for adults with autism.

Darren's early employment history was very inconsistent and he had trouble retaining a job for more than 2 or 3 months. He held jobs as a stock clerk, janitor, bulk mailing clerk, and warehouse worker, but was terminated from all of them because of his behavior problems and inability to stay on task.

It was difficult to find a good environmental job match because many jobs proved to be unsafe for Darren. For example, when he was employed as a janitor Darren attempted to drink cleaning fluids and would suck on sponges and cleaning rags. Staff were aware that Darren had boundless energy that could prove valuable at the right job, but they had difficulty matching his skills and traits to a job.

Description of Company and Job

A job was found for Darren at a national pizza delivery chain delivering advertisement flyers to residences. The company employs several workers who take pizza orders over the phone, make the pizzas, and deliver them. Darren's job is to walk through residential neighborhoods, including apartment complexes, and put advertisement flyers on front doorknobs.

Setting Up the Job

This job as a flyer distributor was considered a good match for Darren for several reasons. First, the job capitalized on a skill that he already had, that is, his ability to walk for long periods of time without fatigue. This provides an excellent outlet for all of his energy. The job also is well suited to a limited attention span; Darren only has to pay attention long enough to hang a flyer on the doorknob—a simple visual-motor task. Finally, the job does not expose him to dangerous liquids.

Establishing Employment Supports

Darren's interdisciplinary team convened to determine the level of support necessary to help Darren succeed at his job.

Determination of Supports Because Darren has pica and sometimes darts into traffic, he requires direct physical intervention from the job coach to ensure his safety. Thus, it was determined that Darren requires continual supervision to safely retain a job in the community. In addition, direct supervision is necessary to ensure that he does his job tasks. Because his problem behaviors are intermittent, Darren's team felt that his job coach could supervise one other worker with autism at the same time.

The team also determined that Darren required instructional support to learn his job duties. Because Darren is nonverbal, has profound mental retardation, and has a high frequency of problem behaviors, the team determined that he would need specialized instruction to learn his task. That is, he is not able to learn his task in the same way that workers without disabilities at the firm are taught their job duties.

Because Darren had high frequency behavior problems, some of which were life-threatening, the team determined that he also needed the support of a behavior management plan at work. The plan was to be developed by a psychologist and the supported employment staff.

Description of Job Coach Duties Darren's job coach has three main job duties: 1) to teach him to put the flyers on doorknobs, 2) to supervise his performance of the task, and 3) to manage his behavior problems. The job coach is also responsible for ensuring his safety in the community.

Description of Behavior Plan Darren's behavior plan was developed by supported employment agency staff in consultation with a psychologist. His behavior plan targeted two important behaviors: 1) staying in location, and 2) eating only food. The goals were to have him remain with his job coach and eliminate pica.

A functional assessment was performed and antecedents and consequences of Darren's darting and pica were pinpointed, as well as his maintaining consequences. It was determined that these behaviors were most likely to occur when Darren was not closely monitored, if he had a lack of staff attention, and if he had an opportunity to perform the behavior (e.g., if he was left unattended near a bottle of ammonia, there was a high risk that he would drink it). The functions of his darting behavior appeared to be to obtain desired items and to obtain increased staff attention. The functions of his pica behavior appeared to be to obtain staff attention and for sensory stimulation.

The plan contained a schedule of positive reinforcement for staying with his job coach, having an empty mouth, and eating only edibles. Reinforcers used were nutritious and other favorite food snacks. Food reinforcers were used not only to strengthen more acceptable behavior, but to provide more acceptable stimuli for ingestion. The plan included the provision of specific instructions on where to walk and frequent praise for cooperation. The purpose of the praise component was to teach Darren that he could obtain staff attention for cooperative behavior, and thereby eliminate the need to misbehave to obtain staff attention. Finally, the plan contained a component that called for his job coach to ensure that his area was free from cleaning fluids and other items that he might ingest.

An important component of the plan for managing his bolting is that Darren always wears a backpack when at work. The backpack is attached over his shoulders and around the waist, and the job coach gently holds the waist strap to prevent darting. This procedure ensures that Darren cannot bolt and be hit by vehicles or grab inedibles. The backpack also gives him a place to store the advertisement flyers, his lunch, his reinforcers, and magazines that he enjoys looking at during breaks.

The job coach was trained to implement Darren's behavior plan and to provide continual supervision to prevent bolting and pica. A behavioral specialist observed his job coach implementing supervision guidelines and provided feedback on how the job coach could improve performance of these essential job duties.

Description of Instructional Procedures Darren has the motor skills necessary to attach flyers to doorknobs; however, he frequently goes off task and needs physical assistance to attach the flyer accurately. Because of this, a program to increase on-task behaviors was developed. This program used a hierarchy of assistance that provided gestural and verbal cues at established intervals prior to resorting to physical guidance. Darren was also praised and given reinforcers for doing his job task independently. With these procedures, Darren became increasingly independent in attaching advertisement flyers to doorknobs.

Outcomes

Darren has remained employed distributing flyers for pizza delivery companies for more than 4 years. He lost one flyer distribution job because of slowdowns in the pizza chain's use of this advertisement strategy; however, he was able to obtain similar employment with another pizza delivery company.

Darren has always earned more than minimum wage on these jobs. With the support of a well-instructed job coach and consistent implementation of his behavior management program, Darren's safety in the community is also maintained.

CHAPTER 10

Jobs in Warehouses

J obs in warehouses and distribution centers can be excellent opportunities for workers with autism. Workers with autism have worked in warehouses and distribution centers that process dental supplies, cassettes and compact discs, housewares, electrical supplies, snack foods and other small items for vending machines, and linens and glassware for party rentals. Warehouse jobs can include a variety of tasks, such as cleaning rental glassware, folding rental party linens, packaging items for display in vending machines, filling orders for cassettes and compact discs, filling orders for electronic parts, and doing inventory. Distribution jobs involve preparing orders for mailing or distribution.

ADVANTAGES OF WAREHOUSE JOBS

Warehouses provide a variety of jobs, which can be suitable for workers of varying skill and ability levels. Some warehouse jobs require the ability to read and count, and entail a great deal of precision. These jobs may be ideal for some workers with autism. Other warehouse jobs, as with some retail stock jobs, require unskilled labor and involve boxing, packaging, unpacking merchandise, and similar tasks. These latter jobs often require no verbal skills and can be performed by individuals with severe autism and severe or profound mental retardation. Distribution jobs are easy to perform and often entail only one-step tasks. Both types of jobs have several advantages for workers with autism.

Work Environment

Warehouse jobs are typically located in environments similar to stockrooms, with the advantages of being larger, generally having more spacious work areas, and not being adjacent to sales floors or retail showrooms. Large work areas are preferred by many individuals with autism because they give them more room to move about. For people with autism who have difficulty remaining in one location or remaining seated at a table, the large work areas in warehouses are an advantage.

Furthermore, because warehouses are not normally adjacent to retail or sales areas, they are ideal for workers with autism who have difficulty dealing directly with the public. These workers' verbal or behavioral repertoires would be considered inappropriate in work areas with customer traffic. The people in warehouses are typically only co-workers who are familiar to the employee with autism and who are comfortable with that employee.

Some workers with autism display behaviors that are disruptive in close quarters, such as screaming, bizarre vocalizations, or even self-injury or aggression. In the warehouse environment, the worker can be somewhat isolated, or at least distanced from co-workers, so that these problem behaviors are not disruptive.

Nature of the Tasks

Many warehouse jobs involve simple, nontechnical tasks, such as packing boxes, unpacking boxes, breaking down boxes, and moving materials from one area to another. These jobs are easily learned and accuracy is not hard to achieve.

Other warehouse jobs are more technical in nature, such as filling orders, which may require reading and counting. These jobs provide appropriate challenges to workers with those skills. If the worker does not have those skills, it is sometimes possible to split the task with a co-worker, so that the worker with autism is only doing a portion of the task. Or, the job coach can provide assistance.

Warehouse jobs often involve gross motor activity, such as carrying and lifting, and involve a great deal of walking. Many individuals with autism who do not do well in jobs that require table work or fine motor work succeed in warehouse jobs because of their propensity toward gross motor activity.

Some warehouse jobs involve tasks that require no verbal language. Because many people with autism have severe problems in communication, these jobs provide an opportunity for successful employment.

There are workers with autism who are not able to work at productivity levels equal to their co-workers without disabilities. Many warehouse jobs have been found that have relatively slow productivity requirements, which allow these workers with autism to succeed. However, other workers with autism work extremely fast, and it is also possible to find warehouse jobs that require a high production level.

Some workers with autism are fortunate enough to obtain warehouse jobs that involve merchandise for which they have a high level of interest. For example, for individuals with autism who are fascinated with the rock music industry, a job in the warehouse of a cassette and compact disc company would be of great interest. One man with autism who is nonverbal and loves potato chips and snack foods was placed in a job in a warehouse preparing snack food trays for vending machines. Because he has a history of noncompliance and self-injury, his behavior plan includes a schedule of positive reinforcement for cooperative behavior. The young man was taught to help himself to chips about every half hour (when his timer rang) if he had worked steadily during that time. He maintained this job, virtually free of self-injury, until separation due to bankruptcy of the company.

Social Requirements

Warehouse tasks can be done with a minimum of social interaction. These jobs work well for people with autism who do not have the conversational or social skills necessary to succeed at jobs that require a great deal of social involvement. Social interactions in warehouse jobs are often casual, and they occur as workers pass each other or during breaks and lunch. Workers with autism can often manage these kinds of interactions well, although they may need some social skills training and assistance to enhance their social integration. Warehouse environments are often tolerant of some deviation from socially expected behavior, so that workers with autism who have occasional behavioral outbursts are not ostracized or fired for such behaviors.

DISADVANTAGES OF WAREHOUSE JOBS

Warehouse and distribution jobs have few disadvantages, but certain aspects of these jobs must be taken into consideration for the worker with autism to succeed.

Work Environment

Warehouse jobs sometimes take place in harsh environments. Some warehouses, for example, do not have adequate climate control, and they are too hot in the summer and too cold in the winter. Some warehouses have high noise levels from machinery or trucks; however, there are workers with autism who can tolerate noise, and, if necessary, be cooperative in wearing headphones to block the noise. Many workers with autism adjust well to these harsh environments.

Warehouses occasionally have large pieces of machinery such as forklifts and trucks going through the work area or nearby. This machinery can present a danger to the worker with autism who darts around indiscriminately. Usually, even workers with profound mental retardation can be taught to stay clear of such dangers. In cases where the worker remains at risk from darting into such dangers, close supervision is needed as part of the support services.

Nature of the Tasks

For workers with autism who have problems with pica, property destruction, or taking property without permission, warehouse jobs may be problematic because workers have access to large quantities of property. Problems with property care can be job threatening. However, property destruction or misuse of property can often be overcome by implementation of a behavior management program that involves positive reinforcement for correct use of property, authorized access to desired items if possible, and prevention of incidents that invoke property destruction. Problems with pica can be overcome by keeping the area swept clear of inedible items the individual might eat, and by providing alternate, more acceptable stimuli (e.g., for an individual who eats small metal objects, providing easy access to chips, pretzels, and nuts as an alternative to buttons, clips, and pins). In most cases where misuse or destruction of property is a concern, as well as in cases of pica, close supervision and monitoring is usually required.

JOBS IN WAREHOUSES

Individuals with autism work in numerous warehouse environments. Even workers who have difficulty keeping jobs due to behavior problems and severe difficulties in social skills have done well in warehouse jobs. These jobs have been the stepping stones to work environments that provide more interaction with the public. Some individuals who initially work in warehouses are able to succeed later in retail jobs where they have some duties on the sales floor. Descriptions of warehouse and distribution jobs held by workers with autism are provided on the following pages.

Inventory Clerk

Job Description: An inventory clerk manages inventory.

Worksite Description: This job is with a small, wholesale bookstore that fills orders for schools. The work takes place in a small warehouse. The company has four employees, including one with autism, who work in close proximity to one another.

Employee with Autism

Worker 1:   Speaks clearly in sentences, low-average cognitive functioning, limited social and language skills, perseveration on inappropriate topics

Job Tasks

* Compare invoice with merchandise received
* Put price stickers on books
* Shelve books by author and title
* Pull specified books from shelves
* Pack books for distribution
* Keep work area clean by throwing out garbage

Equipment, Machinery, and
Hand Tools Needed to Complete Job Tasks

* Books
* Boxes
* Pricing stickers
* Packing tape
* Invoice sheets

Potential Problems in Job Completion

* None

Modifications and Accommodations to Site or Task

* Drop-in assistance from job coach
* Social skills training

WAREHOUSES

Warehouse Worker

Job Description: A warehouse worker manages inventory.

Worksite Description: This job is with a division of a large corporation that distributes lighting fixtures to retail stores. There are approximately 100 workers in the warehouse; 4 work in the same area as the 2 workers with autism.

Employees with Autism

Worker 1: Speaks clearly in sentences, average intellectual functioning, problems with social and language skills, aggression upon provocation, difficulty staying on location, inappropriate verbalizations, loud voice volume

Worker 2: Speaks clearly in sentences, mild mental retardation, self-injury, property destruction, aggression, difficulty with social use of language (including perseveration)

Job Tasks

- Pull ordered items from shelves
- Pack items for shipping
- Price items
- Restock shelves
- Sweep and clean
- Assemble wheelbarrows and other items

Equipment, Machinery, and Hand Tools Needed to Complete Job Tasks

- Boxes
- Tape gun
- Box labels
- Pricing gun
- Screwdrivers
- Hammers
- Broom

Potential Problems in Job Completion

- The job requires performing multiple tasks, making it difficult for the workers to learn to perform all tasks proficiently.
- One worker has difficulty matching stock numbers on invoice sheets with items.

Modifications and Accommodations to Site or Task

- Job coach to assist with training, productivity, and behavior management
- Behavior management plans, including positive reinforcement, self-management, prompt hierarchy, extinction, and procedures for managing dangerous behavior

Stock Clerk

Job Description: A stock clerk manages inventory.

Worksite Description: This job is with a small dental supply company. There are 25 employees; 8 work in the same area as the 1 employee with autism.

Employee with Autism

Worker 1: Speaks in complete sentences, borderline intellectual functioning, yelling, and cursing

Job Tasks

- Pull orders from shelves according to invoice
- Pack ordered items for shipping
- Place shipping boxes in bins
- Enter ordered items into computer
- Restock shelves

Equipment, Machinery, and Hand Tools Needed to Complete Job Tasks

- Order sheets
- Shipping boxes
- Shipping bins
- Computer

Potential Problems in Job Completion

- Difficulty remembering where items belong
- Difficulty following directions

Modifications and Accommodations to Site or Task

- Initial training during job set-up
- Drop-in assistance from job coach

Snack Tray Filler

Job Description: A snack tray filler prepares snack trays for placement in small business environments.

Worksite Description: This job is with a small, family-owned business that distributes snack trays with an honor payment system. The work takes place in a small warehouse that is located in a suburban industrial park. There are 10 employees who work in the immediate vicinity of one another. There are four employees with autism and two other workers who perform the same tasks as the employees with autism.

Employees with Autism

Worker 1: Speaks clearly in complete sentences, mild mental retardation, inappropriate social conversations, speaks too loudly, talks to self, self-injury, aggression, property destruction

Worker 2: Speaks clearly in sentences, borderline mental retardation, limited social and language skills, difficulty following instructions, distracted by visitors

Worker 3: Communicates with sounds and gestures, profound mental retardation, self-injury, aggression, property destruction

Worker 4: Communicates using limited sign language, severe mental retardation, self-injury, aggression, self-stimulation, noncompliance

Job Tasks

- Fill vending trays with snack items
- Break down boxes
- Restock supplies
- Sweep

Equipment, Machinery, and Hand Tools Needed to Complete Job Tasks

- Dollies
- Screwdriver
- Broom

Potential Problems in Job Completion

- Low productivity
- Worksite is a long drive from employees' homes.

Modifications and Accommodations to Site or Task

- Job coach to assist with training, productivity, and behavior management
- Job coach fills in when workers are sick.
- Behavior management plans, including positive reinforcement, self-management, periodic ratings, prompt hierarchy, extinction, and procedures for managing dangerous behavior

Stock Clerk

Job Description: A stock clerk is involved with the distribution of cassettes and compact discs to area stores.

Worksite Description: This job is with a local chain of retail stores that sells cassettes and compact discs. The work takes place in a warehouse from which merchandise is distributed. There are approximately 75 workers in the warehouse, including 2 workers with autism who work in close proximity to about 10 employees.

Employees with Autism

Worker 1: Speaks clearly in complete sentences, low-average intelligence, aggression, limited social and language skills, resistant to learning more efficient ways to perform tasks

Worker 2: Speaks in complete sentences, mild mental retardation, ritualistic behaviors, stealing, eavesdropping, poor money management skills

Job Tasks

- Sort cassettes and compact discs according to destination
- Assemble shipping boxes
- Label boxes
- Pull ordered items from shelves
- Label cassettes and compact discs

Equipment, Machinery, and Hand Tools Needed to Complete Job Tasks

- Tape gun
- Scissors
- Cart for transporting items from the shelves
- Boxes
- Labels

Potential Problems in Job Completion

- Low productivity
- Difficulty labeling cassettes and compact discs

Modifications and Accommodations to Site or Task

- Job coach to assist with training, productivity, and behavior management
- Procedures to fade assistance from job coach
- Behavior management plans, including periodic ratings, positive reinforcement, social skills training, and monitoring to prevent stealing

WAREHOUSES

Laundry Worker

Job Description: A laundry worker launders party rental supplies.

Worksite Description: This job is with a small, family-owned rental catering supply company. There are 11 employees, including 3 workers with autism.

Employees with Autism

Worker 1: Communicates using limited sign language, severe mental retardation, self-injury, aggression, self-stimulation, noncompliance, playing in toilet water

Worker 2: Speaks clearly in sentences, moderate mental retardation, aggression (including hair pulling, lunging, hitting, kicking, scratching, and banging others' heads against walls), property destruction, self-injury

Worker 3: Speaks in complete sentences but speech is unclear, moderate mental retardation, noncompliance, wandering away from tasks, screaming, loud perseverative echolalia

Job Tasks

- Spot-clean tablecloths and napkins with detergent
- Load washing machines with dirty cloths
- Load dryers with clean tablecloths and napkins; set temperature
- Fold tablecloths and napkins
- Shelve dried tablecloths and napkins by size and color

Equipment, Machinery, and Hand Tools Needed to Complete Job Tasks

- Washers
- Dryers
- Tablecloths and napkins
- Detergent

Potential Problems in Job Completion

- Low productivity

Modifications and Accommodations to Site or Task

- Job coach to assist with training, productivity, and behavior management
- Behavior management plans, including positive reinforcement, social skills training, prompt hierarchy, extinction, and procedures for managing dangerous behavior

Warehouse Worker

Job Description: A warehouse worker manages the inventory of food storage containers in a warehouse environment.

Worksite Description: This job is with a company that distributes plastic food storage containers for sales parties. The work takes place in a large warehouse. There are five employees who work in the immediate vicinity of one another, including two workers with autism.

Employees with Autism

Worker 1:   Speaks clearly in full sentences, mild mental retardation, crying, yelling, squealing, task refusal

Worker 2:   Speaks clearly in sentences, high-average cognitive functioning, frequent task and program participation refusal, difficulty relating to employers and others

Job Tasks

- Restock shelves
- Pack merchandise for shipping
- Pick up trash in work area and place in dumpster
- Break down empty boxes
- Sweep work area
- Wipe down desktop when done working
- Put away supplies

Equipment, Machinery, and
Hand Tools Needed to Complete Job Tasks

- Boxes
- Tape
- Broom
- Cleaning rag

Potential Problems in Job Completion

- Low productivity

Modifications and Accommodations to Site or Task

- Job coach to assist with training, productivity, and behavior management
- Behavior management plans, including periodic ratings, positive reinforcement, social skills training, and extinction

Warehouse Worker

Job Description: A warehouse worker prepares plastic capsules containing novelty toys for distribution.

Worksite Description: This job is with a small company that sells candy and novelty items for vending machines. The work takes place in a small warehouse. There are 13 employees who work in the immediate vicinity of one another, including 3 workers with autism.

Employees with Autism

Worker 1: Speaks clearly in sentences, mild mental retardation, self-injury, property destruction, aggression, loud voice, problems with social use of language (including perseveration)

Worker 2: Speaks in complete sentences but speech is unclear, low-average cognitive functioning, screaming, jumping, hand flapping, spinning, rapid verbalizations, inappropriate conversation with co-workers, motor rituals (especially spinning while walking), frequently late for work

Worker 3: Communicates with sounds and gestures, profound mental retardation, self-injury, aggression, property destruction

Job Tasks

- Box plastic capsules
- Roll towels to be used for cleaning vending machines
- Assemble cardboard shipping boxes
- Clean work area
- Heat-seal plastic covering on display boxes

Equipment, Machinery, and Hand Tools Needed to Complete Job Tasks

- Capsules
- Boxes
- Heat-sealing machine
- Plastic

Potential Problems in Job Completion

- Low productivity

Modifications and Accommodations to Site or Task

- Job coach to assist with training, productivity, and behavior management
- Behavior management plans, including periodic ratings, positive reinforcement, prompt hierarchy, extinction, and procedures for managing dangerous behaviors

Dishwasher

Job Description: A dishwasher cleans rental dishes and merchandise and prepares them for distribution

Worksite Description: This job is with a small catering and equipment rental warehouse. Two employees with autism work in the kitchen with five other workers.

Employees with Autism

Worker 1: Communicates using limited manual signs and pictures; severe mental retardation; significant problems with social skills, language, independence, and incontinence

Worker 2: Speaks in complete sentences but speech is unclear, moderate mental retardation, noncompliance, wandering away from tasks, screaming, loud perseverative echolalia

Job Tasks

- Sanitize silverware and glassware
- Dry dishes
- Pack dishes and glassware in boxes
- Sort napkins by color
- Pack napkins in boxes
- Wrap silverware in plastic wrap
- Stack silverware on shelves
- Put away tablecloths

Equipment, Machinery, and Hand Tools Needed to Complete Job Tasks

- Dishwasher
- Sanitizing chemicals
- Towels for drying
- Plastic wrap
- Boxes

Potential Problems in Job Completion

- Problems with productivity

Modifications and Accommodations to Site or Task

- Job coach to assist with training, productivity, and behavior management
- Behavior management plans, including positive reinforcement, voice volume training, prompt hierarchy, and extinction procedures

WAREHOUSES

CASE STUDY #1—MARK
• • • • • • • • •

Employee Description

Mark is a 30-year-old man whose cognitive functioning is in the profound range of mental retardation. His characteristics of autism include severe social withdrawal and serious problems with social skills difficulties, self-stimulatory behaviors, adverse reactions to change, and unusual sensory preferences. Mark is nonverbal but makes his needs known by pointing and using a few essential signs. Despite his problems, Mark enjoys attention, and performs assigned tasks quickly and accurately. Mark has several maladaptive behaviors that can be job threatening. He can be severely self-injurious—he bangs his head, bites his hand, and scratches his skin causing open sores. Of particular concern is the fact that he tends to hit his face very hard around his eyes; he has given himself black eyes. Mark also threatens to injure himself by grabbing a sharp object and holding it above his arm while looking at staff. On the job, he has exhibited public masturbation and poor toileting skills. Mark sometimes defecates in his pants and then smears his feces in the bathroom when instructed to clean himself up. Additional behaviors include pica, noise making, food stealing, self-induced vomiting, and poor attentional skills.

Employee History

Mark's educational services were all provided in institutional or segregated environments. He attended two residential schools before being institutionalized in a state facility for people with developmental disabilities. He then went to segregated special education programs until the age of 16 years when he was enrolled in a prevocational program for people with developmental disabilities. Mark entered a supported employment program for people with autism at the age of 21 years, when his educational funding was terminated.

Mark's employment history is varied. He was employed for almost 1 year as a laboratory assistant where he prepared glassware for laboratory use and did clerical tasks. Later, he was employed as a bulk mailing clerk and then as a stock clerk. He lost all of these jobs reportedly because of slowdowns in the amount of work available, but staff suspect that he was let go due to his behavior problems. For example, at one job Mark was hired to hang clothing prior to display on the sales floor. He would draw blood by scratching his face and the blood would then be found on the clothes that he was hanging.

Description of Company and Job

Mark obtained a job in a warehouse that provided snack trays to local companies and businesses. The vending company was a small, family-owned business that operated in a small warehouse. The warehouse had a work area, a loading dock, and a small office. The company employed five workers, some of whom did the same job as Mark. Mark's job was to fill cardboard snack trays with a variety of snacks. He had to arrange them on a tray in a specific order. Mark was also responsible for stocking the shelves with snacks as necessary. A delivery worker would take the trays that Mark had arranged to local businesses that in turn would sell them to their employees.

Setting Up the Job

Mark has poorly developed social and language skills but good visual-motor skills, so the employment specialist sought a job position that would capitalize on his strengths. Mark's visual-motor skills and visual memory were sufficient to meet the demands of the vending company job. In addition, the job provided a task that kept Mark's hands busy so that he could not engage in continual self-scratching. Furthermore, Mark's previous jobs were in much larger companies and it was hoped that a smaller environment would present fewer problems for him. This job position was considered a good match for Mark except for the constant presence of food, which Mark might try to steal.

Because the snacks needed to be arranged on the trays in a specific order, it was important for the job coach to learn this order before teaching it to Mark. Therefore, the job coach started the job before Mark and wrote a task analysis for filling the snack trays.

Establishing Employment Supports

Mark's interdisciplinary team met to determine the kinds of supports that Mark would need to succeed at work.

Determination of Supports   The presence of dangerous behavior problems was the principal factor in determining the level of support needed. Although very dangerous behaviors, such as head banging, hitting his face around his eyes, and aggression, were infrequent, it was important that staff always be available to manage these behaviors should they occur. In addition, milder forms of self-injury, such as hand and face scratching, posed an ongoing danger to Mark. His public masturbation and pica also necessitated continual supervision. Mark's use of the bathroom was very problematic and it was important that staff supervise him to prevent unsanitary behaviors that would lead to his termination. Concerning his social and language skills, a full-time job coach was considered necessary to act as a mediator between Mark and the social and language requirements of the job. It was also determined that Mark would need a behavior management program and specialized instructional support to learn his new job duties.

Description of Job Coach Duties   Mark's job coach performed a variety of job tasks to support him at work. One main duty was to manage behavior problems when they occurred so that Mark and his co-workers would not be injured. The job coach also supervised Mark in the bathroom and instructed him in toileting skills. In addition, much of the job coach's time was taken with implementing his behavior program. Finally, Mark had difficulty performing work tasks accurately and quickly; therefore, the job coach was responsible for monitoring job performance.

Description of Behavior Plan A functional assessment of the reasons for Mark's problematic behaviors was performed by the consulting psychologist with input from the job coach. The principal reason for many of Mark's behaviors was to provide himself with sensory feedback. This was true for ruminating, pica, self-scratching, noise making, feces smearing, and public masturbation. Severe self-injury and aggression were usually precipitated by unanticipated major changes in the environment. Finally, it was discovered that much of Mark's behavior was motivated by getting attention from others. For example, when he started to scratch his face, the behavior increased rapidly because his job coach would tell him to stop it or to put his hands down.

A behavior plan was designed to address all the functions of Mark's behaviors. The plan called for frequent reinforcers for specific target behaviors. The most important target behavior was using his hands for appropriate activities or keeping them at his side. Reinforcing these behaviors with small amounts of snack foods resulted in decreases in self-scratching, aggression, food stealing, pica, and feces smearing. In addition, it helped to increase his work productivity by focusing on using his hands to do his job tasks. Because Mark seemed to enjoy the sensation of playing with his blood and feces, he was given frequent access to a substitute sensory stimulus—lotion. However, he was never given lotion after a misbehavior because this would only reinforce the misbehavior. Finally, Mark greatly enjoyed attention from others and would misbehave to get it; therefore, he was given frequent attention in the form of praise and conversation for behaving himself.

While at the vending company, Mark showed substantial improvement in his behaviors. Agency staff wanted to maximize his independence on the job but it was believed that he still needed a frequent schedule of positive reinforcement because an attempt to thin the reinforcement schedule resulted in an increase in self-injury. To encourage more independence, a self-management reinforcement program was developed for Mark. He was taught to set a timer to 30 minutes and when the timer sounded he could give himself a reinforcer if he had behaved appropriately and done his work. The reinforcer was a small snack, such as chips from a bag that Mark kept by his work area. This program gave Mark control over his own reinforcement schedule and he maintained the improvement in his behavior.

Description of Instructional Procedures Mark had difficulty maintaining his work quality and increasing his productivity to acceptable employer's standard productivity rates. Instructional procedures were developed to address both of these problems. A prompt hierarchy was implemented to teach

Mark to do his job tasks accurately and independently. His job coach praised Mark for work that was done accurately, especially if Mark also did it independently. Concerning productivity, initial rates of productivity were assessed to determine his baseline levels. Mark then received a reinforcer if he attained rates of productivity that were higher than baseline levels. The differentiated reinforcement of high rates of behavior (DRH) schedule helped Mark attain the acceptable employer's standard productivity rates of productivity.

Outcomes

Mark was employed as a warehouse worker for the vending company for 2 years, then lost the job because the company went out of business due to economic problems. During his employment, Mark's wage was increased from $3.80 per hour to $4.25 per hour, a 12% increase. He has since started a job as a stock clerk earning $4.50 per hour where he has maintained many of the vocational gains made at the vending company.

CASE STUDY #2—SHARON
• • • • • • • • •

Employee Description

Sharon is a 32-year-old woman who has autism and whose cognitive functioning is within the mild range of mental retardation. She can speak in complete sentences; however, she tends to talk very fast with a low voice volume, which makes her speech difficult to understand. In addition, she speaks on only a few topics and does not make eye contact. Also, she rarely initiates conversations with others and is socially withdrawn. Despite her social withdrawal, she occasionally forms close relationships with staff who work with her for a long period of time.

Sharon has a history of job-threatening behaviors—she engages in numerous ritualistic behaviors. Sharon tends to hoard consumable products, such as shampoo and toothpaste, and compulsively steals these items from stores. On occasion, she steals clothes and other objects from stores and takes money out of other women's purses. Sharon also depleted her bank account by spending large sums of money on clothing and other goods, without leaving money for necessities. At work, Sharon sometimes refuses to do her work, works very slowly, and takes frequent trips to the bathroom.

Employee History

Until the age of 17 years, Sharon lived at home and attended segregated, special education schools in her county of residence. She was then placed in an institutional residential school for people with developmental disabilities where she remained for 4 years. At this school, Sharon continued to study academic skills and gained vocational experience working in the institution's laundry. At the age of 21 years, Sharon was transferred to a residential and supported employment program for people with autism.

Sharon began her work career as a bindery worker in a printing company but was laid off from that job due to a lack of work. She then worked at several retail stores as an inventory clerk or stock clerk. Typically, she lost these jobs due to economic reasons; however, a slow work rate, poor social skills with customers, and occasional stealing may have contributed to her termination. Some of these stores stocked goods such as shampoo and toiletries that Sharon would steal.

Description of Company and Job

Sharon now works for a retail music store chain that sells records, cassettes, compact discs, and related products at many different locations. Her work takes place in the chain's warehouse where music products are received and sorted for shipment to individual stores. The company employs approximately 25 people who work in the warehouse. Sharon's job is to label records, cassettes, and compact discs with a store number and to sort these products into separate boxes for each store. When the boxes are full, Sharon takes them to a shipping area where they are put on trucks for distribution to the stores. Sharon is also responsible for filling orders for records, cassettes, and compact discs that are sent in by individual stores. Sharon locates the music products by stock number on storage shelves and boxes them for shipment. Finally, Sharon makes and labels the boxes that she uses.

Setting Up the Job

Sharon's employment specialist thought that her new job in a warehouse for music products was less problematic than her previous stock clerk jobs because she had never stolen any music products and seemed to have no interest in owning them. This new job also makes good functional use of Sharon's ability to read as she has to match store numbers and stock numbers. The job is also good for her because she has only a few job tasks to perform, and those tasks are done the same way each time. It was anticipated that once Sharon was used to the routine and to reading the store and stock numbers she could attain standard employee rates of productivity. Finally, the job presents fewer social demands than previous jobs because she does not have direct contact with customers.

As part of the set-up, the job coach spent several days on the job learning the job tasks prior to Sharon beginning work. The job tasks are multistep, and the job coach needed to learn exactly how to do them prior to teaching Sharon. The job coach also assessed the social demands of the work environment.

Establishing Employment Supports

Because of Sharon's difficulty in maintaining employment, it was anticipated that she would require the full-time support of a job coach. Previous attempts to withdraw job coach support had resulted in Sharon's refusal to work, extreme difficulties related to co-workers and supervisors, and theft of merchandise and money.

Determination of Supports   Upon entering the supported employment program, Sharon's interdisciplinary team recognized that she had no experience in integrated environments. In addition, although she did not have any dangerous behaviors at work, she did steal objects and money, both of which were clearly job threatening. Sharon also had poorly developed social skills and limited language abilities. Her voice volume was very low and difficult to understand. The team agreed that Sharon required full-time supervision by a job coach because of her behavior problems and her poor social and language skills.

Description of Job Coach Duties   The job coach supervises Sharon and one other adult with autism full time during the workday. The job coach taught

Sharon her new tasks and supervises her work performance to ensure productivity and accuracy. The job coach is also responsible for helping Sharon manage her behavior problems and negotiate the social and language requirements of the job.

Description of Behavior Plan   Sharon was in need of a behavior change plan to eliminate her stealing. A psychologist consulted with her supported employment supervisor and job coach to develop a behavior change plan. It was determined that Sharon's behaviors were related to ritualistic behaviors that are secondary to her autism. It appeared that she was stealing to obtain items that she enjoyed having. The goal of the plan was to teach her to budget her money so that she could purchase what she needed rather than steal it.

Each week, Sharon, her job coach, and the residential counselor would develop a comprehensive list of planned and optional purchases for each day of the week. Sharon was allowed to budget for consumable products, such as shampoo and soap, only if in fact she needed those items. Then, each morning her job coach would review with Sharon her expenses for the day and make sure that she had enough money to make these purchases. Sharon was also encouraged to collect receipts for all of her purchases to assist in tallying her budget. At the end of the day, the job coach assisted Sharon in filling out her budget book in which she listed her purchases and a balance of money left over. The job coach also assisted Sharon in counting her remaining money and checking her receipts to ensure that purchases had been made. This budget program served two basic purposes. First, Sharon was assured that she would have enough money to buy what she needed and wanted. Second, her job coach was able to closely monitor her purchases and be in a position to discourage stealing.

Sharon's behavior plan also included a daily rating system on several targeted behaviors. Behaviors that were of particular concern at work were getting permission to use other people's property and following her budget. These rules were written out for her, and at the end of the day Sharon was rated on her performance on each behavior. She was praised for earning positive ratings and, at the end of the week, rewarded with bonus money for engaging in these desired behaviors. Sharon was also trained to rate herself on targeted behaviors. Finally, Sharon was closely monitored at work to prevent stealing. Her behavior plan, including self-management, budgeting, and close supervision, was effective in reducing her stealing.

Description of Instructional Procedures   Because of Sharon's poor social and language abilities, she received extensive training in greeting her coworkers, facing others, and speaking audibly when conversing. Social skills training consisted of systematically practicing the desired social skills with her job coach. Her job coach gave Sharon instruction on the desired social skill and demonstrated how to do it. Sharon then practiced the skill with her counselor, received corrective feedback, and continued to practice the social skill. Generalization training consisted of instructing Sharon on when to use the social skill, prompting her when necessary, and providing praise when she did use it.

Sharon quickly met required productivity rates and was a good candidate for eventually working independently. However, she sometimes stopped working when not supervised, and her stealing behavior threatened to result in loss of her job if it occurred just once. Thus, a goal for Sharon was to work steadily and independently without stealing. Independence training was involved, gradually increasing the amount of time that Sharon worked without the supervision of the job coach.

Outcomes

Sharon has been employed at the music company for more than 3 years with no layoffs. Sharon's salary has increased from $5.00 per hour to $5.75 per hour, and she works about 25 hours per week. Because of her lack of interest in the merchandise she works with, stealing these products has not been a major problem. Although a full-time job coach still works at the music company, Sharon works independently for a portion of each hour. It is anticipated that the length of time spent working independently can be gradually increased. In summary, Sharon has found a job that she seems to enjoy and at which she does well while working toward independence.

CHAPTER 11

Jobs in
Recycling and Delivery

E ntry-level jobs in recycling and delivery provide stable work for some employees with autism who have had difficulty maintaining employment elsewhere. Workers with autism are hired by recycling companies to separate items by color, type, and material; to crush items; and to do general cleaning and pick-up in the work area. They are hired by delivery companies to prepare merchandise for delivery and to deliver it to residents in the community. Workers with autism are also hired by companies that recycle papers, containers, and newspapers. In addition, they work for local newspapers preparing the papers for delivery and delivering them. These jobs are typically easy to perform, and workers with autism with even profound mental retardation are able to perform the tasks independently. Job coaches are required, however, for supervision and behavior management purposes.

ADVANTAGES OF JOBS IN RECYCLING AND DELIVERY

Jobs in recycling and delivery have several advantages for workers with autism who have severe cognitive impairments and who have histories of destructive behavior.

Work Environment

Recycling jobs are often performed in large warehouses or outside of warehouse-type structures. These jobs afford a great deal of personal work space. For workers with histories of severe behavior problems, these environments are advantageous for at least two reasons. First, should behavior problems occur, there is less likelihood that co-workers will be disturbed. Second, it is unlikely that the worker with autism will be disturbed by others.

Recycling environments are often noisy, and this feature is an advantage in the case of workers with autism who are nonverbal and who have unusual vocal habits, such as hooting, loud humming, or screaming. The loud background noise obscures unconventional vocalizations, making them less job threatening. Ernie is a young man with profound mental retardation and autism who often hoots loudly while he works. His hooting behavior would not be tolerated in many work environments—in fact, he has a long history of job dismissals. However, employment in a recycling company is ideal in terms of Ernie's vocal habits. He is free to vocalize without co-workers hearing him. Recycling environments are not only well suited for unusual vocal habits, but for behavior outbursts as well. These outbursts are often less noticeable because of the size of the environment, as well as the general noise level.

Jobs delivering newspapers or advertisement flyers door-to-door are desirable because they take place outside. Many workers with autism prefer being outside, and, for workers who have difficulty remaining in one location, the job is ideal because it involves constant movement from one location to the next. If behavior problems do occur, or if productivity slows for some reason, it is not as critical because there are no co-workers to disrupt.

Nature of the Tasks

Recycling tasks involve crushing, moving items, picking up items, making piles, and other gross motor activities that are easily done by workers with autism and severe or profound mental retardation. These are simple, one-step tasks that do not require fine motor activity or good visual-motor skills. These activities may be of interest to workers with autism who often enjoy the sensory stimulation that such activities provide. Jobs in recycling plants often involve a great deal of movement and walking about, which is advantageous for workers who prefer to move around rather than stay in one area to do a job. Furthermore, these tasks do not require communication skills.

Recycling jobs often do require sorting skills. Papers may need to be sorted by color, texture, or size, and beverage containers may need to be sorted by type of material (e.g., plastic, metal). Workers with autism who have severe or profound mental retardation are capable of such sorting tasks.

Some individuals with autism display property destruction for self-stimulation. For example, Simon is a man with autism and no verbal language who smashes glass; he appears to enjoy the sight and sound that the broken glass makes. Erin is a man with autism who enjoys crushing small objects. Some recycling jobs involve actual destruction of materials, such as crushing cans or smashing bottles. Workers such as Simon and Erin do well in recycling jobs because their problem behaviors are not considered problems in these environments, and they are encouraged to do an activity that provides them with desired sensory feedback.

Delivery jobs also involve simple tasks that can be performed even by workers with profound mental retardation. These jobs primarily involve walking and delivering either flyers or newspapers door to door. For some workers with autism, walking is a pleasurable activity; therefore, they are able to maintain employment in delivery jobs for many years, despite histories of being unable to keep jobs.

Delivery and recycling tasks have the additional advantage of being repetitive. Some individuals with autism have difficulty making transitions from one activity or task to the next. These jobs usually involve engagement in the same task throughout the workday, with little or no need for change or transition.

Social Requirements

Recycling jobs usually require few or no social skills. Because the jobs are solitary and do not involve social interaction with co-workers or customers, they are ideal for workers with autism who lack social skills and who are socially withdrawn. Although there are co-workers with whom these workers can interact, take breaks, and eat lunch, it is advantageous that no social demands are placed on them as part of the performance of their job duties.

Because recycling jobs are often done in large warehouses, there is relatively little need for chatting or social discourse with co-workers. A worker with autism who is socially withdrawn can work comfortably in this environment without any social demands.

Newspaper delivery jobs occasionally involve chance encounters with customers or other people in the community; however, workers with autism can be taught to give verbal or gestural greetings, which is typically sufficient for the job.

DISADVANTAGES OF RECYCLING AND DELIVERY JOBS

Work Environment

Recycling and delivery jobs are often located in harsh environments. They may take place in large warehouses that are too cold in the winter and too hot in the summer. Other recycling jobs are done outdoors, and the worker is directly exposed to the elements. Some workers with severe behavior problems are more likely to display behavior problems when they are hot.

The recycling environment can appear chaotic, with large piles of recycled material, a high noise level, and an erratic flow of large equipment through the area. Because of high noise levels, workers are sometimes required to wear earphones. In addition, the air quality can be poor, which requires workers to wear face masks.

Recycling centers may have a steady flow of trucks, and possibly bulldozers, going through the area in which people work. Individuals with mobility problems may have difficulty keeping out of the path of this equipment. One worker with autism who displays ritualistic spinning while he walks was often found spinning in the path of oncoming bulldozers. This behavior led to his resignation and he found more suitable employment in a manufacturing company in which he is able to work in one area.

Workers in the delivery field are generally walking through the community and, therefore, are exposed to the harshness of the elements. This can be a disadvantage for workers who do not tolerate weather extremes. A related disadvantage is that when the weather is inclement, such as rain or snow, work is canceled. This lack of work can present problems for people with autism who are often dependent on the routine and structure that a job provides. When work is canceled due to inclement weather, filling those hours can be problematic. During these periods, there is a greater likelihood that behavior problems will occur.

Delivery jobs typically take place in residential neighborhoods. Although behavior problems that occur in these environments are not necessarily job threatening, they can serve to bring undue attention to the worker. Workers with autism who have behavior problems such as darting into traffic, running away from staff, or chasing young children must be carefully monitored, and staff must follow positioning guidelines to prevent such behaviors from occurring. Workers with these problems typically require schedules of positive reinforcement to encourage them to remain with staff on the prescribed route. Furthermore, because they are walking about in the community, they must cross streets frequently, which can be problematic for workers who have motor rituals or fears of traffic.

Nature of the Tasks

Delivery jobs are often part-time jobs. In the case of workers delivering a weekly newspaper, they have only 1 day of work per week. Sometimes this type of job can be combined with other part-time delivery jobs to fill up the person's weekly work schedule. Delivery and outside recycling jobs are affected by weather, and in cases of poor weather conditions work may be canceled. Finally, these jobs are entry-level jobs and offer no opportunity for advancement for workers with severe language or cognitive impairments.

Social Requirements

Recycling and delivery jobs often provide very limited opportunities for integration with co-workers. This may be advantageous for workers who have difficulty with social skills, but it is not good for integrating workers with co-workers without disabilities. Recycling jobs are typically solitary jobs and most co-worker interaction is limited to breaks and lunch. Delivery jobs are also solitary. The worker goes to a central location to pick up the newspapers or other items for delivery and then makes the deliveries, with little opportunity for interaction with management or co-workers.

Cognitive Requirements

Workers with profound or severe mental retardation, and some with moderate mental retardation, do well in delivery and recycling jobs. However, workers with higher levels of cognitive functioning and good fine motor skills or other splinter skills are not well suited to recycling and delivery jobs. These jobs do not provide enough challenge for workers with higher ability levels and do not afford them the opportunity to use their areas of strength.

JOBS IN RECYCLING AND DELIVERY

Some workers with autism who have long histories of unemployment are able to maintain steady employment in recycling or delivery jobs. Workers with autism and severe cognitive and language problems who have been unwilling to work in other jobs have proven cooperative in these jobs. Recycling and delivery jobs, although sometimes occurring in harsh conditions with limited opportunity for integration, have enabled workers with severe autism to have steady work in the same kinds of jobs held by people without autism. Descriptions of recycling jobs and delivery jobs that are held by workers with autism are provided on the following pages.

Recycling Worker

Job Description: A recycling worker crushes and sorts by color plastic and metal beverage containers for recycling.

Worksite Description: This job is with a recycling company that has a large warehouse and open yard. The company has about 25 employees, including 3 workers with autism who perform recycling tasks.

Employees with Autism

Worker 1: Speaks clearly in complete sentences, borderline range of intellectual functioning, presents sporadic self-injury and aggression

Worker 2: Speaks in complete sentences but speech is unclear, moderate mental retardation, property destruction, aggression, severe self-injury (including hitting self, head banging, ear banging, arm banging, kicking self, and finger picking)

Worker 3: Speaks in full sentences, moderate mental retardation, aggression, property destruction, problems with social communication (including repetitive questions and standing too close while speaking)

Job Tasks

- Crush plastic bottles
- Separate plastic bottles by color and put them in bags
- Scoop bi-metal cans into piles that are later placed in trash receptacles
- Bail flattened cardboard boxes
- Collect trash
- Sweep

Equipment, Machinery, and Hand Tools Needed to Complete Job Tasks

- Shovel
- Rake
- Trash receptacles
- Bailing machine
- Broom

Potential Problems in Job Completion

- Volunteer job—may not be paid
- Inclement weather
- Self-stimulation slows productivity

Modifications and Accommodations to Site or Task

- Job coach to assist with training, productivity, and behavior management
- Behavior management plans, including positive reinforcement, self-management, alternate sensory stimuli, prompt hierarchy, extinction, and procedures for managing dangerous behavior

Paper Deliverer

Job Description: A paper deliverer folds and puts newspapers in plastic bags for delivery and then delivers them once a week.

Worksite Description: This job is with a company that supplies local newspapers to several communities. The newspapers are distributed to residences in the community. Employees with autism deliver newspapers by themselves or in pairs.

Employees with Autism

Worker 1: Speaks in sentences but speech is unclear, profound mental retardation, prompt dependence, self-injury, tantrums, afraid of dogs, difficulties with communication skills (including loud echolalia and perseverative verbalizations)

Worker 2: Communicates using limited manual signs and pictures, profound mental retardation, shrieking, running away, noncompliance, property destruction, grabbing at others, feces smearing

Worker 3: Speaks clearly in full sentences, mild mental retardation, crying, yelling, squealing, task refusal

Job Tasks

- Fold, rubber band, and put newspapers in plastic bags
- Put newspapers in a canvas delivery bag
- Deliver newspapers door to door

Equipment, Machinery, and
Hand Tools Needed to Complete Job Tasks

- Rubber bands
- Plastic bags
- Canvas bag

Potential Problems in Job Completion

- Lifting the heavy bag of newspapers
- Fine motor tasks of folding, banding, and bagging newspapers
- Safely crossing streets

Modifications and Accommodations to Site or Task

- Job coach to assist with training, productivity, and behavior management
- Job coach assistance provided for difficult aspects of task
- Close supervision and training to cross street safely
- Behavior management plans, including positive reinforcement, alternate sensory stimuli, noncontingent access to reinforcers, liberal snack schedule, prompt hierarchy, extinction, and procedures for managing dangerous behavior

Groundskeeper

Job Description: A groundskeeper works seasonally picking up trash in a warehouse and on the grounds of a waste removal and recycling company.

Worksite Description: This job is with a large waste removal company where garbage trucks are parked in the warehouse and on the grounds. The company employs approximately 100 workers, including 2 or 3 workers with autism who work on the grounds.

Employees with Autism

Worker 1: Communicates using key words, profound mental retardation, noncompliance, refusal to move, severe self-injury (including head banging)

Worker 2: Communicates using sounds and gestures, profound mental retardation, screaming, self-stimulation, aggression, property destruction, noncompliance, lack of independence performing tasks

Worker 3: Communicates using sounds and gestures, severe mental retardation, noncompliance, hooting, rectal digging, feces smearing, aggression (including grabbing others, hitting and biting others)

Job Tasks

- Pick up trash that falls off the trucks that unload garbage
- Wash down waste trucks using a pressure hose

Equipment, Machinery, and Hand Tools Needed to Complete Job Tasks

- Gloves
- Pressure hose
- Trash receptacles

Potential Problems in Job Completion

- Volunteer positions—may not be paid
- Trash needs to be picked up alongside the road, which could be dangerous.

Modifications and Accommodations to Site or Task

- Job coach to assist with training, productivity, and behavior management
- Employees who are in danger of bolting or wandering into the road do not pick up trash along the road.
- Behavior management plans, including positive reinforcement, alternate sensory stimuli, noncontingent access to reinforcers, liberal snack schedule, prompt hierarchy, extinction, and procedures for managing dangerous behavior

Recycling Worker

Job Description: A recycling worker works in a paper recycling plant.

Worksite Description: This job is with a large recycling company. There is a warehouse, a trailer, and a recycling yard where the employees work. The warehouse employs approximately 10–15 workers, 3 of whom have autism.

Employees with Autism

Worker 1: Speaks in sentences but speech is unclear, profound mental retardation, prompt dependence, self-injury, tantrums, unconventional verbalizations (including loud echolalia, perseverative verbalizations, and rocking)

Worker 2: Communicates using key words, severe mental retardation, noncompliance, shrieking, self-injury, ritualistic behaviors leading to tantrums, low productivity

Worker 3: Speaks clearly in complete sentences, borderline range of intellectual functioning, sporadic self-injury and aggression

Job Tasks

- Tear perforated edges off of forms
- Separate different types of paper into bins
- Pick up glossy paper from the floor, which is spread with newspaper

Equipment, Machinery, and Hand Tools Needed to Complete Job Tasks

- Recycling bins
- Gloves
- Earphones to muffle noise

Potential Problems in Job Completion

- Volunteer position—may not be paid
- Very dirty worksite
- Low production due to self-stimulation
- Dangerous environment due to moving trucks and forklifts

Modifications and Accommodations to Site or Task

- Job coach to assist with training, productivity, and behavior management
- Behavior management plans, including positive reinforcement, self-management, graduated guidance, social skills training, prompt hierarchy, extinction, and procedures for managing dangerous behavior

CASE STUDY #1—ALAN
• • • • • • • • •

Employee Description

Alan is a 33-year-old man with moderate mental retardation and autism, which is characterized by extreme social withdrawal, language impairments, and abnormal responses to sensory stimuli. He can be severely self-injurious by picking at his skin, hitting his ears with his hands, banging his arms against hard objects, and kicking his own leg. Alan also grabs people's clothing and refuses to let go. Sometimes he grabs at his job coach while they are driving in a car. He displays many self-stimulatory behaviors. Alan tightly holds onto objects and refuses to let go. He also holds papers and other objects under his chin and arms and small lint balls between his fingers. He tightly wraps his wrists and fingers with rubber bands and strings, thereby cutting off his circulation. Alan also attempts to store food and dangerous objects such as pins, paper clips, and bits of glass in his mouth. Efforts to remove objects from his hand or mouth can cause tantrums, which are characterized by self-injury, grabbing others, and loud yelling. All of these behaviors interfere with Alan's willingness to do job tasks. However, Alan has splinter skills, including the ability to read and write, and some language comprehension.

Employee History

Alan spent several of his early years in segregated local schools for people with developmental disabilities. However, because his behaviors were so difficult to manage, Alan was transferred to an out-of-state institutional school for children with developmental disabilities. During a 10-year period, he was placed in three different institutions. At the age of 21 years, he was transferred to his first integrated program, a supported employment and residential program for people with autism.

In the supported employment program, Alan has held several jobs. Initially, he worked in the recycling industry sorting papers and beverage containers. His first job was a volunteer position that he left in order to obtain paid employment. He worked briefly as a bulk mailing clerk, hardware packer, and food service worker, but lost these jobs due to problem behaviors. For approximately 3 years, he worked part time as a shredding clerk in a county government office. At that job, he worked in a small office separated from other employees. He was eventually terminated from the job due to his screaming at work. It is clear from his employment history that although Alan held some jobs for periods of time, he had not found suitable employment.

Description of Company and Job

The company that Alan works for produces a local weekly newspaper that is distributed in the county where Alan lives. The company employs many workers who do a variety of jobs associated with running a newspaper. Alan's job is to distribute the newspaper to local residences once a week. He binds the papers with a rubber band, inserts them into plastic bags, and then delivers them by walking through residential neighborhoods.

Setting Up the Job

This newspaper delivery job was considered a good match for Alan for several reasons. First, to prevent self-injury it was important to keep Alan's hands busy doing job tasks. This job requires him to wrap the newspapers with rubber bands and then put them into a plastic bag. In addition, when delivering the papers, Alan has to hold a newspaper in his hand, which helps to prevent him from hitting himself. Furthermore, he enjoys holding things in his hands. Second, the work environment is free of tables and other furniture that Alan would bang his arms against. Finally, some of his behavior problems, such as yelling and grabbing others, are less job threatening as he does not work in close proximity to others.

Because Alan's job task is relatively simple, the job coach only needed to develop a task analysis for preparing the newspaper for delivery before Alan started to work.

Establishing Employment Supports

Prior to admission to the supported employment program, Alan was evaluated by agency staff to determine his need for support.

Determination of Supports   It was clear from the frequency and intensity of Alan's behavior problems that he would require direct supervision from a job coach in order to function in a competitive job. In addition, agency staff realized that his job coach would be unable to safely manage Alan and another worker with autism at the same time. His job coach needed to be ready at all times to manage his dangerous, self-injurious behaviors. For these reasons, Alan was provided one-to-one supervision from a job coach.

Description of Job Coach Duties   The principal duty of Alan's job coach is to implement his behavior management plan and to consistently run procedures designed to prevent him from injuring himself. The job coach is also responsible for teaching Alan how to do his job tasks and supervising his work.

Description of Behavior Plan   Because of the numerous functions that Alan's behaviors serve, his behavior plan is quite complicated. A functional assessment revealed that Alan tended to act out when there were changes in the environment, particularly changes in staff. He also acted out if he was not allowed to engage in a preferred behavior, such as storing sharp objects in his mouth. The lack of structured activities and lack of positive attention from others also resulted in self-injurious and self-stimulatory behaviors. Concerning consequences, Alan seemed to enjoy the sensory feedback obtained from many of his behaviors. He liked the pressure of objects in his mouth and hands. He would also scratch his fingers to draw blood or to get medical salves or Band-Aids placed on his fingers. Initially, it was discovered that the more staff said, "Stop it," the higher the frequency of his self-injury; therefore, it was determined that staff attention was a factor in maintaining his self-injurious behavior. Finally, it was discovered that he would sometimes bang objects or his ears to get staff to restrain his arms. He seemed to like the pressure of someone holding down his arms.

Alan's behavior program required that staff provide reinforcers about every 20 minutes for some non–self-injurious and nonaggressive behavior. The target behaviors included using his hands for job tasks, keeping his arms at his side and feet on the floor, having an empty mouth, and keeping his hands on his work materials. These target behaviors were selected to encourage him to use his hands appropriately for anything other than self-injury. Reinforcers had to be selected carefully to provide him with the sensory stimulation that he apparently wanted. Reinforcers included tactile objects, such as rubber balls, cotton, yarn that he was allowed to hold for brief periods of time, hand lotion, and cologne. In addition, his job coach would firmly squeeze his arms or shoulders and praise him when he was involved in an appropriate behavior. Reinforcers were not given within 5 minutes of self-injury or aggression.

Previously, Alan would hit himself and his job coach would hold his hands down for a period of time. This physical contact appeared to be reinforcing. To prevent inadvertent reinforcement of self-injury, guidelines were developed to help his job coach manage dangerous behaviors without reinforcing them. The job coach was trained to block Alan's attempts at self-injury quickly and verbally redirect him back to his job task. This procedure decreased the need for lengthy physical interventions. The job coach also provided Alan with frequent instructions on where he should keep his hands. For example, prior to delivering the newspapers, the job coach instructed Alan to use his hands to hold the newspapers. During car rides, he was instructed to keep his hands in his lap. A final safety feature of Alan's behavior program was hourly checks of his mouth to remove sharp objects and provide a reinforcer if his mouth was empty.

Description of Instructional Procedures Alan was a quick learner, and tasks were taught primarily through verbal instruction and modeling. The reinforcement component of his behavior plan provided motivation for him to remain on task.

Outcomes

Alan has been at his job as a paper deliverer for about 3 years. He is paid a commission dependent on the number of newspapers he delivers. Although the job offers only a limited number of hours, it represents a significant gain for someone with behavior problems as severe as Alan's. This job has proven to be stable because the work environment is such that he is not likely to be terminated due to his behaviors. Alan also works part-time as a shredding clerk and as a janitor, which keeps him busy throughout the week. Alan's self-injury and aggression have decreased substantially from hundreds of incidents of self-injury daily to just a few per month.

CASE STUDY #2—LARRY
• • • • • • • • • •

Employee Description

Larry is a 36-year-old man with moderate mental retardation and with autism. He can speak in complete sentences, although his speech rhythm has a rote quality to it. Most of his speech consists of perseverative questioning. It is possible to ask him simple questions and get a response; however, he typically reverts back to his perseverative questions.

Larry has a history of severe behavior problems. He has hit other people, pulled hair, ripped his clothing, thrown furniture, destroyed property, hit and bit himself, and run away from staff. His aggression has been severe, and on several occasions has resulted in staff having broken bones. He was terminated from his last sheltered workshop because he punched a secretary in the chest who had just returned to work following surgery. On the job, Larry sometimes accosted and grabbed visitors. Larry also paced back and forth constantly and had difficulty attending to his work tasks.

Employee History

As a child, Larry attended segregated schools for children with autism. He remained in such schools until age 21 years. At that time, he was living in his parent's home and was placed in a series of sheltered workshops, from which he was expelled because of his aggressive behavior. At 26 years of age, he was placed in a supported employment program designed for individuals with autism. At the same time, he moved into a group home for adults with autism.

Larry's first job was at a recycling plant where he sorted aluminum and plastic beverage containers for recycling. Larry held this job for 7 months, but was terminated due to his slow pace of work. He then took a job at another recycling center where he removed carbon paper from government forms and sorted papers by color. He resigned to take a higher paying job at another paper recycling center.

Description of Company and Job

The newspaper recycling company that Larry worked for employed about 20 workers, including management staff, truck drivers, and recycling workers. Larry was a recycling worker. His job duties involved walking across the warehouse floor, which was covered with newspapers, and picking up the colored inserts from the black and white newsprint. Larry put the colored paper into a plastic bag that he held. Larry was also responsible for sorting plastic and paper bags.

Setting Up the Job

Because the job task was relatively easy to do, the job coach only had to spend 1 day at the recycling company observing the other workers doing the job and learning about the schedule and the environment before Larry could begin working. This job was considered a good match because Larry had to walk to find the colored paper among the newsprint, and he seemed to enjoy the constant movement. In addition, the job involved a relatively easy discrimination task; that is, discriminating between colored and black and white newsprint, which was something Larry could readily do. Finally, the warehouse was a large open area where other employees worked far enough away that Larry's dangerous behaviors could be managed without possible injury to others and with minimal disruption to the company.

Establishing Supports

Larry's interdisciplinary team met and reviewed his behaviors and skills to determine necessary levels of support.

Determination of Supports The team agreed that Larry required full-time supervision because of his severe behavior problems and because of his language and social skills difficulties. It was clear from his history that Larry required a high level of structure and constant supervision to ensure the safety of himself and others. That supervision would be supplied at work by a job coach. The job coach would supervise him and one other adult with autism full-time during their workday. Larry was paired with another worker with autism who had no dangerous behaviors so that the job coach was always free to manage Larry when he had a behavior problem.

Description of Job Coach Duties The job coach drove Larry to work, taught him his tasks, supervised his work, assisted him in remaining on task and in his work area, and helped him manage his behavior problems. In addition, the job coach was responsible for teaching appropriate social skills and for intervening when inappropriate social behaviors occurred.

Description of Behavior Plan A psychologist consulted with Larry's supported employment supervisor and his job coach to develop a behavior change plan for him. A functional assessment of Larry's behavior was done and revealed several antecedent events. Larry had trouble handling changes in the environment, including changes in staff, normal routine, and the weather. During periods of change, Larry would become agitated, talk about aggressive or destructive acts, and act out. In contrast, he did well in structured environments that presented few changes. Larry also disliked hearing corrections or criticism from staff, particularly if they told him to stop doing something or were harsh with him. Concerning consequences, Larry often got extra attention in the form of conversation and counseling in an effort to calm him down. The purpose of the behavior plan was to assist Larry in exhibiting acceptable behavior at work, with a decrease in bolting, self-injury, aggression, and property destruction, and an increase in more acceptable social behaviors. The plan included hourly ratings on the following targeted behaviors: keeping hands and feet to self (i.e., no aggression), correct use of property (i.e., no property destruction), remaining in his work area, having interesting conversations (i.e., no conversation about aggressive or destructive acts), respecting his body (i.e., no self-injury), and completing his assigned tasks. Because Larry has some reading skills, these rules were written out for him and each hour he and his job coach rated his performance on each behavior. Criteria were set for him to earn a daily soda and a weekly activity reinforcer with a favorite staff person. Additionally, the behavior plan contained guidelines for leading Larry in more appropriate, less perseverative conversation; instructions for preventing behavior outbursts at work; and guidelines on how to handle outbursts should they occur. The plan called for hourly praise and avoidance of a critical, negative tone, which often served as an antecedent for aggression. This behavior plan was implemented throughout each day by his job coach. Because Larry's aggressive behavior could be severe, the job coach was instructed in nonaversive management of aggressive behavior so that he could prevent injury to Larry or others should an outburst occur.

A modification was also made to Larry's work area. Periodically, forklifts would drive through his work area spreading newspapers across the floor. Because Larry often paced back and forth, the quick moving forklifts posed a danger to his safety. To help ensure his safety, permission was obtained from the supervisor to mark off a safe work area for Larry by putting brightly colored masking tape on the floor. Larry was then instructed to remain within the marked off area and reinforced for staying there.

Description of Instructional Procedures Although Larry had the skills necessary to do his job, he frequently wandered off-task and paced aimlessly around the warehouse. To encourage on-task behaviors, an item for completing his assigned tasks was included on his hourly ratings. Larry was given credit for that item if he worked diligently on his recycling tasks. He was also praised for attending to his work and for working quickly. Finally, because Larry had difficulty remaining on task, a prompt hierarchy was used to encourage on-task behavior. Larry was directed back to his task in a noncritical manner. First, the job coach asked, "What's next?" to get him back to task. If he did not return to task within 5 seconds, a specific verbal prompt such as "Pick up the colored paper" was given. If he did not return to working, the job coach then progressed to gestures and finally to light physical guidance if necessary.

Outcomes

Although sporadic problems with aggression and self-injury persisted at that job, there was a gradual decrease in the frequency of those behaviors. In addition, because of the way the work environment was laid out and due to effective management of problems by his job coach, these incidents did not prove job threatening. Larry held this job as a recycling worker for 15 months and then resigned to take a job making more money as a stock clerk in a hardware store. Since leaving this job, Larry's employment history has been varied with occasional interruptions due to periodic increases in the frequency of behavior problems. He continues to need a full-time job coach because of the intensity of his periodic behavior problems. However, his ability to hold down jobs for long periods of time is indeed remarkable given his history of serious destructive behavior and his cognitive and language limitations. When Larry is supervised by a job coach who is structured, gentle but firm, and who runs his behavior plan consistently, he is able to maintain employment with a minimum of problem behaviors. His current employer is pleased with his performance, and the outlook for continued employment at his current job is high.

CHAPTER 12

Jobs in Government

People with autism have been employed by both the local and the federal government to fill clerical, warehouse, library, cleaning, mailing, and printing jobs. Workers in these jobs have performed a variety of tasks, including shredding coupons, filing, cleaning, performing quality control, washing government vehicles, making identification cards, and sorting and labeling books. Some employees with autism work in government jobs temporarily while seeking other employment; others have made government employment a career.

Government jobs occasionally have employment arrangements that are designed to be beneficial for workers with disabilities. For example, the federal government has procedures in place that allow workers with disabilities to bypass certain requirements, such as the need to pass a civil service exam. The employment specialist seeking jobs for workers with autism in federal, state, and local government positions can investigate these types of employment arrangements.

ADVANTAGES OF GOVERNMENT EMPLOYMENT

Government employment is varied and offers jobs in a number of fields. For example, one government employee may work in a library, another may work in a warehouse, and a third may work in a local courthouse. Some government jobs have provided stable employment for more than a decade to employees with autism. Because government jobs vary so much in terms of work environment and types of tasks, the advantages of government employment are a function of the particular job.

Work Environment

Government jobs are located in a variety of environments, including public libraries, courthouses, print shops, warehouses, and offices. The advantages of these environments are specific to the worker with autism. Because some workers with autism display disruptive behaviors in the workplace, some environments are more suitable for these workers than other environments. For example, an employee who sorts and labels books in a library is able to do these tasks in a back room where an occasional behavioral outburst will not disrupt visitors who are in the public areas of the library and cannot see the back rooms.

Some employees with autism work in government warehouses, such as a county liquor control building where they clean bottles and cans and replace damaged beverage containers. This warehouse environment is agreeable to some workers with autism because of its large work area in which employees work near, but not too near, co-workers. This type of work area is free of distractions from customers or visitors to the site. Although some workers with autism enjoy interacting co-workers without disabilities, others are socially withdrawn and prefer work environments that provide some contact with co-workers without presenting overwhelming social interruptions or demands. Other jobs that offer this type of environment are print shop jobs, janitorial jobs in government buildings, and government car washing jobs.

Nature of the Tasks

Because of the variety of government jobs, the demands of the jobs vary as well. Some government jobs include tasks that are easily performed by workers with autism who lack verbal and social skills and who have mental retardation. These workers have been hired by government agencies to do jobs such as light cleaning tasks, collecting materials for recycling, shredding coupons, cleaning bottles, and washing cars. Although these tasks do not require sophisticated social, verbal, or cognitive skills, they do require skills that these workers with autism often have, such as visual discrimination and fine motor abilities.

Some government jobs are clerical, including typing, filing, collating, alphabetizing, and preparing envelopes for mailing. These jobs are suitable for workers with autism who have either reading, word recognition, or fine motor skills. For employees who prefer seat work to work that requires a great deal of mobility, clerical tasks may be appropriate. In these jobs, workers remain in one area and usually do not need to participate in any gross motor activities, such as lifting merchandise or moving boxes.

Social Requirements

Government jobs held by employees with autism can be very task-oriented, rather than interpersonal in nature. For example, one employee with autism who works in a government information office prepares information packets for mailing instead of handling telephone inquiries that come into the same office. Although numerous government jobs involve some kind of interaction with the public, not all do.

Other Advantages

Some government jobs are maintained through contracts between the supported employment agency and the government agency. The government pays the supported employment agency, which in turn pays the workers with autism. This arrangement has some advantages. It provides flexibility in terms of placement of workers. If a worker with autism tries a contracted job and for some reason it is unsuitable for him or her, another worker from the supported employment agency may be placed in that position. Furthermore, the flexibility of some government jobs has allowed these placements to be used as stepping stones for more suitable employment. For example, one supported employment agency has a contract with a local government office that places four workers in jobs that involve sorting items. At various times, a worker from the agency has been placed in one of these positions just until a more suitable job is found for him or her. At that point, the worker moves to a better position and the sorting job is taken by another worker who might be between jobs, in need of additional part-time work, or experiencing a seasonal layoff.

DISADVANTAGES OF GOVERNMENT EMPLOYMENT

Work Environment

Some government jobs are located in offices that are separated from one another by partitions. These offices are typically orderly and quiet, which is suitable for some workers with autism. Employees are free to work without the interference of co-workers. However, for workers with autism who display behavioral outbursts, these partitioned offices are not adequate at filtering out the disruption of co-workers. The partitions are typically not high enough or thick enough to protect co-workers from possible screaming or banging. These sorts of disruptions in this type of environment can cause a worker with autism to lose his or her job.

Cognitive Requirements

The numerous clerical jobs available in the government may not be available to workers with autism because of cognitive disabilities. Often, these jobs require some academic skills.

Other Disadvantages

As mentioned previously, some government jobs are arranged through contracts between the government and the supported employment agency. This process, although often beneficial, can also be a disadvantage because it is a fairly complex arrangement to negotiate. The supported employment agency must have the knowledge, connections, and skill to find such employment arrangements, negotiate them, and oversee them. The application process for a government job can be protracted and complicated and may take months or longer to complete. Although these placements can provide long-term stability and good job matches, the administrative requirements are more complicated than those simply between an employer and a worker with autism.

Another administrative disadvantage in government employment is that certain government jobs have regulations that restrict the supports a supported employment agency can put into place. For example, there have been difficulties with placing job coaches in federal jobs.

Although there are workers with autism who have had paying positions with government agencies for years, there have also been situations in which workers with autism are contracted to work as volunteers. Occasionally, there is an initial understanding that the position will be a paid position, but payment is never arranged and the employee continues to work without pay.

Finally, government contracts between supported employment agencies and the government must be negotiated annually. In some cases, this annual renegotiation is smooth, and stable employment is provided for many years; however, if there is any dissatisfaction on the part of the government manager, the annual renewal process can be used to terminate employment. This process is sensitive to changes in managers, changes in the goals of the contracting agency, and political concerns.

JOBS IN GOVERNMENT

Workers with autism have enjoyed long-term employment in government jobs. Some workers have used government jobs as a stepping stone to more suitable employment, as interim employment between jobs, or as temporary employment during seasonal layoffs. Government jobs come in a variety of environments and involve a wide range of tasks. These jobs have proven to be well suited for individuals with autism of varying cognitive, language, and behavior skills. Descriptions of government jobs held by workers with autism are provided on the following pages.

Janitorial Worker

Job Description: A janitorial worker collects material for recycling from offices and does janitorial tasks.

Worksite Description: This job is in a large county office building. There are more than 1,000 workers in the building. The three workers with autism and their job coach work throughout the building.

Employees with Autism

Worker 1:   Communicates using limited signs and pictures; profound mental retardation; property destruction, aggression, noncompliance, rocking, self-injury (including head banging)

Worker 2:   Communicates using limited manual signs and pictures, severe mental retardation, significant difficulties with social skills, language, independent task completion, and toileting skills

Worker 3:   Speaks clearly in sentences, moderate mental retardation, self-injury, yelling, echolalia, perseverative speech

Job Tasks

- Collect paper for recycling
- Collect cans for recycling
- Dust stairwells
- Wipe down elevators
- Pick up trash around dumpster

Equipment, Machinery, and Hand Tools Needed to Complete Job Tasks

- Rolling cart
- Dustpan
- Dust rags
- Dumpster

Potential Problems in Job Completion

- The job involves going outdoors frequently, which makes work difficult during bad weather.
- The job requires crossing streets with heavy traffic, which can be dangerous.

Modifications and Accommodations to Site or Task

- Job coach to assist with training, productivity, and behavior management
- Constant monitoring to ensure safety and task completion
- Behavior management plans, including positive reinforcement, prompt hierarchy, alternate sensory stimuli, extinction, and procedures for managing dangerous behavior

GOVERNMENT

Office Clerical Worker

Job Description: An office clerical worker retrieves and mails publications requested by customers.

Worksite Description: This job is with a large federal government agency that informs and protects the public on issues related to food and drugs. The agency employs more than 1,000 workers, 35 work in the same division. There are four workers with autism.

Employees with Autism

Worker 1: Speaks clearly in complete sentences, borderline range of intellectual functioning, sporadic self-injury and aggression

Worker 2: Speaks in full sentences, average intelligence, difficulties with social skills (including not asking for help when needed, interrupting others, and asking inappropriate questions)

Worker 3: Speaks clearly in full sentences, mild mental retardation, swearing, aggression, stealing, urinating in inappropriate places, leaving the office without asking, undressing in public, inappropriate sexual behaviors

Worker 4: Speaks clearly in sentences, high-average cognitive functioning, frequent task and program participation refusal, difficulty relating to employers and co-workers

Job Tasks

- Retrieve publications from shelves as requested
- Place publications in envelopes
- Apply address labels to envelopes
- Operate copy machine
- Miscellaneous errands

Equipment, Machinery, and Hand Tools Needed to Complete Job Tasks

- Stamping machine
- Xerox machine
- Envelopes
- Address labels

Potential Problems in Job Completion

- Low productivity

Modifications and Accommodations to Site or Task

- Job coach to assist with training, productivity, and behavior management
- Behavior management plans, including periodic behavior ratings, positive reinforcement, social skills training, prompt hierarchy, extinction, and procedures for managing dangerous behavior

Office Clerical Worker

Job Description: An office clerical worker collects information regarding the use of public school facilities.

Worksite Description: This job is with a small county agency responsible for coordinating services used by the county public school system. There are five employees, including one with autism.

Employee with Autism

Worker 1:   Speaks clearly in full sentences, average intelligence, self-injury, limited social and language skills, repetitive inappropriate conversations, invades other people's personal space and privacy (including reading personal written material)

Job Tasks

- Alphabetize forms
- Put forms in numerical order
- Label forms
- Fill out building use forms
- Ask for assistance with forms missing information
- File forms
- Check work

Equipment, Machinery, and Hand Tools Needed to Complete Job Tasks

- Forms
- Labels

Potential Problems in Job Completion

- Problems relating to co-workers

Modifications and Accommodations to Site or Task

- Social skills training
- Self-management

Janitorial Worker

Job Description: A janitorial worker cleans a small courthouse annex.

Worksite Description: This job takes place in a county courthouse building that has been vacated for renovations.

Employees with Autism

Worker 1: Communicates using limited signs and pictures, profound mental retardation, property destruction, aggression, noncompliance, rocking, eating and hoarding garbage, self-injury (including head banging)

Worker 2: Communicates using limited manual signs and pictures; severe mental retardation; significant problems with social skills, language, independence, and toileting skills

Worker 3: Speaks clearly in sentences, high-average cognitive functioning, frequent task and program participation refusal, difficulty relating to employers and co-workers, excessive phone use during work hours, frequently late for work

Job Tasks

- Clean bathrooms
- Mop floors
- Vacuum floors
- Empty trash cans and take trash to dumpster
- Sweep floors

Equipment, Machinery, and Hand Tools Needed to Complete Job Tasks

- Mop and pail
- Broom
- Vacuum cleaner
- Dust rags

Potential Problems in Job Completion

- Low productivity

Modifications and Accommodations to Site or Task

- Job coach to assist with training, productivity, and behavior management
- Behavior management plans, including positive reinforcement, alternate sensory stimuli, periodic ratings, prompt hierarchy, extinction, and procedures for managing dangerous behavior

Janitorial Worker

Job Description: A janitorial worker cleans a county courthouse.

Worksite Description: This job is with a county agency that provides janitorial services to county buildings. The work takes place in a county courthouse. There are 50 workers in the agency; 5 work in the same building, including 1 with autism.

Employee with Autism

Worker 1:   Speaks clearly in full sentences, mild mental retardation, self-injury, property destruction, aggression, bolting from moving vehicles, yelling

Job Tasks

- Clean bathrooms
- Wipe down benches

Equipment, Machinery, and Hand Tools Needed to Complete Job Tasks

- Rags
- Buckets
- Cleaning products

Potential Problems in Job Completion

- Problems relating to co-workers

Modifications and Accommodations to Site or Task

- Job coach to assist with training, productivity, and behavior management
- Behavior management plans, including periodic ratings, positive reinforcement, extinction, procedures for managing dangerous behavior, and guidelines for riding in cars

Office Clerical Worker

Job Description: An office clerical worker completes clerical and other miscellaneous tasks.

Worksite Description: This job is with a county department of transportation. The work takes place in a conference room in a large office building. There are 20 employees, including 3 workers with autism.

Employees with Autism

Worker 1:   Communicates with sounds and gestures, profound mental retardation, self-injury, aggression, property destruction

Worker 2:   Speaks in complete sentences but speech is unclear, moderate mental retardation, noncompliance, wandering away from tasks, screaming, loud perseverative echolalia

Worker 3:   Speaks in sentences but speech is unclear, moderate mental retardation, crying, self-induced vomiting, toilet stuffing, urinating and defecating in clothing

Job Tasks

- Tear used taxi coupons to destroy them
- Put inserts in envelopes for mailing
- Label envelopes
- Prepare promotional materials, including blowing up balloons and packing toys in bags
- Collate
- Collect mail from other offices

Equipment, Machinery, and Hand Tools Needed to Complete Job Tasks

- Pump to fill up balloons
- Labels
- Envelopes
- Bags for packing toys

Potential Problems in Job Completion

- Low-quality work

Modifications and Accommodations to Site or Task

- Job coach to assist with training, productivity, and behavior management
- Behavior management plans, including positive reinforcement, prompt hierarchy, voice volume training, extinction, and procedures for managing dangerous behavior

Coupon Shredding Clerk

Job Description: A coupon shredding clerk shreds coupons as well as does various clerical tasks.

Worksite Description: This job is with a small division of a county transit service department. There are 10 employees, including 1 with autism.

Employee with Autism

Worker 1:   Speaks in complete sentences but speech is unclear, moderate mental retardation, property destruction, aggression, severe self-injury (including hitting self, head banging, ear banging, arm banging, kicking self, and finger picking)

Job Tasks

- Tear transportation coupons
- Bundle bus schedules
- Stack bus tokens
- Operate copy machines
- Sort papers

Equipment, Machinery, and Hand Tools Needed to Complete Job Tasks

- Copy machine

Potential Problems in Job Completion

- Loose staples in the work area are dangerous because the worker eats them.

Modifications and Accommodations to Site or Task

- Job coach to assist with training, productivity, and behavior management
- Behavior management plans, including positive reinforcement, prompt hierarchy, alternate sensory stimuli, guidelines to prevent screaming, extinction, and procedures for managing dangerous behavior

Beer Breakage Warehouse Worker

Job Description: A beer breakage warehouse worker is involved in quality control of alcoholic beverages before they are distributed to the public.

Worksite Description: This job is with a county agency that provides quality control of alcoholic beverages. There are 50 workers in the warehouse; 2 employees with autism work alone in a separate area.

Employees with Autism

Worker 1: Speaks clearly in sentences, mild mental retardation, self-injury, property destruction, aggression, problems with social use of language (including perseveration), drinks bottles of beer while working, displays incidents of taking off clothes in bathroom and returning to work undressed

Worker 2: Speaks clearly in sentences, average intellectual functioning, difficulties with social and language skills, aggressive upon provocation, curses loudly, frequently hangs around administrative offices bothering staff members

Job Tasks

- Clean beverage cans and bottles
- Attach six-packs of cans with plastic rings
- Replace damaged bottles and cans

Equipment, Machinery, and Hand Tools Needed to Complete Job Tasks

- Rags
- Plastic rings
- Beer bottles and cans

Potential Problems in Job Completion

- Forklifts constantly moving around the work area are dangerous.

Modifications and Accommodations to Site or Task

- Job coach to assist with training, productivity, and behavior management
- Behavior management plans, including periodic ratings, positive reinforcement, self-management, social skills training, prompt hierarchy, extinction, and procedures for managing dangerous behavior

Bindery Worker

Job Description: A bindery worker is involved in various steps in the production of printed matter.

Worksite Description: This job is with a county mail service and printing agency. The work takes place in a large room in a multistory office building. There are 25 employees, including 2 workers with autism.

Employees with Autism

Worker 1:   Speaks clearly in full sentences, average intelligence, self-injury, limited social and language skills, repetitive inappropriate conversations, invasion of other people's personal space and privacy (including reading personal written material)

Worker 2:   Speaks in full sentences, borderline cognitive functioning, poor personal grooming, limited social and language skills

Job Tasks

- Separate books
- Collate and bind bulletins using collating machine
- Cut paper using paper cutting machine
- Operate drill press
- Operate hole punch
- Staple using foot stapler
- Glue stacks of paper to make pads
- Pack orders for mailing

Equipment, Machinery, and Hand Tools Needed to Complete Job Tasks

- Collating machine
- Drill press for making pads
- Foot stapler
- Hole punch
- Padding glue and brush

Potential Problems in Job Completion

- Problems with productivity

Modifications and Accommodations to Site or Task

- Job coach to assist with training, productivity, and behavior management
- Social skills training

Office Clerical Worker

Job Description: An office clerical worker completes various clerical tasks.

Worksite Description: This job is with a large federal health care agency. The work takes place in a building where there is an office and a warehouse. Fifteen employees work in the warehouse; the worker with autism works alone in the office.

Employee with Autism

Worker 1:   Speaks in full sentences, mild mental retardation, task refusal, property destruction, sulking, aggression

Job Tasks

- Prepare requisitions
- Make charge plates
- Laminate sign cards

Equipment, Machinery, and Hand Tools Needed to Complete Job Tasks

- Purchase orders
- Charge plate maker
- Laminating machine

Potential Problems in Job Completion

- Low productivity

Modifications and Accommodations to Site or Task

- Job coach to assist with training, productivity, and behavior management
- Behavior management plans, including positive reinforcement, written schedule, prompt hierarchy, extinction, and procedures for managing dangerous behavior

Book Sorter

Job Description: A book sorter sorts books, which come from 25 county libraries, into bins according to destination.

Worksite Description: This job is with a medium-size county library. The work takes place in a book sorting room separate from other offices. There are approximately 100 employees who work for the library; 2 employees work in the immediate area, and the library employs 3 workers with autism.

Employees with Autism

Worker 1:   Communicates using complete written sentences but is electively mute, average intellectual functioning, self-injury, noncompliance, ritualistic calculating during which he is unresponsive to verbal instruction

Worker 2:   Speaks in full sentences, borderline cognitive functioning, poor personal grooming, limited social and language skills

Worker 3:   Speaks in complete sentences but speech is unclear, severe mental retardation, nose picking, rummaging in trash for food

Job Tasks

- Sort books and reserve materials into bins by destination
- Load bins onto trucks

Equipment, Machinery, and Hand Tools Needed to Complete Job Tasks

- Bins

Potential Problems in Job Completion

- Lack of work while waiting for shipments to arrive
- Co-workers uncomfortable around workers with autism
- Too much work on days following holidays
- Sorting area is crowded and noisy; this causes one worker to leave his work area.
- Some workers have difficulty reading alphabet codes used for sorting books.

Modifications and Accommodations to Site or Task

- Job coach to assist with training, productivity, and behavior management
- Behavior management plans, including periodic ratings, positive reinforcement, written schedule, social skills training, prompt hierarchy, extinction, and procedures for managing dangerous behavior

CASE STUDY—GEORGE

Employee Description

George is a 27-year-old man with autism and severe mental retardation. He has good receptive language but is nonverbal, communicating his basic needs with a few signs. George is severely withdrawn and prefers to be alone. He also has difficulty handling environmental changes, particularly changes in staff, to whom he becomes easily attached. Although George can attend well to tasks, he has several behavior problems, including sporadic aggression, property destruction, and self-injury. George's self-injury can be severe—he hits himself with his fist and bangs his head against hard objects. He is sometimes noncompliant and repeated prompts can lead to self-injury. Finally, George engages in self-stimulatory behaviors, such as rocking and hand flapping.

Employee History

George spent his early education in segregated, public special education centers. He also received respite residential care in an institution for people with developmental disabilities. At the age of 14 years, because of the severity of his aggression and self-injury, George was placed in an out-of-state, segregated residential school. He returned to his home state when he was 19 years old and attended a community-based residential and educational program for adolescents with autism. Other than living at home, this was his first integrated life experience. At the age of 21 years, George was transferred to a supported employment program for adults with autism.

Description of Company and Job

George's employment specialist found him a job working for the local county government as a custodian in county government buildings. When George first obtained this job, it had been worked out as a contract between the supported employment agency and the county government. Today, the job would be obtained through the supported employment agency responding to a request for proposals put out by the local government. Under either arrangement, the government pays the supported employment agency, and the agency in turn pays George.

George began this job about 1 month after entering the supported employment program. The job involves performing a variety of cleaning tasks in large county office buildings. Job tasks to be done include cleaning bathrooms, mopping floors, vacuuming floors, dusting furniture, sweeping, and emptying the trash. George is also responsible for collecting and separating paper and beverage containers to be recycled.

Setting Up the Job

Because this job position has several different tasks, the job coach needed to learn each task individually and to learn the sequence of tasks over the entire week. George had difficulty handling changes and transition; therefore, the job coach needed to be aware of these problems so that George could be informed of upcoming job tasks. The job coach spent about 1 week learning the job before George started working.

The job as a janitor was considered a good choice for George because he has better gross motor than fine motor skills. He demonstrated an ability to do cleaning tasks in his group home, and he seemed to enjoy them. Finally, janitorial work is done alone and requires little need for ongoing socialization. One problematic aspect of the job is that it requires frequent changes in task and location, something that George had difficulty with in the past.

Establishing Employment Supports

It was clear that George would require ongoing support at work to function in competitive employment. George's interdisciplinary team determined the necessary level of support by evaluating his behavior problems and instructional needs.

Determination of Supports Due to the severity of George's self-injurious behaviors, it was anticipated that he would require constant support and supervision on the job. Because George is nonverbal and has profound mental retardation, his team determined that he would not be able to learn his job tasks and his job schedule by the county's normal employee training procedures. Rather, he would need training provided by someone who is proficient in training workers with autism who have no language skills and have severe mental retardation.

The team did not feel that George required one-to-one supervision. He was capable of learning and performing multistep tasks and his behavior problems, although severe, occurred only sporadically. Therefore, it was determined that his job coach could supervise another worker with autism as well as George provided that the other worker did not also display any dangerous behaviors. It was important that his job coach be free to manage dangerous behaviors should they occur.

Description of Job Coach Duties The job coach is responsible for teaching a variety of janitorial tasks to George and for implementing necessary behavior strategies. The job coach is also responsible for assisting and supporting George when changes occur because they are especially difficult for him.

Description of Behavior Plan A functional assessment determined that George's self-injurious behaviors are often related to changes in the environment and to being told to do a task. Problems with environmental changes are handled by telling him about his schedule in advance, keeping his weekly routine as consistent as possible, and informing him of any necessary changes.

Over time, George has become very familiar with his work routine and can anticipate the next task. Self-injury is sometimes a response to being rushed, especially by new staff; therefore, his behavior program requires that staff always give adequate notice prior to changes in task, and that he be given time to comply with requests. Staff were cautioned against rushing him or repeatedly prompting him. George is also provided with social reinforcers in the form of praise, conversation, or attention about every 30 minutes for any behavior that is incompatible with self-injury or aggression. Special attention is paid to reinforcing work-related behaviors, such as initiating job tasks and working independently on job tasks. With these procedures, problem behaviors have been substantially reduced at work.

During work, George began to collect trash, such as paper and drink cans, and stuff them into his pockets. He would often return from work with his pockets full of papers and pens that he had taken from trash cans. He became agitated and self-injurious if his job coach prevented him from collecting trash or took the trash away from him. A functional assessment determined that the function of collecting trash was to obtain paper items and pens to keep in his pockets. To assist in eliminating this behavior, George was provided with similar, but clean, items to carry in his pockets. Now, each morning before he leaves for work, he is given his choice of objects that he can carry if he chooses to. These include sections from recent newspapers and pens. George usually takes a few of these objects and puts them into his pockets. At work, when he tries to collect items from the trash cans, he is redirected back to task. Because he already has the other objects in his pockets, he accepts the redirection. When George returns from work, he is praised if he only has the objects that he selected that morning in his pockets.

Description of Instructional Procedures   George's self-stimulatory behaviors sometimes interfere with completing tasks in a timely manner. He often rocks back and forth rather than do his work. In addition, if he is rushed to do a task, George may self-injure. Because of this, a hierarchy of prompts is used to promote on-task behaviors without unnecessarily rushing him. If George rocks for more than 2 minutes, a general prompt of "What's next?" is given. After 5–10 seconds if he fails to return to work, a more specific prompt, such as "Mop the floor," is given. If this does not work to get him back to task, a gestural cue is paired with a verbal prompt. If this is also unsuccessful, the job coach provides gentle physical guidance for him to return to work. George is never forced to do a task that he resists. With the prompt hierarchy, George is consistently redirected back to task in a structured, nonhurried manner that does not cause behavior problems. Gradually, George has become independent in doing his tasks.

Outcomes

George has now worked as a janitor for more than 5 years. His starting wage was $3.35 per hour and he now earns slightly more than $5.00 per hour for 25 hours of work each week. He has adjusted to the changes involved in doing a variety of tasks and even anticipates the next task. Dangerous behavior problems have decreased substantially, but they still occur when there are major environmental changes, particularly when familiar job coaches leave. Because of the presence of these dangerous behaviors, as well as the fact that he remains nonverbal with severe mental retardation, George still requires the full-time supervision of a job coach.

CHAPTER **13**

Advances and Future Directions

ince the mid-1980s, tremendous advances have been made in the vocational instruction and vocational accomplishments of people with autism. These accomplishments have cut across all aspects of vocational development for this population. Adolescents and adults with autism have begun to leave their segregated environments and enter the community. Some of these people have entered the community as workers, and have been able to earn salaries and work alongside employees without disabilities. Advances in instructional technology, behavioral technology, and the supported employment technology have enabled these individuals to become productive workers. The world of work has opened up to people with autism, and strides have been made in the variety of jobs they hold, the variety of environments in which they are employed, and the stability of their employment. This chapter reviews these gains and summarizes the advances that have made them possible. It also discusses future directions in employing people with autism.

WORKERS WITH AUTISM

In the past, the phrase "worker with autism" was a contradiction in terms. Individuals with autism have not had the same training and vocational opportunities as people with other developmental disabilities. When students with developmental disabilities were included in public education, students with autism were often considered uneducable and sent home. When young adults with developmental disabilities were served in day programs, young adults with autism often failed to meet the standards of behavior and again were sent home. When adults with developmental disabilities were given the opportunity to earn money in sheltered workshops, their peers with autism were considered unmanageable and were excluded. When adolescents and adults were given the opportunity to work in integrated, competitive environments, their peers with autism were considered unfit and, therefore, were excluded. In addition, an unfortunate segment of the population could not even enjoy the community integration afforded by living with their families because many individuals with autism have been housed in out-of-state residential schools or at institutions for people with mental illness or mental retardation.

Despite all of these setbacks, a major advance has been made in successfully employing people with autism. Since the early 1980s, individuals with autism have become workers with autism. Although they have been underrepresented in supported employment initiatives, there have been people with autism who have successfully worked and earned wages. This accomplishment, if only by a small percentage of individuals with autism, has implications for all people with autism.

This advance of employability has not been limited to so-called "high functioning" individuals with autism. People with all levels of autism, and all levels of cognitive, social, and behavioral functioning, have successfully held paid positions. Many people with autism who are mildly affected by the disorder and do not have mental retardation have been able to hold jobs without the support of job coaches. People with autism who have moderate mental retardation have been able to hold jobs with varying levels of support, depending on their social and communication skills and the presence of challenging behaviors. People with autism and profound mental retardation, without language skills and with challenging behaviors, have also had successful employment experiences with the support of trained job coaches.

This advance of workers with autism into the workplace cannot be appreciated fully without some word about salaries. Whereas, in many cases, people with autism entered the work force with trepidation and sometimes as volunteers, they have proven themselves to be wage-earners. Workers with autism have worked at salary levels ranging from below minimum wage (with a special worker's certificate) to salaries that are more than double minimum wage. There are some cases of workers with severe autism and mental retardation earning more money per hour than their job coaches. Therefore, although only a small percentage of individuals with autism have been employed, they have demonstrated that autism is not incompatible with earning wages.

VARIETY OF EMPLOYMENT ENVIRONMENTS

An additional advance made by workers with autism concerns the variety of environments in which these workers are successfully employed. Workers with mental retardation have long been relegated to jobs in food service, custodial, and horticultural environments. Stereotypes associated with autism could have lent themselves to creating a similarly restricted range of choices of employment. For example, because of the rigidity associated with autism as well as the sensitivity to certain stimuli, it has been a generally accepted notion that people with autism need quiet environments with rigid routines and few distractions. These notions could have hampered job searches significantly. Fortunately, the majority of workers with autism have not been confined to a certain industry, environment, or job type. Workers with autism have managed to avoid jobs that emphasize their weaknesses in language and social skills and find employment under numerous job titles in a variety of industries. Workers with autism have been employed in the retail industry, warehousing, manufacturing, distribution, delivery, recycling, as well as by government, small businesses, large businesses, family-owned enterprises, and national chains. Workers with autism have branched out within the different industries to work for such companies as children's clothiers, women's clothiers, toy stores, linen suppliers, rental outlets, greeting card manufacturers, venetian blinds manufacturers, dental supplies manufacturers, electronics manufacturers, housewares stores, discount department stores, discount clothiers, newspaper recycling companys, business card printers, and various warehouses. Table 13.1 shows the affiliation, ownership, and nature of business of companies that employ workers with autism.

Workers with autism hold such diverse positions as venetian blind assembler, microficher, women's and children's clothing stocker, computer cable manufacturer, computer board assembler, electronic component assembler, greeting card producer, printer, and furniture refinisher. They also work in a

Table 13.1.   Types of businesses employing workers with autism

Affiliation	Nature of business
Federal government	Bulk mailing
Local government	Catalog sales
Private for profit	Construction
Private nonprofit	County, community newspaper
	Electronics manufacturing, repairing, and testing
Ownership	Food service
Corporation	Government
Family business	Health care
Individual owner	Linen and laundry service
Public organization	Manufacturing and assembly
	Hotel chains
	Printing
	Public health information and advocacy
	Recycling
	Rental equipment
	Research, development, and high technology industries
	Retail sales
	Vending and snack distribution
	Video monitoring and transcription service
	Warehouse and distribution
	Waste removal

variety of environments, including stockrooms, warehouses, salesrooms, restaurants, kitchens, courthouses, libraries, airports, and shopping malls. Table 13.2 lists job titles that are held by employees with autism.

Although an individual's pattern of strengths and weaknesses plays a large role in the job selection process, workers with autism have not been confined to any particular industry, environment, or job description. Rather, their choices are almost as broad as those of their co-workers without disabilities, who are also limited to some extent by their patterns of strengths, weaknesses, and educational backgrounds. So, although only a small percentage of the population of adolescents and adults with autism work, those who do work have demonstrated that workers with autism need not be restricted to one particular niche in the workplace.

ADVANCES OF SUPPORT SYSTEMS

Many individuals with autism cannot obtain and keep a job without a support network of auxiliary services and support personnel. Advances in the provision of auxiliary services during the past 2 decades have played a major role in the employment success of these workers. Specifically, advances in behavior management, instructional technology, auxiliary services, and staff training have made valuable contributions.

Table 13.2.   Job titles of some workers with autism

Advertisement flyer distributor	Laminator
Assistant subassembly worker	Laundry worker
Beverage warehouse worker	Manufacturing worker
Bindery worker	Microfilm reproducer
Book sorter	Newspaper deliverer
Bulk mailing clerk	Office clerical worker
Car washer	Order filler
Computer cable assembler	Packager
Conference material assembler	Personal computer board tester
Dishwasher	Poster roller
Electronic component assembler	Radio monitor and transcriber
Food service worker	Receiving/stock clerk
Furniture finisher	Recycling worker
Greeting card manufacturer	Shredding clerk
Groundskeeper	Silk screen printing worker
Heating/air conditioning assembler	Snack tray filler
Inventory clerk	Vending company warehouse worker
Janitorial worker	Venetian blind assembler
Laboratory assistant	Warehouse worker

Behavior Management

Autism can be associated with poor social skills; stereotyped behaviors; and severe behavior problems, such as self-injury, aggression, and property destruction. Additionally, pica, toileting problems, bizarre vocalizations, and verbal and motor rituals can be present, all of which can impede employment. These behaviors have presented challenges to parents, teachers, and other staff who are working with the individual with autism.

Initially, attempts to treat the challenging behaviors associated with autism were limited to simple contingency plans—either attempts at positive reinforcement schedules or schedules of punishment. There were several problems inherent in this simplistic approach. First, events that were chosen as reinforcers were often not reinforcing. For example, teacher praise would be chosen as a reinforcer, but for the individual concerned, the praise was not reinforcing. The same problem occurred with attempts at using punishment. Stimuli that were chosen as punishers were in fact sometimes not punishing, such as adult reprimands, removal from the room, and time-out.

A second, possibly more important, flaw to ineffective behavioral interventions was their lack of adequate foundations. Although many behaviorists prided themselves on the fact that their techniques were based on research and founded on the principles of behavior, their interventions were not founded on a functional assessment of the individual's behavior. That is, intervention plans were driven by technique rather than purpose. If the therapist favored the use of positive reinforcement, plans for behavior change centered on positive reinforcement. If the therapist was inclined to use punishment, plans were built around punishment.

A focus on the role of functional assessments has resulted in great strides in behavior change. By determining the functions or causes of the individual's unacceptable behavior, and then using that information to select interventions, the effectiveness of the overall plan is greatly enhanced. Many individuals with autism who have succeeded in the work force have benefited from behavior planning based on functional assessments of their behavior. Rather than being based on the therapist's biases or on shot-in-the-dark techniques, behavior plans have been based on a full functional assessment. These advances in intervention planning have resulted in many cases of rapid and startling changes in behavior. These behavior changes have allowed many workers with autism, who otherwise would have failed, to succeed in the workplace.

An additional boon to behavior management has been the proliferation of procedures that are feasible in integrated community environments. When individuals with autism were confined primarily to institutions or segregated schools, behavior management procedures were often cumbersome and obtrusive. Showy charts, elaborate token economies, extremely dense schedules of positive reinforcement (e.g., reinforcers provided every minute), and cumbersome data collection procedures could be and were implemented in segregated or research environments. These same procedures would now bring undue attention to the individual with autism in the workplace. They are impractical in integrated, competitive employment environments. Fortunately, a variety of unobtrusive and practical but powerful procedures have emerged that have resulted in behavior change in integrated environments.

Related to the advances made in the feasibility of behavioral procedures are advances made in the acceptability of behavioral procedures. Procedures that were considered acceptable in segregated environments are considered unacceptable in integrated environments. These procedures are primarily those classed as punishment procedures. The research and history of behavior change and autism is replete with interventions based on punishment. Punishers of many types were used, including removal of positive reinforcers; activity punishers, such as forced exercise; and presentation of aversive stimuli, such as aversive tastes (e.g., pepper sauce, shaving cream in the mouth), aversive smells (e.g., ammonia capsules crushed under the nose), and aversive tactile stimuli (e.g., electric shock).

Punishment procedures have generated objections both on moral and scientific grounds. Both arguments have merit. An equally compelling objection, which arises with their use in the integrated work environment, is their lack of acceptability to the public. Applying electric shock to a child with autism in the "privacy" of the classroom might be considered acceptable by some classroom staff and even parents. However, applying electric shock to a worker with autism on the sales floor of a toy store would be considered unacceptable by the worker's fellow employees, management, and the public. If behavior management was dependent on the use of such techniques, it is likely that workers with autism and serious behavior problems would be unwelcome in the workplace, not so much because of their behaviors (those have already been accepted in many workplaces), but because of the interventions that would follow.

Fortunately, an array of procedures are being used in integrated work environments that are effective in the management of even severe forms of self-injury and aggression, including cases of high frequency occurrence (up to thousands of times per day). These procedures, as discussed in Chapter 4, have proven to be not only feasible and unobtrusive, but acceptable to the public (in those cases in which the public notices). In fact, the job coach who implements a well-designed behavior plan that is centered on unobtrusive, nonaversive procedures merely appears to onlookers to be a support person who has an extremely positive relationship with the worker with autism.

Instructional Technology

Autism has been referred to as the ultimate learning disability. Individuals with autism often have a great deal of difficulty learning in conventional ways. Once a task is learned, there can be difficulty generalizing from one environment to another, one teacher to another, and even from one type of material to another similar type. Once training is terminated, there can be difficulty with the worker maintaining gains made during the learning phase.

Fortunately, behavior management procedures have been developed that have enabled individuals with autism to become competent employees. Strategies that reduce the need for generalization, strategies that enhance generalization, and procedures for maintenance have been developed and applied not only in classroom environments, but in integrated work environments as well.

Auxiliary Services

In the past, autism was considered to be a failure of social development rooted in poor parenting. During the past 2 decades, autism has been acknowledged as being a neurological disorder rather than an environmentally caused disorder. During the period of time when autism was considered to be an environmentally based disorder, there was a lack of effective auxiliary services. Auxiliary services, such as parent or child therapy, were aimed at healing the faulty relationships or faulty psychodynamics that were presumed to underlie the disorder. These services, given their incorrect bases, could not cure or mitigate the effects of autism and often reduced the parents to states of frustration and depression. When these services failed, the result was often the recommendation to institutionalize the child.

Since the early 1980s, auxiliary services gradually improved and are now being provided within the framework of autism as a neurological disorder. Rather than focusing on parent–child dynamics, auxiliary services have evolved that seek to ameliorate the characteristics of autism. Therapy provided to parents, teachers, and supported employment staff focuses on development and implementation of behavior management strategies. In addition, rather than have the therapy directly applied from the therapist to the person with autism, behavioral consultation has become the preferred modality. This means that the behavioral consultant assists parents, teachers, and other direct service personnel to implement strategies that can ameliorate some of the learning and behavioral features of the disorder. Although this auxiliary service does not signify a cure for autism, it can result in significant strides in social and vocational development.

Some people with autism have benefited from individual counseling. Changes in the methods of individual counseling—away from a psychodynamic approach, which sought to cure underlying causes of the disorder, and toward a practical, skill-building approach—have resulted in gains in social, emotional, and vocational development for people with autism. Therapists who are skillful at providing individual counseling to people with autism are in great demand, and new procedures have improved the benefits of counseling.

Occupational therapy is another field that has evolved to provide useful auxiliary services to people with autism at work. Occupational therapists assess the needs of the person with autism in relation to the demands of the job. For example, Janet is a woman with autism whose job required frequent stooping and lifting. She often engaged in task refusal, and she took frequent breaks from her task. An occupational therapist evaluated Janet at work and determined that she was lifting improperly, causing undue stress on her back and unnecessary fatigue. Additionally, the occupational therapist diagnosed muscle weakness that contributed to the problem. She prescribed strengthening exercises for Janet to perform and taught Janet more efficient ways of lifting. Her services were instrumental in helping Janet adjust to the demands of her job.

The field of psychiatry has developed also in relation to autism in recent years. Initially, psychiatric input was of limited value, especially given the original and erroneous identification of insufficient parenting as the cause of the disorder. Although many adults with autism, and even severe behavior problems, do not require psychiatric services, some people with autism have benefited from psychopharmacological treatments provided by psychiatrists. Those psychiatrists who have expertise in treating people with autism have made significant contributions to the well-being of their patients and to their success at work. The case of Jackson provides a good example. Jackson has moderate mental retardation and severe autism. During his first several years in a supported employment program, he had continuing problems with aggression and property destruction. In fact, several job coaches suffered broken bones from Jackson's assaults. Behavior management plans decreased the frequency of Jackson's aggressive outbursts significantly; however, serious episodes did still occur. Often, they occurred when he was supervised by substitute staff, a situation that could not always be prevented. Jackson lost several jobs due to these outbursts. The services of a psychiatrist were sought, and Jackson was placed on a low dose of a neuroleptic medication. This resulted in an immediate improvement. For the past 3 years, Jackson has remained in the same job and has had no outbursts of aggression. Again, many people with autism do not need psychotropic medications, but at times this treatment can be valuable when provided by a psychiatrist who has expertise in the field of autism.

Another auxiliary service that has benefited people with autism is speech and language services. Traditional, less effective means of improving language used to center around deskwork in which language was taught out of context of the individual's routine. However, in recent years, traditional speech and language services have given way to more effective strategies that stress teaching functional language in the individual's environment while the individual performs activities of daily living. Teaching is practical and relevant because it is incorporated into the individual's daily activities. Speech and language therapists have made valuable contributions by helping establish appropriate goals for the individual and by developing strategies that are geared to the needs of the work environment.

Speech and language services have also shifted from the language therapist being the primary provider of services to the individual's support staff providing the services under the training and supervision of the language therapist. The speech and language staff person often targets appropriate goals; develops strategies; and then teaches support personnel, such as the job coach, to implement those strategies in the course of the worker's day.

Staff Training

The direct support of the job coach is instrumental in the successful employment of many working adolescents and adults with autism. Advances made in staff training have enhanced the ability of job coaches to make such a positive impact on employment. Good staff training systems have been developed that meet two important functions. First, they can prepare the job coach to effectively support the worker with autism. Second, they can compensate for the disruption that can be caused by staff turnover.

Prior to the development of good staff training procedures, job coaching often did little to retain employment. Merely providing a job coach to teach the tasks and then monitor or supervise the person with autism was usually not sufficient to keep that person employed. Because of the severe learning, language, and behavior problems often involved, the job coach needed to become an expert in how to teach a person with autism, how to communicate with that person, and how to relate to that person to minimize the likelihood that interfering behaviors would occur and to maximize the likelihood that job adjustment would take place.

A primary reason for the failure of many job coaches to provide adequate support is that they did not receive adequate training. They may have degrees in psychology, rehabilitation, or even special education, but their educations may not be enough to prepare them to be job coaches. Traditionally, direct care staff for people with autism were given little formal training upon employment. There may have been a brief orientation session and some didactic training in autism or behavior modification. Then, the job coach was sent out to support a person with autism. Often, the result was failure. In cases where the job coach did provide adequate support, the employee with autism was still in jeopardy of losing his or her job if that job coach resigned and a replacement was provided.

Staff training systems have evolved that combine didactic and hands-on training. These systems normally include didactic training in autism, normalization, policies and procedures, communication, supported employment, and behavior management. Then, individualized training is provided about the workers with autism whom the job coach will serve. This training includes information about the background of the workers and the implementation of instructional and behavioral procedures. Next, on-the-job training is provided by working with experienced personnel, and by demonstration and feedback. This on-the-job training covers the implementation of instructional and behavior plans, the details about the worksite, and training on-the-job tasks that the worker with autism was hired to do. Finally, ongoing monitoring of the job coach and periodic training updates related to the job are provided. Advances in staff training ensure that workers are adequately supported and that the effects of job coach turnover are minimized.

EMPLOYMENT STABILITY

In the early 1980s, when supported employment of people with autism became a viable option, job turnover was high. Agencies providing supported employment to people with autism were often able to obtain jobs, but keeping them was problematic. It was not unusual for a person with severe autism to go through several jobs within a 1- or 2-year period. In recent years, there has been an increase in the stability of employment of people with autism. Workers who only used to be able to keep a job for several months are now able to work on a long-term basis. This increase in stability is most likely due to several factors, including more expertise on the part of support personnel, a greater acceptance by the business community of workers with disabilities, and the improvements in behavior and productivity of workers with autism.

CHANGES IN PUBLIC POLICY

Recent changes in the service delivery system offer new opportunities for funding supported employment programs. These changes remove some of the historic disincentives and contain incentives for providing supported employment for people with autism.

Changes in federal laws have opened doors for individuals with autism in many ways. PL 101-336, the Americans with Disabilities Act of 1990 (ADA), provides access to public facilities. This federal law, which is best known for the changes required in public buildings and facilities to make them accessible to people with disabilities, mandates that child care centers can no longer refuse to serve children because they have a disability. This means that students with disabilities are included from the time they enter nursery school until they are adults. This is an important new provision for children with autism because socialization experiences between them and children without disabilities at these early ages are beneficial for both. The ADA also prohibits discrimination in employment on the basis of disability. This law encourages employers to hire people with autism as well as other disabilities.

The Individuals with Disabilities Education Act (IDEA) Amendments of 1991 (PL 102-119) require that all students by the age of 16 years, or younger if they are more severely disabled, have a transition plan and services. Transition services include community experiences, independent living, instruction, supported employment, and other activities leading to outcomes promoting the movement of the student from school to adult life in the community. IDEA benefits students with autism by exposing them to integration and job experiences while still in school.

An additional benefit of IDEA is the expansion of the list of related services that school systems may be required to provide. Therapeutic recreation, social work services, and rehabilitation counseling are some of the services that have been beneficial to people with autism that are now included as special education and related services by IDEA.

These amendments to IDEA also require the addition of autism to the list of disabilities that identify children eligible for special education and related services. In the past, children with autism were identified and considered part of larger disability categories, such as serious emotional disturbance or mental retardation. Now that autism has a separate designation, it is possible to determine how many students with autism are participating in supported employment and related integrated experiences. This information can then be used to plan activities that promote such inclusion.

Changes in rehabilitation law are also expected to benefit people with autism. The Rehabilitation Act Amendments of 1992 (PL 102-569) require that rehabilitation professionals presume that all individuals are eligible for employment, regardless of the severity of their disability. The assessment process is being redesigned to actually place individuals in jobs to determine the environment and supports that are needed for them to achieve and maintain employment. This legislation also removes time limits on the supports provided through this federal program. These changes are too new to have made an impact on the lives of people with autism, but they hold much promise for the future.

FUTURE DIRECTIONS

People with autism have demonstrated that they can be valuable workers. In addition, despite continuing limitations, the fields of education and habilitation have demonstrated an ability to support people with autism in their employment efforts. However, employment as a lifestyle for people with autism is a relatively new effort, and there are a variety of directions that the disability field can take. Increases in self-management, improvement in support determination, expansion of opportunities, and increased accessibility to supported employment are all future directions that can have a positive impact on people with autism.

Increases in Self-Management

Many individuals with autism have required behavior management plans that help them keep their jobs. Implementation of behavior management plans requires trained personnel. Experience has demonstrated that even minor errors in plan implementation can result in a resurgence of behavior problems. An increased use of self-management plans would have a positive impact on the employment of people with autism.

Increasing the use of self-management has several immediate benefits. First, the worker gains more control over his or her programming. Second, many workers with autism have expressed a preference for self-management, rather than behavior management by others. Third, when workers can manage their own behavioral control plans there is less of a need for experienced support personnel.

The use of self-management can be expanded in at least two directions. First, self-management has proven effective in a variety of ways with people with high levels of cognitive functioning. Yet, many of these people have not been provided with the opportunity to use self-management. They are either dependent on informal systems of control, such as repeated prompting and reprimands, or they are dependent on formal behavior management plans. To the extent possible, these people should be provided with the opportunity to benefit from self-management technology. Second, there has been limited use of self-management with people with severe autism and mental retardation. Although these plans are often used in conjunction with other controlled behavior management plans, they still allow the worker a window of independence and self-control. More workers with autism who are severely limited in their functioning need to be given the opportunity to use self-management procedures to the extent of their abilities. Third, the technology of self-management for people with autism needs to be expanded to benefit those with more severe behavior problems and with greater degrees of autism.

Improvement in Support Determination

A major reason for job loss and underemployment of people with autism is a failure to properly determine support needs. Support needs can be miscalculated both in terms of a staff to worker ratio and in terms of the type of support that is needed. Often, failure to keep a job is ascribed to the person with autism, rather than to an insufficient amount of support. However, too much support consigns the worker to a state of dependence that might be unnecessary given the worker's capacities. Therefore, an important future direction is the development of reliable and valid methods for assessing the support needs of people with autism.

An issue related to assessing support needs is the current emphasis on natural supports. There may be cases in which workers with autism have been oversupported and a more sophisticated support determination technology could help alleviate the problem. Trimming the quantity and intensity of supports can benefit a worker. An increased reliance on supports inherent in the workplace can also be beneficial; however, there must be reliable, valid methods available to determine the support needs.

Many workers with autism are, for the first time, benefiting from supported employment. Because the technology of their support is still evolving, the dismantling of this support comes at some risk. Yet, some future directions in transferring to natural supports can be considered. One direction includes developing methods for transferring job coaching functions to co-workers. Some workers who are initially supported can do well if supports are gradually transferred to in-house personnel. In addition, some people with autism need no external support and can do well with a little extra help from the employer. Future efforts in the arena of natural supports can be directed toward preparing workers with these potentials to work with as little external support as necessary without jeopardizing their jobs by removing necessary supports prematurely. The mechanisms established to achieve these aims will need to be carefully investigated and the possible effects of their use carefully weighed prior to eliminating or reducing supports that are currently helping the worker maintain employment.

Related to the issue of transferring support to co-workers is the issue of identifying the exact nature of supports used when people with autism do not have job coaches. It is not uncommon for a person with a developmental disability to work well in a job without the use of a job coach, then to abruptly begin to fail. The cause is often the withdrawal of natural supports that had developed and were not noticed or acknowledged. Usually, this withdrawal occurs when a supporting co-worker or supervisor is transferred out of the employee's job area. Because the supporting co-worker or supervisor provided support discreetly, a gap in services results when that person leaves and the nature of this gap may not be readily known. To prevent a relapse into dependence on job coaches, and to promote more widespread use of company-sponsored supports, mechanisms need to be established to help supported employment agencies identify natural supports as they evolve.

A final future direction in the area of support is the delineation of criteria that render people capable of working without the supervision of trained job coaches. Some workers with autism will always need external support because they require constant monitoring for safety purposes that transcend vocational goals. Other workers are able to work without their job coach after initially learning the job. Others never need a job coach. Development of criteria for decision making helps ensure that no worker fails at employment because of an underestimation of support needs, and that no worker is provided with more support than is necessary.

Expansion of Opportunities

Workers with autism manage well in entry-level jobs in a variety of occupations; however, most of these workers remain in those entry-level jobs for the duration of their employment. Upward mobility is rare with workers with autism. The barriers to upward mobility should be examined so that change can be brought about and goals for achieving upward mobility can be established.

Related to the issue of upward mobility is that of more skilled employment. Although some workers with autism are hired in skilled positions, most work in unskilled positions. Unskilled jobs appear to be good matches to their strengths and interests; however, it is possible that many people with autism could obtain and keep more skilled employment. A future direction in the employment of people with autism is to undertake an examination of this issue and make a determination of the possibilities of attaining more skilled employment for more workers with autism.

A final area in need of examination is the opportunity to expand on the kinds of jobs workers with autism can obtain. People with autism have worked in an impressive variety of environments and have done well in fields that have traditionally not been accessed by people with developmental disabilities. The splinter skills that are often associated with autism have made this possible, as well as instructional and behavioral technologies. Yet, there is still a need for expansion, especially in rural areas and areas experiencing high rates of unemployment. The more occupational flexibility these workers have, the greater their likelihood of getting and keeping a job in depressed economic conditions or in areas with restricted occupational opportunities.

Increasing Participation in the Work Force

Workers with autism have worked in a variety of occupations with a wide range of job titles. Unfortunately, gains in employment have been made by an extremely small number of people with autism. For the most part, supported employment has not included people with severe disabilities, such as autism.

Those individuals with autism who have benefited from supported employment are more realistically viewed as models than as representatives of the population as a whole. The relatively small number of people with autism who are employed demonstrates that people with autism can work and that even severe autism is not a barrier to employment. They have demonstrated that people with autism and no verbal language can work, that people with autism and destructive and injurious behaviors can work, and that people with autism and profound mental retardation can work. Most of these workers have demonstrated that they can achieve some level of social integration at work; that they enjoy work; and that they can earn wages, pay taxes, and make a valuable contribution to their companies. Some of these people have demonstrated that people with autism can work faster than their co-workers without disabilities, that they are reliable workers, and that they can remain devoted to the same job for many years. A few of these people have shown that they can work independently of professional supervision and that they can succeed with support systems that are naturally occurring in their workplace.

Workers with autism have been able to make impressive gains for themselves in the workplace, given the opportunity and sufficient support. For most people with autism, the opportunity has never been presented, and for many for whom it has, support has been insufficient. Therefore, while some workers with autism go to work, earn wages, and pay taxes, the majority of them are consigned by their disability to segregated environments in which their problems are magnified, their strengths obscured, and their earning power unrealized. The most pressing needs in employing people with autism are to provide more people with autism the opportunity to work and to provide those workers with sufficient support to remain in the work force.

REFERENCES

Americans with Disabilities Act of 1990, PL 101-336. (July 26, 1990). Title 42, U.S.C. 12101: *U.S. Statutes at Large, 104,* 327–378.
Individuals with Disabilities Education Act Amendments of 1991, PL 102-119. (October 7, 1991). Title 20, U.S.C. 1400 et seq: *U.S. Statutes at Large, 105,* 587–608.
Rehabilitation Act Amendments of 1992, PL 102-569. (October 29, 1992). Title 29, U.S.C. 701 et seq: *U.S. Statutes at Large, 106,* 4333–4388.

Index

Page numbers followed by *t* and *f* denote tables and figures, respectively.